T0323691

Underwriting Commercial Real Estate in a Dynamic Market

Underwriting Commercial Real Estate in a Dynamic Market

Case Studies

Christian L. Redfearn
USC Price,
Los Angeles, California
USA

ACADEMIC PRESS

An imprint of Elsevier

Notices
Knowledge and best practice in this field are constantly changing. As new research and experience broaden our understanding, changes in research methods, professional practices, or medical treatment may become necessary.

Practitioners and researchers must always rely on their own experience and knowledge in evaluating and using any information, methods, compounds, or experiments described herein. In using such information or methods they should be mindful of their own safety and the safety of others, including parties for whom they have a professional responsibility.

To the fullest extent of the law, neither the Publisher nor the authors, contributors, or editors, assume any liability for any injury and/or damage to persons or property as a matter of products liability, negligence or otherwise, or from any use or operation of any methods, products, instructions, or ideas contained in the material herein.

Library of Congress Cataloging-in-Publication Data
A catalog record for this book is available from the Library of Congress

British Library Cataloguing-in-Publication Data
A catalogue record for this book is available from the British Library

ISBN: 978-0-12-815989-7

For information on all Academic Press publications
visit our website at https://www.elsevier.com/books-and-journals

Working together
to grow libraries in
developing countries

www.elsevier.com • www.bookaid.org

Publisher: Candice Janco
Acquisition Editor: Scott Bentley
Editorial Project Manager: Susan Ikeda
Production Project Manager: Paul Prasad Chandramohan
Cover Designer: Mark Rogers

Typeset by SPi Global, India

Dedication

To the memory of John Quigley. John was my advisor at Berkeley and more than any other person responsible for putting me on the path to writing this book, which is essentially about enjoying the rewards of curiosity. John still reminds me how much can be learned by asking one more good question.

Contents

Part II
Extending the Framework: Commercial Leases

Part III

Framework, Deal Structure, and Risk and Return

Part IV

Iteration and Integration: Development and Redevelopment

Case 20. Do Cycles Die of Old Age? Or Is 10 the New 6?

Acknowledgments

This is my first book and while I have 18 years of alumni to ask for real estate help, I had only two people to help turn this idea into a book. Scott Bentley and Susan Ikeda are my editors at Elsevier. While I feel slightly short-changed that I never had one of those Hollywood scenes in which we argued about deadlines or secondary sources. I have thoroughly enjoyed learning from them and am hopeful that the rest of the acknowledgments fit under the allocated word count. Thank you.

In terms of helping shape the book's content, allow me to begin by thanking the largest and, perhaps, most essential group of contributors to this book: my USC Dollinger Master of Real Estate Development students over the past 18 years. I like experimenting in class and my students have not only allowed this but have become willing co-conspirators in throwing curve balls at subsequent cohorts. After a few years working in the MRED program, I started telling incoming students at orientation, "Everyone passed the comprehensive exam last year, so it must have been too easy." The students groan but invariably accept the challenge and each year we work together to get more out of the program. The cases in this book are one outcome of that collective process to improve real estate education. I would not have taken the cases in this direction and ultimately to this book without my students. Thank you.

The second group I would like to thank is the real estate faculty at the USC Sol Price School of Public Policy. This is an eclectic group of tenure-track and adjunct faculty whose expertise spans product types, submarkets, firms and the roles within them. Some among them are also keen to point out that there is significant variation among them with regard to the number of real estate cycles they've survived, but all of them share a commitment to help students. They are extraordinary professionals in their own right, and they have helped me by always pushing critical thinking. This means that students readily buy in to the case approach to teaching. Moreover, this group enabled me to translate how I thought about cities as an urban economist to how I should best approach educating real estate professionals. I benefitted from countless breakfasts and lunches with USC faculty. I have been grateful for their support from Day One. As busy as they are, they are a uniformly generous group whose typical response to a request from me has been: "Of course, how can I help?" Thank you.

Every one of the cases in this book are from drawn from real world deals as described by real estate alumni and faculty. I would like to acknowledge the case sponsors (whose deals are the inspiration for these cases) and the readers (who have helped me vet them) by name. These include: Tyler Carlson, Eric Clapp, John Drachman, Jeff Dritley, Liz Falletta, Damian Gancman, Iain Gulin, Greg Heller, Alon Kraft, Jeff Kreshek, John Loper, John Menne, Joe Nelson, Gary Palmer, Shlomi Ronen, Scott Scharlach, Justin Shapiro, Ryan Shea, Wil Smith, Adam Weinbaum, and Elliot Weinstock. Several others were very helpful, but preferred to remain anonymous. Thank you all.

My experimenting with cases accelerated after I met Al Borstein. Al is a graduate of the Harvard Business School who has three sons who are real estate professionals, two of whom are graduates of USC. Al enjoyed learning through cases at HBS and wanted to support case development within the MRED program. The Borstein Family Foundation endowed the cases series, allowing me to expand the number of cases and their use. These cases have been instrumental in advancing both how we teach at USC and the careers of countless alumni. I am grateful for the Borstein gift, and I am also deeply grateful to Al for his active support of my efforts. He is not a passive donor. We meet frequently and he is more than happy to challenge and improve my thinking in the same way that I challenge my students. My pride in these cases and in this book cannot be separated from his role in supporting them. To Brenda, Craig, Loren, Eric, and Alan, thank you.

Though space is limited, I am compelled to also thank Peter Gordon and Raphael Bostic who have been great friends and colleagues, but also my two predecessors in running the MRED program. When I was a little lost at the beginning of my time at USC, Peter helped me find my people by getting me to teach real estate finance in the MRED program. Both Peter and Raphael were relentless in pushing quality and when I wanted to experiment with my classes, both only asked how it would improve the program. When I took over the program, thanks to them I inherited one that was already well-positioned to thrive. I would also like to thank Richard Green, whose support for creating our Bachelor of Science in Real Estate Development degree was instrumental. Now, the Borstein cases are now being used across the two programs. Thank you.

The glue that binds real estate together at USC is Sonia Savoulian. Sonia has been the chief administrator of the real estate programs at Price since well before Raphael and Peter were directors. All of my ideas about changing the curriculum and industry—including the cases that resulted in this book—were vetted, stretched, challenged, and improved by countless conversations with Sonia. She is unique in her commitment to creating the environment in which we can best help our real estate students and the real estate industry. Thank you.

Finally, because I see this book as about embracing and enjoying curiosity, I can't help but acknowledge my family who must have found a way to embrace and enjoy the curiosity I've been for all these years. They are wonderful. Among them is my wife, Jen, who has read and edited every word of this book. For everything, thank you.

CLR

The Borstein Family Foundation

The Borstein Family Foundation was founded in 1998 by Alan and Brenda Borstein. From its inception, the vision and focus of the foundation has been to support the advancement of medical research, medical care, providing educational opportunities for underserved children, and to promote education.

The Borstein Family Foundation continues to support organizations, both locally and nationally, that are focused on such causes that are consistent with the vision of the foundation. Some of the charities that the foundation supports are: Alzheimer's Association, Cedars-Sinai, City of Hope, Crossroads School for Arts & Sciences, Harvard University, HomeAid Los Angeles, Jewish Federation, John Wayne Cancer Institute, Los Angeles Jewish Home, Los Angeles Regional Food Bank, Los Angeles Ronald McDonald House, Mattel Children's Hospital UCLA, More Than Words, Operation Mend, Operation Smile, P.S. Science, The Rape Foundation, The YMCA, USC Lusk Center for Real Estate. The foundation also helped establish the Borstein Family Endowed Professorship of Real Estate, which Prof. Redfearn now occupies, and endowed the Borstein Real Estate Case Study Series, which are at the heart of this book.

Introduction: The Returns to Effort and Expertise

"Brain damage" is one of my favorite colloquialisms in real estate. It refers to complexity, as in "We passed on the deal. It was too messy, too many moving parts, and just too much brain damage." For some, complexity implies risk and is something to be avoided. But experienced developers and investors know that complexity is in the eyes of the underwriter as much as it is in the real estate being underwritten. In assembling the cases in this book, I hope to help readers overcome fear of complexity and see how, if well-underwritten, complexity can be used to create or capture value. These case studies are meant to complement the many good real estate finance textbooks that are comprehensive in their treatment of the essential building blocks of real estate and real estate finance. Individually, none of these essential building blocks are particularly complex relative to the "brain damage" that can arise from their interactions, especially in light of the varied contexts in which they take place: the many product types and their different manifestations, the enormous complexity of the neighborhoods and cities in which buildings are located, the diversity of tenants within them and leases they've signed, and the various capital sources that can be used to acquire them. Given that this heterogeneity is inherent to real estate, it is clear that underwriting is less about finding "The Answer" and more about assessing, balancing, and managing risks and opportunities. This book is about embracing complexity and enjoying the returns associated with effort and expertise; it is about helping real estate professionals underwrite commercial real estate in a dynamic world.

It may be easiest to demonstrate this process by thinking about underwriting a Class A, core office building being marketed for sale. A good broker will have prepared a credible—if optimistic—forecast of future cash flows. He will have selected a number of plausibly optimistic rent and sale comparables. And he'll make use of some standard valuation tools that will suggest that his client's property is worth quite a bit. This is his job. As an analyst on an acquisitions team, your job might be to propose a bid. You could then assemble a bunch of reasonable estimates for operating cash flows, rent growth rates, consensus estimates for exit cap rates, preliminary debt and equity terms, etc. But what if the building isn't typical along these dimensions? What if it has a rent roll that has an average lease term that is short and average rents that are now below-market? Would you then think of this as a value-add play? Can you turn the impending lease rollover into a significant bump in NOI? What if the same anchor tenant whose lease is about to expire isn't interested in signing a new lease or simply can't? If the anchor tenant leaves, should you demise the space or wait for another big tenant? Should you lower rents to generate some leasing activity? Who would pay to demise the space? And who's going to pay for the leasing commissions and tenant improvements that go along with filling the vacant space? These are just the starter questions. If you become the owner of this property, then you will have a lot to think about, and so too would your equity partner and lender. If you weren't viewing this deal from the sponsor's perspective and instead worked for the lender, you wouldn't like the sound of vacant space and would likely offer either a very low LTV loan or want to set up some sort of sweep account to ensure that your loan can be serviced. As an equity partner, you may respond to the perceived vacancy risk and want to structure a joint venture agreement that perhaps gives away some upside return in exchange for priority in distributions. All of these stakeholders have to agree with the purchase price, the leasing strategy, and the capital stack. This means many conversations among current tenants, potential tenants, equity partners and lenders, and continuing these conversations until some form of consensus can be formed. This complicated, real life process is why cases have come to play such a large role in our real estate programs. The first thing we do with cases is unpack and discuss the language, structures, and stakeholders—like those in the paragraph above. These are as important as the time-value of money. Once these basics are understood, the first layer of complexity will lift and we can move onto the others. Cases are an excellent way to learn about underwriting, and the questions listed above *are* the stuff of underwriting. It really can be complicated and it will make you understand why the real estate industry likes colorful terms like "brain damage." But this sort of complexity should not necessarily be viewed as a reason to abandon a deal. Instead, it could be seen as an opportunity to find value.

In fact, this sort of complexity is what I find so compelling about real estate. I am an urban economist at heart, but have spent almost 20 years teaching real estate students and then hanging out with them as they advance in their professional careers. I like to think hard about how cities work and how neighborhoods change within them, and so do my students and graduates. But they have an essential next step, which is to act on their understanding of real estate markets and their dynamics. Indeed, for many, career success will largely depend on their ability to assess value accurately and to recognize good opportunities to buy or sell as fundamentals change. This is true whether they are acting as sponsors, equity partners, lenders, or providing services to any of these groups through advisory, brokerage, and appraisal work. Embracing complexity is rewarding both professionally and personally. My graduates and colleagues talk less about money and more about the deals that they were able to make work by seeing what others did not. In a world as dynamic and as heterogeneous as real estate, this means constantly rethinking one's approach to underwriting. My students learn to do this reflexively and my goal in assembling the cases in this book is to help others do so, too.

The hypothetical building I introduced above can be found in Case 6: "Bayview double take." I was first introduced to the Bayview Corporate Center (BCC) when one of the real estate faculty told me about how it had fallen out of escrow as asset prices fell in 2008. A great question that we contemplated was how much someone ought to pay for a property when no one was sure about how much further asset prices would fall. It had been considered a gem just 2 years earlier, but even at a significant discount to the 2006 valuation, it had just fallen out of escrow. We asked students to make use of standard tools and make reasonable assumptions to value the BCC, and they realized quickly that one could justify an enormous range of values, each supported by something resembling market-based underwriting. The first version of the case was as a nuts-and-bolts exercise in leasing and debt choices, but the case really came to life when we started interacting these basic questions with the students' perceptions of how the larger office market would recover and how important a premier location was at different points in the cycle. The students explored various future outcomes and various strategies for operating the property. It was through this exercise that a range of plausible outcomes became clear. Some choices were obviously suboptimal and could be eliminated. This allowed the students to focus on refining the more plausible options. Students were then able to provide a bid and guidance for a number of key operating decisions. In the end, the range of bids from the students were distributed right around the actual sale price. While I was pleased with their performance (at least relative to how the market had priced the BCC), I was much happier with the level of conversation about trade-offs, about risk, about mitigating those risks, about debt and leasing strategies, and ultimately about the bid. The exercise over several weeks produced an extraordinarily rich conversation that significantly advanced their thought process about underwriting at the same time that they were also getting more comfortable with the basic tools and, honestly, having a lot of fun. I had tinkered with cases before then, but it was the Bayview Corporate Center that really made it clear how powerful cases could be to help students both master basic skills and also deepen their understanding of underwriting by introducing some of the complexity inherent in real estate.

Since then I've been building cases every year, picking new ones to update and fill holes in the curriculum. Most cases begin with hearing back from alumni who found some "cool deal" they wanted to share with me. Generally, if they found it interesting and found themselves stuck at a particular decision point, then other students would benefit from sitting in their shoes for a while and trying to address whatever issue they faced. The case series has matured and I see it as accomplishing numerous goals in every real estate class we offer, from a basic principles class to an advanced case class. First, real estate has its own dialect. I am a native speaker of English, but when I went to my first real estate conferences it was hard to be sure I was fluent. All the cases in this book are based on real deals with USC MRED alumni and faculty. I spent time trying to capture their character and language as much as the essence of the case itself. One of the first hurdles students face when they graduate is speaking like a real estate professional; the cases here should help them see how real estate professionals think about and discuss their challenges. Another hurdle facing students is grasping the real estate industry itself and understanding how they might fit into it. I've used "real estate" repeatedly so far and in each case it's been meant to refer to a very large group of assets, firms, and professionals who are far from homogeneous. Across the cases, students will get a chance to try on playing different roles in different firms. Students will first discover that "the answer" to most questions depends on who you and your firm are as much as any real estate fundamental. The cases may also help students discover an interest in pursuing a particular market, product type, or firm. Each case also offers the opportunity for practice. All the cases have enough data to start underwriting, but each can also be "dialed up" or "dialed down," so that an introductory class can practice the basics of building a pro forma, while an advanced class can practice choosing from among institutional JV structures. Finally, the cases are effective at developing intuition. Once students start exploring different scenarios for future cash flows, they begin anticipating management choices that go along with different states of the world. They will start to see that they may not have a choice about market rents, but they have a lot of control about how to act in light of the market.

The best way to read these cases is to imagine yourself in the role of the protagonist, because each case is based on a real human who sat where you are now. Each main character had to think well and deeply about real estate, to learn to make decisions, and to support and advocate for their choices. Once students take ownership of the role, the assignment is less about homework and more about imagining themselves as real estate professionals. Because it is easy to search and find information about real estate deals, I've masked most of the particulars. Early on I discovered that clever students would find a deal and then reverse engineer their underwriting to echo the market outcome. To be clear, the market is not always right and just because an established real estate professional was willing to pay top dollar for a deal in 2007 doesn't mean they were right. Among the cases in the book, there are several properties that can be found on line, but those that have been masked retain all the same key issues facing the protagonist. You might be able to figure out something about the actual property, but I recommend that you resist this impulse. There will be no answer to find online when you are sitting at your first job. Take the opportunity to practice now, when the cost of your mistakes is minimal.

The best way to teach a case is to let students read the case and then bring them into class to talk through all the issues: language, structure, data, stakeholders and their influence, motivations, risk tolerance, etc. Then create an assignment to fit the needs of the class. It could as simple as asking students to consider the follow up questions found at the end of each case. It could be to ask the students to underwrite an updated case based on a class conversation.

I routinely change numbers in the case when students argue that market assumptions have changed. When one of the students with a background in lending says "You'll never get that LTV today" we talk about lending and the changing world of debt, and then we agree to explore those changes by using new debt terms. It's common to start with some standard assumptions to calibrate the models, but then let the students turn to the market for alternative scenarios.

One of my favorite exercises is assigning students to different roles and allowing them time to see if they could work together to find a deal. Each student is told to take the perspective of a lender, equity partner, sponsor, or property owner. As a class, we talk through the priorities of each and how these roles differ. I then jokingly tell the students that they'll be fired if they're too aggressive in getting a deal done and also that that they'll be fired if they're too conservative and can't close a deal. Then students not only see how hard it is to find a deal in a competitive world, but they also have a chance to explore their own risk tolerance and expectations for returns in ways we likely wouldn't see from traditional assignments. In general, the more students invest in this kind of exercise, the more they'll learn and the more fun they'll have.

Several final bits of advice that I relay to my students is accumulated wisdom from the graduates and faculty of the real estate programs at USC. I'll credit Wil Smith, Damian Gancman, and Tyler Carlson for repeating this when they visited my class as alumni: "The only thing you know for sure about your pro forma is that it's wrong." That might be true, but the logical conclusion is not that we should dump forecasting: do you want to invest your capital based on guessing? Do you want to assume that markets are efficient and that every property is fairly priced given its risk? A significant challenge for some students is learning to let go of the hope of certainty. Most real estate deal involve uncertainty and risk. If you are looking to avoid both, you won't close many deals. Finding a good deal is about finding a good return given the risk. Many of these cases include instructions from a boss to follow. You don't have to agree with your boss, but be mindful that it's easier to disagree if you've done a good job defending your position. And, explicitly or implicitly, there is always an imperative to understand and quantify risk, to determine whether risk can be mitigated against or potentially compensated for with high returns. This is the essence of these real estate cases, doing your best with incomplete data and insufficient time to get more. It means there no one right answer, just good and bad underwriting.

One final note on risk, which I've mentioned often without establishing how one might measure it. One common approach to assess it is sensitivity analysis, in which one variable is changed up and down by, say, 10% to assess impacts on returns. Early on I found sensitivity analysis to be good for identifying the most relevant assumptions, but wholly inadequate for assessing actual risk: in what state of the world do rents fall by 10% when concessions, vacancy, and cap rates stay fixed? I started experimenting with scenario analysis in which various narratives about the property and local fundamentals would lead to many variables changing that were consistent with the narrative. But it was Stan Iezman who helped me push this further—when I asked him how many scenarios he ran at his firm to assess risk, he answered, "As many as you need." Consider exploring an "optimistic" scenario and a "pessimistic" scenario for bidding on a grocery-anchored retail center in which the anchor is 2 years from the end of its lease. In the "optimistic" scenario, the anchor accepts market rents and stays; in the other, it leaves. If the probability of staying is 50/50, someone will average the two very disparate returns and call this the "expected" return. This might be appropriate if this identical deal could be repeated 1000 times. But, in reality we get only one outcome and it appears that this "expected" outcome isn't even among the two scenarios being underwritten. Another approach might explore a third scenario that offers discounts to market rent to ensure that the anchor stays. It could be arranged for ahead of bidding on the center and would mean greatly reducing the downside risk. Stan's advice should be kept in mind: if there are more uncertain issues that are relevant, then explore more scenarios. This is just an example of how students can start to see how to add value through embracing complexity and seeing it as an opportunity to underwrite well. Good luck.

Part I

Developing a Framework

One major theme for this book is that context matters for underwriting real estate. This is obvious, but can be difficult to fully grasp while focusing on the basics. The first five cases in this book include multifamily properties because I wanted to allow students to focus on developing their frameworks for underwriting while holding as much constant as possible. In these cases, the lease terms are not explicitly defined because they are so broadly standardized that 1-year leases are generally implied when month-to-month leases are not called out. This has several important implications for underwriting. The property must be retenanted every year so that changing fundamentals in the apartment market will constantly be transmitted into the value of the asset. This contrasts with longer-term commercial real estate leases, which can cause distortions between the leased value of a property from what short term fundamentals might otherwise suggest. The five cases in the next section focus on the multiple impacts of long-term commercial leases. Across the cases in this section there is more than enough variation to start developing a framework that would allow a common approach to underwriting.

Beginning with apartments is also helpful because many students are familiar with them. Other product types are introduced after students begin mastering other sources of variation. The cases in this section span metropolitan areas and the submarkets within them. They include old and new properties, institutional investors and first time entrepreneurs, as well as numerous different protagonists. The contrasts are instructive. In each of the cases there are ample opportunities to explore market analysis, model building, debt and equity options, and scenario analysis, with each challenging the students to grapple with a key strategic decision facing the protagonist. Across these cases, it will become abundantly clear that one-size-fits-all underwriting will lead to mistakes. As such, students will have to learn which valuation tool is most appropriate given the circumstances and given the questions being asked. This is what I mean by "framework": a systematic approach to underwriting that is rigorous but not formulaic. In some cases, quick and dirty valuations are best, being effective enough and inexpensive in terms of time and data. In other cases, full-blown pro formas will be required and employed in multiple scenarios in order to get a sense risks and opportunities. The first three cases are terrific examples of how professional real estate investment in multifamily can work in practice—an important point being that there is no one "best" way. I included the last two cases to stretch people's thinking about multifamily underwriting. The case in Detroit represented a novel and courageous bit of entrepreneurial inspiration that outperformed many other real estate investments over this horizon. Finally, the fifth case on "Little Data" was borne out of an undergraduate class and a simple offering memorandum. It started as a pro forma building exercise, but quickly spiraled out into a richer conversation about how to choose both the tools of valuation and the data used in them. While holding much constant, these five cases should help students build intuition as to how context matters and how it might influence their approaches to underwriting.

Case 1

Vista View and a Second Shot at Ownership

"I don't know. Maybe I'm just too attached to this one."

I. Voicemail

"Hi Gil. I just wanted to follow up with you about the Vista View property. We're going to be looking for a best and final offer of at least $57 million. But you saw how much interest there was and I expect the winning bid to be a bit more than that. Bids will be due next week sometime. I'll call later with details." This was how Gil Herron started his morning, and it was not a great way to start. He had already invested a significant amount of time underwriting this deal; he had even spent time building rapport with the broker. But he didn't even get a direct call from the broker with the news. Instead the broker had called his office phone, and called when he wouldn't be there. The message was clear: Gil may have made a good impression, but the winning bid would have to involve more than that. He would have to figure out if there was any room to improve his bid. And while this sort of price escalation was routine in later-cycle deals, getting to $57 million—or more—was going to be tough.

It was perhaps overly optimistic to think that the broker was calling him about being selected as the buyer after his last bid. But Gil had still hoped for this because he had more than just a deal riding on it. This deal—the Vista View Apartments—was the first he had brought to his new investment committee. Gil had been with Moorage Capital Partners for only a month. He had been hired by Moorage to help expand their footprint on the West Coast—actually, to make its first footprints: Moorage owned no units west of the Mississippi. Based in Boston, Moorage Capital Partners has owned between 20,000 and 40,000 apartment units at various points over the last decade—most of them along the eastern seaboard. Gil was one of two people who had opened the first West Coast office last month. The team had been given a seemingly simple dual mandate: to place capital and to make good risk-return investments. Since then he had combed through dozens of multifamily offering memoranda, but this was the first deal he had felt really good about. In fact, he was enthusiastic enough to write a brief memo about the property to members of the investment committee several weeks ago. The memo was met with the same enthusiasm, and he felt his

Underwriting Commercial Real Estate in a Dynamic Market. https://doi.org/10.1016/B978-0-12-815989-7.00001-X

start at Moorage was heading in the right direction. Unfortunately, the seller had been happy enough with the pool of bidders to push for a higher price.

Gil had been planning to tour three properties that afternoon in northern San Diego but rescheduled them. This morning he felt he really needed to see the Vista View property again, to review his underwriting, and to decide what he would do with Vista View: should he break the news that he and Moorage had not won the deal or suggest that Moorage would need to write a larger check so that it could remain in the running to acquire the Vista View Apartments? In either case, Gil knew he wouldn't be calling the East Coast at off times in hopes of finding his managing director's voicemail. It might be an awkward conversation, but it would be better to just do his homework today and be ready for whatever questions were coming his way when he did call the office in Boston. While he would need to be able to address the details, they had hired him so that he could answer one question in particular: "What investment would you recommend?"

II.   Moorage Capital Partners and Its New SVP

Moorage Capital Partners is a 25-year-old private equity firm that was born of the wreckage of Boston's housing bubble and bust in the late 1980s. The founding partners had been veterans of earlier real estate cycles and retained a great deal of confidence that the long-term fundamentals warranted continued investment. In the small world of real estate, the founding partners of Moorage had known each other for years, partnering or competing over numerous real estate deals in New England. All of them had seen cycles before and saw that the downturn was the right time to buy. But in 1991 each of their own firms had decided to slow their acquisitions until there were more obvious signs of strength. They had been frustrated having to watch good real estate trade at what they felt were below their "true" value. So they left their respective firms and formed Moorage Capital Partners to act on these beliefs.

Raising capital for a new firm in a downturn was a challenge, so they developed an approach that could be described as "solid investments in stormy seas." The firm's name followed the business plan: a mooring is a safe place to anchor a ship, and Moorage was able to raise funds by acquiring well-located apartment buildings that were largely occupied. These investments were marketed as "shelters from the storm" because they had demonstrated a durable history of high occupancy. What had been marketed as a defensive strategy proved to be quite successful when the recovery brought both higher rents and higher asset values. Happy with their results, Moorage and their partners began to reinvest their returns back into more multifamily properties.

Twenty-five years from that start, Moorage Capital has replicated this strategy through every cycle. They sell assets when they feel prices are high enough, but otherwise remain interested in holding good assets for the longer-term. While they have expanded to units along the eastern seaboard and select submarkets inland, the same conservative mindset kept them from heading west. But for so many reasons, this year senior management has finally decided to test the waters of the West Coast. Gil was one of two people hired to run Moorage's new office in Los Angeles. Moorage Capital is a firm that few brokers will know west of the Rockies, but one that has an exceptional reputation among national lenders and a lot of expertise with operating apartments. While they would be new players to these markets, Moorage would not be seen as rookies.

To help understand both local markets and players, Gil Herron has been hired as the senior vice president of acquisitions for the West Coast office. With only two people in the office, titles are largely ceremonial as each of them do whatever is needed to find potential acquisitions. This means reading through lots of offering memoranda, setting priorities among them, and spending a lot of time trying to understand the properties and the fundamentals that support their valuations.

Gil had worked for an investment bank throughout the housing bubble and bust. He was one the few who kept his job during the downturn because he had embraced taking on numerous roles, one of which was handling the real estate assets it owned. It was then that he realized just how thinly financial markets had understood real estate. During the recovery, many of his peers moved away from real estate as it had become an impaired asset class, but Gil found the ground-level stories about individual assets much more compelling than the high-level approach he'd taken to real estate while at the bank. With the financial sector remaining a challenge, he took a risk and found a job with a top-50 apartment owner. While he'd only taken a single real estate principles class in school, he got a rich education in the first years of the recovery. Early on every valuation was up for grabs; all the certainty that had been part of the bubble was gone. Gil was still learning how to underwrite individual apartment properties, but then so too was everyone else during the recovery.

Gil had enjoyed his time with his previous firm. But its senior management team was well-established and it could be a generation before he had the chance to play more senior role. When Moorage Capital inquired about his interest in building something new, he jumped at the opportunity.

A full month into his new job, the adrenaline had not worn off. He was very excited about building a presence on the West Coast. As part of his interview with Moorage, he had emphasized both his real estate skills and reputation, but he also sold them on the opportunities for investment on the West Coast. To many it now felt late in the real estate cycle, and multifamily deals felt relatively expensive but he still thought the western half of the United States and the key metropolitan areas within it would continue to outperform. He had spent time at school on the East Coast and had grown to understand its attraction, but he was from Los Angeles and simply saw the future as brighter here. He certainly had been enthusiastic about the opportunities at the Vista View Apartments when the price had been at $54 million. At $57 million—or maybe even more—he was less excited.

III.   Vista View and Local Fundamentals

The Vista View Apartments are in Mission Viejo, California. Located in Orange County, this vibrant submarket has long since shed its earlier reputation as a bedroom community for Los Angeles. Indeed, where once the majority of real estate in Orange County was residential, providing housing for commuters to the major employer to the north, a significant motivation for this investment is the fact that now there isn't enough housing for the employees who have come to Orange County for jobs here. While Orange County benefits from being part of the most vibrant metropolitan areas in the United States, its local economy has evolved into a unique and thriving submarket unto itself. The Orange County office market now has over 1.6 million employees and an unemployment rate of less than 3.5%. The Orange County office market stands at approximately 100,000,000 sf and is growing. Near the Vista View Apartments, the Irvine Spectrum and surrounding South County office markets total close to 20,000,000 sf and vacancy here has fallen to below 8%.

One of the constraining factors to this growth is the cost of housing, which has been rising well above rates of inflation in recent years. In fact, prices and rents now surpass the peak pricing of the housing bubble years in 2006 and 2007. This is impressive given the size of the downfall then, when unemployment rose past 10% and office vacancy was approximately 25%. Orange County had been one of the primary centers for the subprime mortgage industry, which had been devastated with the housing bust. There was pain from 2008 to 2010 as deals unwound, development stopped, and extend-and-pretend was a dominant strategy for many owners.

Orange County has since found other economic engines and has succeeded in bringing jobs and incomes back to the region. The County now hosts some of the largest names in tech, design, automotive, and biotech, among other industries. The attractive weather, high-quality schools, ample open space, and diversity of amenities can equate to an extraordinary quality of life if one can find housing at a reasonable cost. For a variety of reasons, state and local policies have left the state underhoused for decades. This has allowed owners of housing to charge ever-increasing rates; those with particularly good locations have been able to charge much more. And while there has been some development and redevelopment, it has been mild relative to a typical recovery in which housing leads the economy back. Certainly housing supply has not kept up with to the economic growth in the region. There have been numerous efforts at "solving the housing crisis," but these aren't serious and are unlikely to lead to a strong housing supply response that might be a source of falling rents in the foreseeable future. Gil could only find two similar projects in the surrounding area built in the past 20 years. To him, the primary risk in investing in Vista View is overpaying for it.

Beyond the larger fundamentals at work in the region, there are plenty of additional reasons to believe that bidding will be aggressive. Vista View is located in a strong submarket with regard to demographics, and there are few apartment complexes nearby. In some of Moorage's east coast markets, single family homes have been a serious competitor to apartment owners. This is something the investment committee will want to know about. However, median household annual incomes here are approximately $100,000 (higher than the Orange county median of $78,000), but houses around the Vista View apartment nearby averaging prices of about $900,000. Gil would need to run the numbers but thought there is good reason to assume that no new direct competitors will arrive soon even if rents rise. Importantly, the Vista View Apartments are largely designed as townhomes and are likely to attract households that aspire to own in the same neighborhood at some point. Indeed, all of the two- and three-bedroom units are townhome style with two car direct access garages; the one-bedroom units are flats that have either direct access or detached garages in each unit. While a little dated, these units are not the generic boxes typical of earlier housing booms.

Despite the high pricing for the Vista View property, the broker had marketed it as a value-add deal. His pitch rested largely on the interiors of the units, which are mostly original with laminate countertops. Some of the units have stainless steel appliances, but most of the units still retain the legacy of what was trendy when they were built in 2002.

IV. Options

The broker had been smart to market the property as a value-add deal. While inflation showed some signs of picking up, treasuries remained quite low and there is a lot of capital looking for safe assets that could earn a reasonable spread over them. The broker had also been smart about being vague as to what "value-add" would mean. He would, of course, want as many bidders as possible to "see the dream." He had been right to be vague because this would allow all the prospective bidders to find their own optimism about what constituted a successful and optimal renovation program.

The broker provided his own underwriting of the cash flows and, not surprisingly, Gil found hopeful assumptions in key places in the broker's pro forma. Gil started with the broker's numbers but then considered assumptions he thought more realistic, refining his own model as he went. The broker had baked in some optimism looking forward, but mostly created an attractive cash flow by rolling forward some of the favorable trailing numbers from the property's cash flows over the past months. At the same time, there might be some reason to be optimistic: both Gil's sense of the market and the rent comparables suggested there was room to push rents higher. Once Gil had built his estimated current cash flows, he did not even download the rest of the broker's pro forma numbers, preferring to work from his own assumptions about rent growth, vacancy, and operating expenses.

Moorage Capital had a long track record of such renovations but they were entirely based on properties thousands of miles away. While they understood the principle of it, they knew that the cost-benefit economics must be local. That's why they hired Gil—they would be looking to him to put together a business plan for the renovation. Gil assumed that he would have to renovate 85% of the units at an average cost of $8700 per unit. He also intended to invest funds in modernizing the common areas and landscaping. There had been a significant swing toward interest in and use of shared space in last 10 years as key amenities for residents. At Vista View, the current common areas were tired and seem to be wholly unused. The total cost for the renovations of the units and common areas came out to $10,700 per unit. Gil thought he could get through the renovations over the course of 2 years.

The outcome of these renovations would be an updated and current property in a great location. Gil thought he was being conservative in assuming that the blended average of renovated units would earn a premium of 15% over the blended average of the current rents. And from there Gil expected high occupancy and relatively robust rent growth. But because of Moorage's conservative approach, Gil used the rent growth forecast he had been given by a local market analysis firm. Moorage wanted a good return, but more than that they wanted to buy a piece of property that would outperform when the market turned down. With the renovation, the Vista View Apartments would be the best product in the submarket while charging a rent that Gil thought was more than fair given the amenities both inside and outside the units.

Along with solid underwriting, Moorage avoided using too much debt. Gil had an ongoing relationship with a lender who would be happy to provide up to 60% of the total costs of the acquisition and renovations. In exchange, the lender would charge a 1% origination fee and offer a 7-year fixed 4.25% annual interest rate loan. As with many standard loans, it would amortize over 30 years but be due at the end of 7 years. The lender required a minimum debt service coverage ratio of 1.25 throughout the loan term.

At $54M, Gil thought this standard loan would have been a good fit: relatively low cost, relatively long term, low risk from inflation, and no recourse. At a bid of $57 million, it would mean lowering already thin equity returns. Gil wanted to explore a way to use more debt to keep the equity returns a bit higher. At his previous firm, they had begun using a GSE (government sponsored enterprise) loan program that would allow both a higher LTV, a lower DSCR, and possibly a longer amortization period.

The GSE loan program was designed to encourage reinvestment in existing assets. To qualify for the program, an owner needed to invest no less than $10,000 per unit. There were more rules, of course, but Gil wanted to know first if the program's economics would be helpful before digging deeper into the other terms. For now he assumed that the GSE program offered up to 90% of the stabilized value of the property, a stabilized DSCR of no less than 1.15, and a 35-year amortization period. Gil underwrote the hold period as 7 years, but with Moorage's inclination to hold good real estate for longer terms, the GSE's option for loans up to 35 years could also be important. While the interest rate was marginally lower at 4.20% per year, it was the other terms that compelled Gil to spend some time considering it as a debt option.

Beyond the standard rent, vacancy, OpEx assumptions, and the decision to pursue the GSE loan program option, Gil would also have to argue that their expected returns would be fair relative to the risk to their equity investment. At the higher asking price, Gil would be nervous. He would have to run the numbers, of course. Maybe he had set his price expectations about buying apartment buildings during recovery when asset prices were much lower. And maybe there was, in fact, that much more demand out there, and that $57 million (or more) could prove a fair price to pay.

While trying to get comfortable with the new pricing, an idea came to Gil about a different approach to investing in Vista View. Gil thought the price might be too high to own the property outright. However, he had recalled his mandate to make good risk return investments. He wanted to own this property, but didn't want to overpay. What if Moorage became an equity partner in the firms that were willing to meet the new higher asking price? He knew two of the other firms who would likely to make final and best offers. Gil wondered if it would be best to contact one of them and offer mezzanine finance to them. That is, Moorage could become a senior equity partner rather than the sole owner of Vista View. The advantage to the prospective sponsor, of course, would be likely lower cost capital and thus a better return on their equity. The advantage to Moorage was a good coupon and very low risk. If the world did blow up, asset prices fell, and Moorage ended up becoming the owner of the property, they would essentially be acquiring Vista View at a price at which they would be happy to own it for the long-term. If there were no downturn, Moorage would be paid a healthy return on its investment.

This would require some phone calls both to the Boston office and to some people here in Southern California, but Gil thought he would start by proposing to contribute 50% of the equity in exchange for a preferred return of 8% with a return of the initial capital investment at the end of 7 years. In this structure there would be no upside, no promoted return, but it would satisfy the dual mandate and allow Gil to notch his first deal with Moorage. Gil canceled his morning tours in San Diego so that he would have enough time to rebuild his pro formas, check his returns, and think about his options. Then he would send an email to his managing director in Boston and set up a phone call for the morning to make sure he could lay out his thought process and provide some guidance.

V.   Deliverables

Like most real estate deals, this will likely be an iterative process to underwrite the Vista View apartments. It would take some time and thought to wade through the implications of each assumption on the others. If Gil was willing to push rents higher in his underwriting, he certainly could create more theoretical value on paper. The same could be said of assuming lower operating expenses or reserves, using a lower exit-cap rate, or imposing more debt at lower rates. Moorage Capital had plenty of analysts on the East Coast who could create fantasy numbers as well. Gil's role here is not to be an oracle, but rather to provide a good sense of risk and return based on the various options he wanted to bring back to the investment committee. Both Gil and the investment committee wanted this deal to work, but it was getting hard to be objective. He thought to himself, "I don't know. Maybe I'm just too attached to this one." This can be dangerous and lead to fantasy underwriting, but can also lead to a deeper look at value when others walk away. To be sure, Gil would be asked by the investment committee if it was time to move on. If not, then why hadn't he been more aggressive in his underwriting before? Was there still a good value at the higher bid? Was there another way to earn a good return while still being in the equity slice of the capital stack?

VI.   Questions/Issues to Explore

a. Why has Moorage decided to "head west"? Why locate in Los Angeles? Why now? Is the dual mandate enough guidance for Gil? How would he answer these questions, if it had Gil heading west on his own to start his own multifamily business, without Moorage's track record?

b. What are the big fundamentals that shape the apartment business? How would you summarize Moorage's business plan with this effort with Gil and his colleague in the new office in Los Angeles? Gil seems to be spending a lot of time traveling to tour apartments. Is the plan a tactical one, to find bargains? Or is it a strategic one based on broader and longer-term trends?

c. Gil has accumulated a fair amount of data in this underwriting of Vista View. Is there a good way to inform his decision-making using any of the numbers in a "quick and dirty" fashion? It takes time to build a discounted cash flow. Is there a short way to value Vista View? Do your best and estimate the value of the property without building a discounted cash flow model and explain your assumptions. Note that between the broker and Gil, there are a variety of numbers that seem to suggest there is uncertainty about even lagged numbers. We know there will be forecast errors, but there seem to be different ways of looking back at the part performance at Vista View. What is the "right" way to interpret the cash flow numbers in the "Trailing Data/ Year 1 Pro Forma Numbers" below?

d. Build a pro forma for a 7-year holding period. Using Gil's numbers, what are the estimated unlevered IRR and unlevered equity multiple? Again, be clear about which numbers you choose and why. Is there a material difference in terms of these return numbers if you use different starting numbers from the cash flow tables below? Do your best to choose the most defensible numbers and annotate your choice.

e. Are these returns "good enough" given the risks? What are the primary risks faced at the Vista View property? Is there another property or investment that you think offers a better risk return trade-off? What should the unlevered return be? What price can you pay for Vista View to hit this number?

f. How should Gil underwrite the renovations? That is, Gil will need to have vacant units in order to undertake the renovations. How should Gil account for the renovation costs and subsequently higher rents in the future? Clearly there can be many levels of precision regarding the schedule; does it matter whether this timeline is monthly, quarterly, or even annually?

g. Clearly Gil's assumptions both about the market rent and its future growth rates after the renovations are guesses, but this is true of every multifamily deal. Do you think Gil made good assumptions given information he has? What do you make of the rent forecast he makes? Should he use the third-party rent forecasts he has be given? And, given all the assumptions Gil has had to make in putting together his business plan and pro forma, how robust do you think his expected returns are to these assumptions? Are there any variables that are highly influential of the unlevered return?

h. Should Gil make use of the GSE loan program? What are its strengths and weaknesses? To be sure, there will be more research needed on the specifics of the program, especially eligibility. But, do the economics of the loan suggest doing this additional research?

i. Given the risk-return trade-offs associated with paying the higher price to become the owner of the Vista View property, what do you make of Gil's idea to offer mezzanine debt? Would you want to try something novel like this for your first deal with your new firm?

j. Or, should Moorage seek out a mezzanine equity provider so that Moorage can be the sponsor/owner?

k. Recall the dual mandate Gil received. Then understand that he may be nervous about suggesting that Moorage meets the higher price, but his mandate also requires him to place capital. Having gone this far, should he press ahead? Should Moorage say yes to the higher price?

l. In making your recommendation, what are the three most significant risks Moorage faces? Can you mitigate them? If not, do you think the expected return is high enough to compensate Moorage for the risk?

Please compose a brief and articulate memo to communicate your suggested plans. Please include any relevant exhibits you think support your memo. You may need to make some assumptions of your own. Do so as needed, but explain and annotate them.

Vista View Rent Roll.

Unit type	Bedrooms	Bathrooms	Number of units	Size sf	Total size sf	Current rent	Broker pro forma rent
1a	1	1	18	674	12,132	1,692	1,824
1b	1	1	14	712	9,968	1,691	1,840
1c	1	1	19	755	14,345	1,703	1,854
2a	2	2.5	27	1,190	32,130	2,241	2,539
2b	2	2.5	43	1,325	56,975	2,314	2,650
3a	3	2.5	27	1,400	37,800	2,611	3,021
Totals			148		163,350		
Averages				1,104		$2,142	$2,418

Rent comparables

Property	Year built	Units	Avg size	Avg rent	Rent/SF	Occupancy
Los Alisos	2014	320	831	$2,081	$2.50	96%
Siena Terrace	1988	356	824	$1,876	$2.28	96%
Madrid	2001	230	940	$2,093	$2.23	96%
Avalon Baker Ranch	2015	430	988	$2,407	$2.44	94%
Shadow Oaks	2001	210	1,252	$2,983	$2.38	96%
Total/Average	2004	1,546	946	$2,249	$2.38	
Vista View Apartments	*2002*	*148*	*1,104*	*$2,355*	*$2.13*	

Sales comparables

Property	Year built	Sale date	Units	Price	Price/unit	Avg size	Price/SF
Madrid	2001	Sep-17	230	83,000,000	360,870	992	364
Amerige Pointe	2005	Sep-16	292	115,000,000	393,836	978	403
Elan Overlook Laguna	1989	Jul-16	100	41,100,000	411,000	1,025	401
Elan Huntington Beach	2015	Jul-16	274	131,000,000	478,102	900	531
Total/Average	2003		224	92,525,000	410,952	974	

Summary of Bid Assumptions.

Acquisition	
Price	57,000,000
Number of units	148
Year built	2002
Gross rental area	163,350
Closing costs	$500,000
Initial capital expenditures (per unit)	$10,700
Moorage acquisition fee (% of price)	1.00%
Management fees (% of total income)	2.75%
Tax inputs	
Millage rate (on purchase price)	1.06%
Property tax rate growth (per year)	2.00%
Assessed land value	$21,844,017
Assessed building value	$35,155,983
Disposition	
Exit cap rate	4.50%
Cost of sales (on sale price)	3.00%
Loan terms	
Loan to value	57.50%
Amortization period (years)	30
Annual interest rate	4.25%
Loan term (years)	7
Minimum debt service coverage	1.25
Origination fee (on loan amount)	0.75%

Trailing Data/Year 1 Pro Forma Numbers.

	Trailing 3 months	Trailing 12 month	Moorage year 1 pro forma	Broker's year 1 pro forma
Gross potential income	4,250,330	3,673,344	4,374,587	4,552,418
Economic loss				
Vacancy	(211,465)	(280,943)	(217,626)	(232,848)
Loss to lease	(160,684)	(130,585)	(147,233)	–
Loss to concessions	(16,880)	(10,976)	–	–
Office/model units	–	–	(12,994)	(35,549)
Employee units	(35,504)	(33,207)	(15,159)	–
Bad debt	2,469	1,504	(21,223)	–
Total economic loss	(422,063)	(454,207)	(414,235)	(268,397)
Total rental income	3,828,267	3,219,137	3,960,351	4,284,021
Ancillary income	16,966	14,212	14,932	–
Garage/storage income	8,964	7,176	7,467	7,323
Utility income	119,020	117,493	119,819	115,167
Other income	97,404	79,160	81,535	93,160
Total other income	242,354	218,041	223,753	215,649
Total income	4,070,621	3,437,178	4,184,104	4,499,670

	Trailing 3 months	Trailing 12 month	Moorage year 1 pro forma	Broker's year 1 pro forma
Operating expenses				
Real estate taxes		444,928	604,200	604,200
Property insurance		53,066	68,849	43,935
Utilities		141,270	146,978	137,133
Management fees		79,453	124,156	91,205
Variable expenses				
Administrative		62,697	49,735	53,831
Landscaping		44,585	47,314	44,370
Leasing & advertising		32,535	33,511	35,888
Payroll		310,629	305,662	319,692
Repairs & maintenance		104,837	62,858	58,000
Security		3,653	3,687	3,580
Unit turnover expense		43,730	40,912	43,500
Total variable expenses		602,665	543,679	558,861
Replacement reserves		43,065	42,630	35,525
Total operating expenses		1,364,447	1,530,492	1,470,858
Net operating income		2,072,732	2,653,612	3,028,812

Area Apartment Forecast.

Period	Annualized rent growth	Changes in area occupancy
1Q18	3.51%	−0.08%
2Q18	1.57%	−0.69%
3Q18	1.79%	−0.14%
4Q18	2.95%	0.36%
1Q19	2.91%	0.03%
2Q19	3.31%	0.20%
3Q19	3.81%	0.60%
4Q19	3.91%	0.50%
1Q20	3.31%	0.00%
2Q20	2.91%	−0.4%
3Q20	2.31%	−0.8%
4Q20	2.11%	−0.7%
1Q21	2.71%	−0.4%
2Q21	3.21%	0.20%
3Q21	3.41%	0.60%
4Q21	3.21%	0.50%
1Q22	2.91%	0.20%
2Q22	2.41%	−0.5%
3Q22	2.11%	−0.8%
4Q22	2.41%	−0.9%

Case 2

Altitude and Perspective: Let the Fund Guide Investment?

30,000 feet may be the right altitude to see the bigger picture, but down here I'd invest differently.

I. Mapmaker and Finding New Territory

Final bids for both properties would be due next week. Gail Hideki hoped that winning one of the two auctions would end this chapter of Mapmaker's Fund IX. Even if she wanted to, she wouldn't be allowed to submit aggressive bids for both, so she needed to pick the one she thought would win and still allow Mapmaker to hit its returns. Three months ago, the fund manager had asked Gail to target good multifamily properties in the Washington, DC metropolitan area. Gail had been working with the Fund IX manager for long enough to know the written and unwritten rules for buying apartments, so as she looked at close to 60 offering memoranda she immediately eliminated half of them because they didn't meet some basic fund selection: too small, too large, too old, too ugly, etc. Mapmaker Real Estate was now in its ninth fund and all nine had focused on value-add investment, but each with a slightly different business plan in mind. For each, raising the fund was an iterative process that involved many conversations with many potential investors while at the same time being mindful of other market opportunities. Of course, at the heart of these conversations with the new investors was a general sense of expected returns and the types of risks a fund strategy would expose investors to. But these had been challenging conversations for more than a decade.

When Mapmaker formed in 1997, it had marketed itself as a firm that would out-perform and out-execute. A common thread among the senior management was that all of them had spent time earlier in their careers in property management, asset management, and acquisitions. Management was a grind, but they had all seen the rewards from paying attention to the day-to-day business of owning apartments. This had been a key part of what they saw as a strategic advantage: they knew how to buy a good building because they could anticipate how it would perform, and they would keep rethinking how the building was positioned relative to its submarket. While this "blocking-and-tackling" approach

Underwriting Commercial Real Estate in a Dynamic Market. https://doi.org/10.1016/B978-0-12-815989-7.00002-1

19

to apartments was how Mapmaker thought it would be branded, it also developed a reputation as smart, maybe even a step ahead of the market.

But internally, the surprisingly high returns from the first two funds were a bit mysterious. While Mapmaker had executed on its plans, the returns were far better than just from what might be expected from working hard. It retrospect, interest rates had continued to fall, making debt cheap and exit cap rates lower than they had assumed. Mapmaker had an easy time raising their third fund in 2001, but return expectations for the fund were higher. Come late 2006, they felt lucky that they had been able to get approval to sell most of the Fund III assets as the bubble crested. The last two properties they held onto by accident. They were not best-in-class properties, but had been cash cows and Mapmaker had held out for higher pricing. But waiting took them into the downturn and both deals fell out of escrow in late 2007. Both properties held up very well: rent growth stopped, but occupancy stayed close to 100%. Their investors and lenders were thrilled to have something good in their portfolios, earning solid yields. Despite this, Mapmaker continued to hunt for a buyer but could not find a decent price through 2008. Capital markets had just been too spooked by real estate as an asset class. This experience would shape how Mapmaker changed its strategy in the years ahead.

The market's changing perception of risk and in the pricing of risk revealed something important to Mapmaker's senior management. It began to think more deeply about capital markets as a primary driver of asset values. Mapmaker had traditionally approached a deal by thinking first about local fundamentals and meeting tenants' needs. Their belief was that if they found a good real estate deal, then capital would follow. But in the recovery, Mapmaker thought it had discovered that it might be maybe as important to think about capital markets' needs first. In 2009, capital needed safety.

As the real estate market and larger economy fell apart in 2008, capital scrambled to find safe havens. The 10-year US Treasury rate fell from just over 5% in the summer of 2007 to less than 3.5% a year later. By the end of 2008, it had fallen to almost 2%. The price of these safe havens had skyrocketed. At the same time REIT yields rose dramatically. Real estate had been at the center of bust and prices had plunged broadly. But the last two properties of Fund III continued to pay rent; NOI actually increased as some of their expenses declined. It seemed to Mapmaker could provide investors an alternative to low interest treasury bonds.

What Mapmaker saw in its firm was the ability to produce safe assets. It had an excellent track record in owning and operating high performing apartment buildings. As investors got more confident that the bust had hit bottom, they began looking beyond treasuries and would become grateful for the safety and additional yield of apartment investments. Mapmaker had finished raising capital for its Fund IV, but had held off from investing in 2007 and 2008. In 2009, Mapmaker executed its thesis that the best apartments were almost as safe as government bonds, but were not priced that way. They bought core assets in core markets and simply held them, proving rents and occupancy. Markets quickly bought into these properties as solid investments to earn yields that were significantly better than treasuries, but without much more risk. Lenders were slow to agree and Mapmaker had to put up significantly more equity in each of the Fund IV deals. While Mapmaker did little to change the physical assets, it still saw itself as a value-add firm. In the case of Fund IV, it viewed senior management's willingness to put their own equity in to close deals as their value add: "More than anything, these are great assets. We're going to help them be seen as such."

Funds V and VI focused on more traditional light value-add acquisitions, buying intrinsically high-quality properties that had been managed badly during the downturn. The "value" that was added in these funds addressed some minors renovations, but mostly getting rents to back to market and operating the properties professionally. There had been ample opportunities by 2010 to find good buildings in great locations that had owners who—while caught up with other distractions—were ignoring the tenants and units, or owners who had insufficient capital to address either. Mapmaker was able to acquire a sizeable portfolio of these properties.

As the market believed the bottom had passed, and as they saw the relatively high and stable cash flows in these lightly renovated and professionally managed apartment properties, the risk premium associated with them fell. Each of these three funds experienced both higher than pro forma rents and lower than pro forma exit cap rates. These funds were home runs for Mapmaker. In Funds VII and VIII, the same basic investment theses was applied, but now Mapmaker had assumed it could find marginal assets that could be repositioned to safe assets in secondary and, in some cases, tertiary markets. Mapmaker had been among the early movers into gentrifying neighborhoods: Williamsburg after Brooklyn was too expensive, Ballard after Downtown Seattle was too pricey, and the Navy Yard after pension fund advisors became comfortable investing in Washington, DC's once-marginal neighborhoods. Beyond these famous examples, Mapmaker had also found good properties in Nashville, Denver, Austin, and Raleigh—decidedly not gateway cities, but each with a solid investment thesis about urbanizing and improving neighborhoods.

In relatively short order, the market responded to the same changing geography of fundamentals that had worked to Mapmaker's benefit, and it became harder for it to find any bargains in core markets. So in Fund VII, Mapmaker found new territory in either Class B buildings in Class A locations or Class A buildings in Class B locations. And in Fund VIII, it pursued properties that were both physically and locationally Class B or B-. In both funds, acquisitions were internally thought to be purchased at bargains because the market remained overly concerned about risk. Mapmaker continued to attract investors because of Mapmaker's return record and because its continued investment thesis of "building safe assets in world that has a shortage of them" struck investors as the right strategy. Even through today, their investors, like Mapmaker, felt that the recovery would deepen and an urbanizing America would be looking for more upgraded apartments in improving neighborhoods.

II.   An Evolving Investment Thesis for Fund IX

Mapmaker has now fully invested Fund VII and VIII and the investors were eager for more—hence Fund IX. Once more Mapmaker began conversations with potential investors about the new fund's business plan and about types of properties and returns that could be expected now that the real estate cycle was maturing. Given Mapmaker's track record, it had great leeway as to which opportunities to pursue. It could, for instance, return to buying core assets which remained in demand, but were now perhaps "priced to perfection." Indeed, Gail was more worried about overpaying for a core asset than she would be about any the value-add or core-plus deals in her final 10 OMs she had found in and around Washington, DC. At current core prices, she thought there was only downside for equity holders. While she didn't foresee any large correction and widespread foreclosure, it was getting harder to see how much rent growth could realistically be assumed. And it was also clear than it would be a mistake to assume that yields and spreads could fall much more, if at all.

Mapmaker Real Estate would not undertake ground-up construction and the investors were largely not ready to embrace what was being called "opportunistic" real estate. So the broad categories left were core-plus and value-add. These had always been a moving target, but now it felt late in the cycle and offerings with these labels had begun to fray further. It seemed that the number of core assets had grown dramatically during this recovery. Cap rates below 4% could be found in lots of places where they certainly were not in 2009, and more importantly, the spread between similar assets in these locations relative to prime locations had closed significantly. In 2009, "core" meant the highest quality buildings in the best neighborhoods and in only a handful of gateway cities. All these buildings would have been considered Class A and all of them would have performed well throughout the downturn. These kind of properties had "bulletproof" cash flow stories to go with them that resulted in the low cap rates. But as the recovery took hold, the definition shifted so that properties that used to be considered "core plus" were being priced a bit more aggressively and approaching core pricing. Even some neighborhoods that were seen as so risky early on they had been labeled (and priced) as "opportunistic" were getting closer to core-plus pricing. The shifting definition of these properties had pronounced implications for returns.

In this regard, Gail had adopted some thinking and language from school. One of her professors had been particularly hard on some capital providers as being too attached to "their boxes." He was referring to a conceptual box that included those properties that defined what was worthy of investment and what was not. His favorite example was the use of Millennials to justify investments. He had found many investors appealed to them to buy apartments that were too small, underparked, and still were expected to yield high rents. After all, they would say: "Millennials didn't need a car because they would use ride-sharing; they didn't need a living room because they'd be happy hanging out in

Starbucks, and they wouldn't ever own a home because they were comfortable renting in the heart of the city." So, if there was evidence of a growth in this demographic around a property, the "Millennial box" got checked, and that allow investment committees to sign off on new projects. Now with rents softening in some downtowns now despite more Millennials living there than ever; he would say: "What do you know? It turns out that both demand AND supply matters as well."

On the other hand, Gail's professor had also told a story of a veteran developer being unable to find funding for an entitled hotel parcel in coastal California in 2010. He would repeat the developer's story: "I was told everywhere I looked that hotels are an 'impaired' asset class. I couldn't get a dime." Had the developer been able to close that deal and build the hotel, he would have been able "to buy for an all-in return on cost of 10 percent!" and "…be selling a seasoned, gem of a hotel at a 5 percent cap rate!" While hotels were doing badly at that time, the land was already entitled, the location was an obvious long-term draw, and the low basis suggested a solid return even if things went sideways for years. Despite a strong case for investment, the hotel was not in capital providers "box." Gail's professor would run on about how real estate to was too heterogeneous to use such simple rules. Their "boxes" meant good assets got punished because they'd been lumped in bad asset classes.

But for Gail, this explained what might have contributed to Mapmaker's extra-normal returns. When the "box" shifted, expanding to allow institutional capital to invest in a previously impaired real estate segment or submarket, cap rates would fall—and they had fallen significantly across five of Mapmaker's funds. Gail's firm had been buying apartments in properties or locations that were just outside the "box" of institutional capital. They would then renovate in anticipation of the change in capital flows into the newly expanded "box".

This strategy was successful enough to create competitors who would attempt to replicate it. In the short term, this both validated Mapmaker and improved returns. But all those renovated units and an increasingly busy development pipeline was creating a lot of new supply. Gail recognized that "a lot" was a relative term and it didn't really mean that housing had been overbuilt in aggregate, but rather that a handful of submarkets were seeing many more units. The problem for Mapmaker was that much of the new supply was occurring in the same submarkets they'd been eager to enter. Gail had visited the West Coast recently and had seen cranes all over the downtowns of Los Angeles and San Francisco, but both places continued to experience housing shortages.

After some discussion, the fund manager had secured commitment from investors by articulating a strategy that would find value-add targets in "primary and key secondary markets that offered good risk adjusted risk-return investments." Gail thought this was marketing-speak for continuing what it had been doing, but being willing to accept a lower return. The fund manager disagreed, arguing that there were more opportunities for value-add and that because of their expertise and experience, Mapmaker would be able to find them and be able to pay more because they could mitigate risks and control costs the way others would not be able to. In any case, her fund manager was expecting "mid- to high-teen" levered IRRs over a 7-year hold after acquisition. Gail was less sure that would be possible without taking on more risk.

III.   The Debate

Well through the Fund IX investment window, Gail has been tasked with executing on the plan: finding a deal in greater Washington, DC that would follow the fund strategy and still earn the expected return. Gail had found 10 properties that were close worthy of her attention, and ran some basic numbers with the fund manager. She and Gail shared an evolving approach to finding a bargain. The two of them quickly became focused on a pair of assets that would offer enough obvious challenges to keep the number of bidders on the lower side. Their basic approach was identifying enough complexity or enough hair in the deal to shake off the crowds. It meant that there were opportunities to earn an extra normal return from effort and good thinking. While they agreed which properties were the two finalists, they did not agree on which one to pursue. Looking for some way to tilt the argument her way, Gail emailed the senior analysts and junior VPs she knew at Mapmaker:

> *Here is a situation that I'm working on right now in real time. Two deals in DC. One is a 1990 vintage deal in Arlington that's in a killer location and an awesome physical asset. However, there's been a lot of supply in DC and so there has been very little rent growth over the past few years. It's a sub 5% cap rate and appears to be an obvious value-add candidate based on the finishes of the units. There is a decent rent gap vs. the comps, but the comps are all 15 years newer and high rises with beautiful finishes. So, it's tough to say just how much upside there really is. You'd also have to spend $11,000 per unit on the property in capital just to make the property competitive, so there's a lot of execution risk. But from 30,000 feet this one seems to meet our investment thesis. On the flip side, we are looking at a deal in Wellington, VA which is a working class suburb 45mins-1 hour from DC. This deal is a mid-6 % cap tax credit deal that rents only to tenants who make no more than 60% of the area median income. The rents are at the maximum allowable so there is no repositioning. You'd have to spend almost nothing in capital to reposition the asset and clip a monster coupon once you put full leverage on it for doing basically nothing. Also, the tax credit restrictions burn off in 15 years so you'll get some benefit on the back end when you go to sell it. The area median income in this submarket is projected to grow 2.8%, which is decent. Down on the ground this one looks like a better return. It just seems to be a bit of a stretch with regards to the acquisition criteria. I'm not sure either of the deals clearly meet our written rules, but the unwritten thesis was to make good risk/return investments for the fund. I'm stuck here.*

Gail knew which way she was leaning, but was sure the fund manager was going to instruct her to pursue the other.

IV. Deliverables

You were one of those to receive Gail's email, along with her summary notes and exhibits. How do you respond? Which deal was Gail leaning toward? Why? On what basis did Gail assume that the fund manager would push back? Recognizing that Gail had cc'd the fund manager in the same email she sent you, would you change your response? To be sure, there were several levels of analysis you could pursue. The fund manager may follow up with specific instructions, but be sure to respond with your thoughts and some thoughtful underwriting. If you're looking to impress your bosses, you might want to provide something detailed.

V. Gail's Notes

The Arlington

The Arlington (the "Property") is a 376-unit, 367,352 sf multifamily rental property built 25 plus years ago in Arlington, Virginia. The property has been institutionally maintained since opening but has not undergone any significant upgrades since construction. As such, the property offers a new owner the opportunity to increase value through the renovation of unit interiors, reconfiguring the amenities spaces and reclaiming office space currently used for the ownership's regional offices. Walkable to numerous shops, restaurants and entertainment, the Property presents an urban environment just a 5- to 10-min commute from the Pentagon and the District of Columbia, respectively. The DC market has remained robust since the economic downturn and shows little signs of slowing down.

Physically, much of the Property's amenities and features are showing signs of becoming obsolete. Kitchens feature black appliances and Formica countertops in a submarket where most competing property have granite and stainless-steel appliances, among other upgrades. The current ownership operates its main offices from the second level of the clubhouse, presenting the opportunity to reposition that space for community amenities.

The Property's community room, adjacent to the fitness center, can be reconfigured into a more dynamic community area or combined with the fitness facilities, while an underutilized racquetball court adjacent to the fitness center can be reclaimed and incorporated into a revamped fitness center. The numerous courtyards throughout the property could be improved with the addition of grills and outdoor furnishings.

By comparison, newer apartment communities in the area command considerably higher rents than the Property, so it is possible that renovation and redesign may close some of this gap. However, its dated structure and general layout cannot be mitigated completed.

The Property is currently 96% occupied and features a mix of one-, two-, and three-bedroom units. While the Property's one-bedroom, two-bedroom, and three-bedroom units fetch an average of $1735, $2233 and $2568 per month, respectively, comparable properties earn $2000, $2600 and $3900, respectively.

The Property's location is objectively excellent. Being just 10 min from the nation's capital Washington, DC ensure a continued demand from renters, despite the age and condition of area properties. Transportation such as the nearby I-395 and bus depot make commuting quick and easy for commuting residents. For those who have their own vehicles, the Property has 545 garage spaces available for resident and guest use. The nearby, pedestrian-friendly retail and entertainment, comprised of movie theaters, award-winning restaurants and a mix of everyday and luxury shopping, further increases demand.

In general, the Property's location is in high demand and will continue to be so. However, rents have hit a ceiling as new, amenity-rich communities are the ones commanding the highest market rents. While renovations and redesign efforts will never likely lead to top-of-the-market rents, they will likely close the considerable delta between the Property and its newer competition.

The broker for the Arlington provided some starter numbers. The historical numbers were interesting, but it would be up to Gail to vet the Year 1 numbers and think through her assumptions about future growth rates. Certainly, northern Virginia, like Washington, DC had experienced a great run in recent years, but there was now a lot more supply. The broker thought rents would continue and suggested 4.5% rent growth would be "fair." The deal would probably trade at a 4.5% cap rate or maybe a bit higher. Gail and her fund manager agreed that they could probably bump rents by 10% if they invested an average of $11,000/unit to get them up to current standards. She was not sure what this would do to rent growth rates after the bump.

Lenders would be happy to provide a first mortgage on this property. Gail assumed that she could find a 65% LTV 7-year loan that would include 65% of the acquisition price and 65% of the renovation costs. Given the year-long leases, she thought they could complete the renovations over three years, maybe two if there were aggressive. Gail assumed loan terms would include a 4.35% annual interest rate, amortized over 30 years and a 0.75% origination fee.

The Arlington				
Units	376			
Total SF	367,352			
Avg. SF/units	977			
Income	2016 actual	2017 actual	Annualized 2018 actual	Pro forma year 1
Gross rent	9,037,536	9,135,894	9,208,561	9,536,129
Vacancy	(540,770)	(331,610)	(301,567)	(476,806)
Discounted units	(159,960)	(166,784)	(168,785)	(81,294)

Net rental income	8,336,806	8,637,500	8,738,209	8,978,029
Parking income	284,589	303,828	303,343	312,443
Storage income	6,079	8,118	9,271	9,549
Miscellaneous income	332,665	446,081	485,127	434,312
Effective gross income	8,960,139	9,395,527	9,535,950	9,734,333
Expenses				
Payroll	616,293	668,395	659,817	532,356
Marketing	102,253	98,505	94,611	97,449
General & administrative	350,284	324,463	322,155	274,899
Repairs & maintenance	57,480	59,684	55,183	56,838
Retananting costs	102,496	106,174	99,096	94,000
Management fee	317,142	337,471	342,941	243,000
Net utilities	85,831	57,481	35,351	36,411
Insurance	107,821	85,702	81,693	84,144
Real estate taxes	1,224,068	1,171,342	1,182,116	1,248,627
Total expenses	2,963,668	2,909,217	2,872,962	2,667,725
Net operating income	5,996,471	6,486,310	6,662,988	7,066,608
Reserves	-	-	-	94,000
NOI after reserves	5,996,471	6,486,310	6,662,988	6,972,608

The Wellington

Wellington, VA

The Wellington (the "Property"), is a 245-unit, 10-builing, 244,265 sf multi-family rental property located in Gainesville, Virginia, within the Washington, DC metropolitan area, home to 18 Fortune 500 companies. Since 2000, the Wellington region has seen a 250%+ increase in its population and boasts an average household income of $145,000. Area rents have reacted positively to these demographic trends and occupancies remain at all-time highs. The Property is currently 98% occupied up from 96% 2 years ago.

Built 15 years ago, the community features a swimming pool, state-of-the art fitness center, business center, community clubhouses, and on-site management.

Each unit is equipped with energy saver appliances, full-size washer and dryer, open kitchen plans, private balcony or patio, walk-in closets, central A/C, and gas heat.

The Property has also benefitted from its location and proximity to area shopping (two major malls within 1.7 miles), 10 public golf courses within the County and a pedestrian-friendly streetscape lined with restaurants, retail and recreation. There are major highways and interstates within minutes away. Finally, there are numerous national and multinational corporations and governmental entities, employing hundreds of thousands of people—the property is near the 12th largest business district in the United States. Less than hour away is Washington, DC, which alone is home to 785,600 jobs and 124.4 million sf of office space.

The Property's immediate submarket has a population of 95,878 people with a median age of 34 years old and an average household income of $69,438. The young, financially stable demographic has allowed analysts to project occupancies levels of 95% or higher though the next several years. Additionally, supply remains stable with only one comparably sized property opening this year and another scheduled for delivery next year.

However, while Property greatly benefits from the wealth of the area, the owner must offer restricted rents for all units to individuals or households earning less than 60% of the Area Median Income (AMI). There are 12 years remaining on this restriction. On average, an affordable two-bedroom unit now experiences a $150 reduction in rent per month and an affordable three-bedroom unit experiences a $225 reduction in monthly rent. But, AMI there has risen well above inflation due to the strong economy and changing demographics.

Over the last 3 years effective rents have increased 3% per year and are on-track to do so for the next several years ahead. Occupancy too has trended upward—from 94% in the DC metro area 2 years ago to a projected 96% next year. From a rent comparable-basis, the Property's market rate unites are almost $100 below the average of like properties, likely due their slightly smaller size. The Property's affordable units, while smaller on average (by 100 sf) than the competition average on par with comparable properties.

In general, the Property is well-maintained and in a strong area positioned to continue its steady upward trend, bolstered by its proximity to the nation's capital. However, with plain vanilla amenities and average units, one might consider this community somewhat of a commodity. Finally, should applicable tenants continue to reside at the Property, the affordability restriction will greatly impact cash flow.

Gail had again been able to get some basic broker numbers to look at. She would need to think through how best to forecast future cash flows, but did find a lender who gave her some loan terms he thought reasonable: a 10-year loan with a 67% LTV, using a 4.55% annual interest rate (using a 30-year amortization period). This loan would likely require a 0.5% origination fee.

The Wellington				
Units	245			
SF	244,265			
Avg unit size	997			
Income	**Actual trailing 12 Mo**	**Annualized trailing 6 Mo**	**Anualized trailing 3 Mo**	**Pro forma year 1**
Gross potential rent	3,890,628	3,903,846	3,909,050	3,981,367
Vacancy	(59,324)	(58,802)	(67,876)	(79,628)
Concessions	(576)	(639)	(639)	(3,981)
Bad debt	(9,425)	(1,894)	10,833	(7,963)
Net rental income	3,959,953	3,842,511	3,851,368	3,889,796
Utility reimbursement	3,750	6,107	7,403	3,862
Cable RUBS	48,917	94,694	38,451	50,384
Other income	242,784	305,788	252,833	267,434
Effective gross income	4,255,403	4,249,101	4,150,055	4,211,476
Expenses				
Repairs and maintenance	114,948	114,948	114,948	118,396
Payroll	335,556	335,556	335,556	345,622
Administrative	58,970	58,970	58,970	60,739
Marketing	42,271	42,271	42,271	43,540
Janatorial	67,899	67,899	67,899	69,936
Utilities	234,050	234,050	234,050	241,072
Taxes	440,316	440,316	440,316	453,525
Insurance	42,913	42,913	42,913	42,875
Management fee	159,273	159,273	159,273	121,519
Total expenses	1,496,195	1,496,195	1,496,195	1,497,224
	-	-	-	-
Net operating income	2,759,208	2,752,905	2,653,860	2,714,252
Capital reserves	73,500	73,500	73,500	73,500
NOI after reserves	2,685,708	2,679,405	2,580,360	2,640,752

Case 3

Apples and Oranges: The Strengths and Weaknesses of Being a Generalist

I.   Entrepreneur Helping Entrepreneur

Across a continuum of capital sources for real estate deals, "family and friends money" is often the starting point for the first couple of acquisitions. From there a little success might allow one to move up to "country club money" as the "family and friends" investors start talking about how well these first round of real estate investments are doing. If this momentum continues, one might be able to enter the big leagues of "high net worth investors" or "institutional capital." For some, being able to obtain institutional funding for real estate deals represents a benchmark that "they've made it." For others, partnering with institutional capital is just a great way to lose control of a property and a chance to cede much of the value they've created to the "money partner."

Over the last decade, Isaac Gilliland had touched the full spectrum of capital sources. He began in real estate at the high end, working on trophy projects but touching only them only lightly. As an architect at a nationally renowned firm, he had played a small role in these large-scale developments. He'd sat in with the developer and the team of institutional capital providers, but at the back of the room and only understanding bits of the conversation. While he was adding value as a service provider, he had essentially no control over projects and essentially captured none of the value that he created in the process. He felt well removed from the things that he found most compelling about design, and far from the bigger reasons he had pursued a career in architecture. He began to believe that it was the developer who was best positioned to build great real estate, because it was a developer who had the final say—even over the "starchitects" at his firm. Isaac wanted a more direct route to making an impact on the built environment and larger community, so he decided he wanted to become a developer.

Isaac returned to graduate school to retool, focusing particularly on his blind spots—particularly market analysis and finance. While he understood a great deal about real estate, especially the physical plant and its functional role, he knew very little about capital markets or about Excel and pro forma modeling.

Underwriting Commercial Real Estate in a Dynamic Market. https://doi.org/10.1016/B978-0-12-815989-7.00003-3
© 2019 Elsevier Inc. All rights reserved.   **31**

Once back in graduate school, he let no detail about these subjects escape his grasp. He even refused to let the finance wizards on his teams build the models when he had group assignments. This focus turned into a passion, and over the course of the program he became perhaps the most sophisticated modeler in his class and certainly the cleanest. "It's not rocket science; it's just about a relentless attention to detail. Something you really get drilled on in architecture." His new Excel tool kit would prove an essential component for him becoming an entrepreneur, but his design sensibility would be the characteristic that enabled him to get started. He was very good at the numbers, but he was even better at thinking about them and communicating them.

While he was looking for his own deals he started consulting with other developers, helping them construct their financial models. In graduate school, it had seemed to Isaac that everyone knew how to build a pro forma and he was playing catch up. But once he started modeling for others, he found a deep pool of clients who needed both basic pro forma skills and help communicating what these numbers meant. From then it was only a short time before he started playing many roles for real estate entrepreneurs: serving as their analyst, their marketing team, and with great frequency, their CFO. Typically his clients may have had good instincts about a deal, but they often couldn't easily get past their big idea and into the details. Most often, Isaac was tasked with helping develop the "pitch book" used in raising capital to fund their deals.

There is a durable myth in real estate about "doing a deal on the back of the napkin." And it may be that some real estate deals start that way, but in Isaac's experience "no one should expect to get a bank loan or significant equity using anything scribbled on a napkin." Among his clients, some would tell war stories that felt like a version of the legendary "napkin" deals. Ironically, early successes of this sort often ended up causing them to hire people like Isaac; as their subsequent deal sizes grew, so too did the need to attract more formal capital sources and these typically required more formal underwriting.

One of Isaac's first clients was Jeremy Potts, who had graduated from family and friends money to a version of country club money that Jeremy called "high net worth" investors. Jeremy had been a long-time director with an owner-operator who built and owned some office product, but mostly had accumulated a largely West Coast industrial portfolio. Jeremy's firm had been happy to let deals it didn't want to pursue be passed along. If a deal was too big or small, in the wrong submarket, or had the wrong rent roll, Jeremy could pass these opportunities along to his high net worth investors. It had given Jeremy a second cash flow stream, and the firm benefitted because it also brought more investors into their orbit.

While being an industrial specialist, Jeremy had seen the downside of being narrowly focused during a cycle early in his career when he had nearly lost his savings that he had invested in two of his industrial deals. When the tenant who was going to lease both failed, both the value of his equity and his annual bonus disappeared. The investments recovered somewhat, but he wouldn't again invest so much in a single bet. After that, he started looking to diversify and began to bring what he found to his high net worth investors. They were a smart group and would ask hard questions, but ultimately trusted Jeremy's suggestions. Jeremy found it hard at first to become more of a generalist in a world of specialists, but was happy to be diversifying. Moreover, he felt if he had stayed a specialist, he would've forced himself to be idle in down markets or be willing to make promises he wouldn't be likely to keep if he had continued to raise capital. That was a risk he would not take.

So Jeremy moved his focus to where markets had been—in his words—"forgotten." Certainly there were some bumps along the way, but it was easier to find a good deal when most of the capital world was looking somewhere else. Jeremey turned to Isaac to help him develop and communicate his preliminary ideas about two potential apartment deals. Jeremey's potential investors were people who could write large checks, and all of them had diversified portfolios and diversified tastes in investments. They were eager to create "lifecycle" wealth and would follow Jeremy's lead if his underwriting was rigorous and sound. Jeremy had helped them find good returns before by looking in the weeds for alternative investments, but it had been a bit of work to get them on board. These had been nontraditional investments in which showing both rigorous and sound underwriting was a challenge. While the two multifamily deals Jeremy was now considering bringing to them were in many ways standard real estate deals, each would offer some wrinkles to examine carefully.

II. Optics and Optionality

By 2009, Jeremy had been quick to realize how valuable multifamily properties would become in the years after the housing bust. Not only were the demographics heavily in its favor, with the population distribution tilting toward 18–30-year-olds in the peak of their family formation lifecycle, but there were now more types of households looking for apartments. The Baby Boomers' kids were trying to leave home, and the new empty nesters were showing signs of moving back into urban areas (where some would become renters). The other significant new renter demographic was those who had lost their homes due to foreclosure. These groups varied markedly by metropolitan areas, but would certainly add to aggregate demand for apartments.

The investment thesis that urban apartment would be in demand had been accepted in institutional capital circles, but not in all markets and not all multifamily properties. The large majority of institutional investors wanted to invest in Class A buildings in "global gateway cities," those handful of metropolitan areas that were large enough to provide ready liquidity and those also likely to experience robust growth. In the United States, they might be considered Boston, Chicago, Los Angeles, New York, San Francisco, and Washington, DC. This particular definition remains open to debate—for example others might include Houston or Miami on this list. The early movers in these markets did very well and now the question was had these markets reached equilibrium or was there more appreciation ahead? Had gateway cities simply been the cutting edge of a broader trend toward urbanism, in which demand for city living might increase more broadly? It was an essential question for real estate investors. In the global gateway cities, cap rates had compressed considerably in the last several years. They had widened some during the last downturn, but asset prices in these markets were already beginning to approach pricing late in the last cycle. There seemed to be many investors providing good reasons to justify further cap rate compression, but it was making some nervous.

If investors found the yields too thin in the core markets they could, of course, look into secondary and tertiary markets. Places like Portland, Charlotte, Memphis, and Denver had all experienced a renaissance of sorts in recent years, and there was palpable enthusiasm in cities like these. But at this point institutional capital had only begun to explore other options on a broader scale. For Jeremy, this looked like an opportunity. He felt confident that more capital would look for multifamily properties and would begin to look outside core areas because the apartment investment stories there had been so successful. Jeremy thought there would be similar stories in other submarkets that were not yet priced as such.

To find his deals, Jeremy typically turned to talking with a dozen or so brokers he had made friends with over the last 20 years. He was looking for deals they didn't want; they only got paid when a deal closed and they saw lots of deals that were going to be hard to sell. This was great for Jeremy: he didn't want to compete with well-marketed deals that would generate significant interest. That meant higher prices and lower returns for him and his investors. After a number of breakfasts, dinners, and golf with this group, he was handed two deals that had been viewed as problematic. They were apples and oranges.

The first property was a surprise. It was Block Seven, 260 newly constructed apartment units located in Denver. The offering memorandum (OM) was filled with all of the features today's young urbanists seem to want in a multifamily property: ample and well-appointed common areas, a bike storage and repair facility, pet cleaning area, a bocce-laden rooftop veranda for use during the summer months, and a brewpub style happy hour area downstairs for year round use. Jeremy was surprised that his broker had passed on this property. It seemed to check all the boxes his client usually looked for. But when Jeremy studied the map to see where the property was in Denver, and he realized that he had assumed wrongly that it was in LoDo (Lower Downtown Denver) or some other submarket aspiring to be LoDo. Instead, he found himself trying to find Westminster, Colorado on Google maps. Westminster is in fact part of a larger Denver metropolitan area, but it was decidedly not urban (or least not yet) and likely would not be for some time. Jeremy could see why this might be an opportunity. Most of the candidate buyers would be excited by Denver as an up and coming metropolitan area—not a global gateway city, but getting more interest. They might be that much more interested by the marketing material and its urban elements. But then they would likely end up discovering it was in Westminster and would not pursue it. At the same time, Block Seven would be an expensive acquisition for noninstitutional buyers, so Jeremy thought there was a chance to buy an almost new property at a reasonable price. And, Jeremy thought Denver did make sense for a longer hold. His high net worth investors might want to find private equity capital to provide the rest of the equity needed. Actually, it occurred to Jeremy that some of his investors would be happy to have to have meetings with some of the blue chip firms who could provide this sort of partnership.

The second property was very far from the image of the hipsters at Block Seven, those bearded and tattooed, fixie-riding Millennials. Instead the second candidate property was Les Fontaines, three distinct buildings built on the same property over the course of 10 years spanning 1958–67. It was called Les Fontaines, apparently, because of the rather sad fountains in its center courtyard. The style of the buildings looked every bit as old as the dates of construction suggested. All three were two-story walk-ups, there was no covered parking, and the only common space amenity was a modest kid playground area. The play area seemed be well-maintained but dated. Overall, the property was clean and seemed to have been run fairly well, with adequate maintenance and a long history of lower than average turnover and high-occupancy. Given the vintage, the submarket, and the design it certainly would not attract a lot of attention. Though almost twice the number of units, Les Fontaines would sell for much less than Block Seven. Jeremy and his high-net worth investors were able to invest a total of approximately $10M in equity. If the deal was quite good, they might be able to arrange for a bit more, but this would be a big investment for them. They could use it to pursue either, both, or neither of these two deals. It would be up to Jeremy to make the recommendation, but it would be up to Isaac to help him navigate the underwriting and the pitch book, if it was warranted.

III.   Apples and Oranges? Apples or Oranges?

Jeremy turned to Isaac to help. He was looking for both formal pro formas he could share with his high net worth investors, but he was also asking for help underwriting. Before it went to the investors, Jeremy wanted to think about the cash flows he might expect. Jeremy dumped his work into an email to Isaac.

I'm pretty sure I've got at least one winner here, but maybe two. Can I ask you to replicate the brokers' numbers to make sure we understand how it's being sold? But more than that, I'd love some time from you exploring these two deals. I don't see Les Fontaines being anything but chugging along, but maybe with some good debt the overall return might be good? Let me know what scenarios you think are good starting points. And see what kind of CapEx surprises might hurt us. If you see something else worth talking about let me know.

On the "Denver" property (and you'll see why that's in quotes), it'd be a bigger ask of the investors, but we'd have to do that or turn to other equity sources. I can call my buddy at a private equity shop for loose terms. I had some place holders in my notes (attached). Look into the broker numbers, but I'm feeling like we'll have to look at NOI growth and the equity options at the same time. If we aren't pretty sure about getting a stronger rent roll, it might be too expensive to go the private equity route.

You always find something I missed. Please find those things this time! Make a recommendation for both – about pricing, capital stack options, and advice about business plans if something strikes you beyond the obvious.

Yours, JP

These sorts of assignments were Isaac's favorite, better than doing pitch book layouts. Now his job was to see what he could find in Jeremy's notes and documents and write a short memo, including the broker's model, his top three scenarios for each property, and how he interpreted the numbers. For his last three assignments, his suggestions had essentially all been adopted. On the fourth, his client couldn't close the deal when his loan was denied, something Isaac had anticipated. His consulting work was proving a great test lab for the day Isaac would go out and pursue his own deals.

IV. Deliverables

Jeremy made a generic request of Isaac to get help underwriting these deals, building and stress testing the financials, thinking about debt and equity choices, and about expected returns. Isaac could do this, of course, but he would also be looking for red flags. Two of his calling cards in his underwriting were making solid assumptions about what might be expected in terms of a property's cash flows, and also providing a section in the write up that explicitly called out what could go wrong—and how it could be mitigated against or at least be priced appropriately in setting a bid.

In this case, you will take the role of Isaac: you will first start playing the role of analyst and build the pro formas. Then you will get to be the asset manager and think about how to maximize the value of the properties if they were to be purchased. And finally you get to play the role of CFO and be forceful in assessing whether the returns you find more than compensate Jeremy and his investors for the risks they will be taking. If these deals are worth pursuing, you will then play the role of marketing staff and build the pitch book. It reality, this sort of work would pay well, but the reward for Isaac was the chance to sharpen his underwriting as he looked forward to playing the role of developer. He would start with replicating the broker's numbers and then think about how to adjust them and then learn what he could to help Jeremy.

Questions/Issues to Consider.

a. Neither of the seller brokers gave guidance for going-in or going-out cap rates. Isaac and Jeremey called around and heard that good starting points for where pricing will end up will be 5.1% and 6.0% for the Block Seven going-in and going-out cap rates, respectively. For Les Fontaines, they heard that going-in and going-out cap rates would be 6.5% and 7.0%. Using these estimates and the broker's assumptions, what is the unlevered and levered IRR and equity multiple for Block Seven and Les Fontaines? Use a 10-year holding period as the starting point for your underwriting.

b. Which of the two debt options for both Block Seven and Les Fontaines would you choose and why?

c. How do you define "best"? Would your recommendations be acceptable to the lenders? Assume the debt service coverage ratio for Block Seven is 1.20, while for Les Fontaines it is 1.25. What is the debt yield for these loans? Would lenders be happy with these loan terms?

d. If Jeremy and his high-net worth investors are interested in keeping their maximum total investment close to $10 million dollars, can they pursue either or both of the deals using first loans and their own equity? If not, explore using the additional capital sources for each. In the case of Les Fontaine, Jeremy has found a debt fund to provide a second loan, while for Block Seven, he found a private equity firm to participate. Preliminary terms for both are below in the exhibits. With both now in your pro formas, what are the returns to Jeremy and his partners? Calculate both the IRR and equity multiple on their invested capital. Note that the private equity firm can structure the waterfall in many ways. The simple version waterfall Isaac sketched assumes:

- During the holding period, that the private equity firm ("the EP") will get 100% of any cash flow after debt service to pay its preferred return or unpaid preferred return.
- Second, any remaining cash flows after the preferred return has been paid is split 25%/75% to the EP and Sponsor, respectively.
- At sale, the private equity firm ("the EP") will receive 100% of any cash flow after debt service and loan repayment until the EP's original investment is repaid.
- Second, after the EP's original investment is repaid, any remaining cash flows is split 25%/75% to the EP and Sponsor, respectively.

e. What do you think of the brokers' forecasts and cash flow assumptions? Do you see any systematic optimism from the brokers' assumptions? Which ones come to mind as worthy for more investigation? Test how sensitive the returns to Jeremy and his partners to changes in the brokers' assumptions. Which ones are the most influential?

f. What economic narrative to you have in mind that would make your change the brokers' assumptions? Are they lower in your model just because you know you don't want to pay up the broker suggests? Or are they lower because your view the various fundamentals at work in them don't justify the broker's optimism?

g. What would you recommend for the bids? What would the highest you'd be willing to pay for either of the two candidate properties? To formulate bids, you'll have to make some assumptions about future cash flows, as well as cap rates. Do your best to justify these. And, with these expected cash flows in place, what risks are associated with the two properties. As part of your bids, note the top three risks Jeremy faces. Can the risks be mitigated? If not, do you think the expected return is high enough to be well-compensated for the risks?

h. If you suggest skipping both of these two properties, where do you think you're find a better deal? Is this even relevant? Should your bid choices be about other deals or should Jeremy define a general lower threshold for the deals he brings to the high net worth investors?

i. Please provide Jeremy a brief but effective memo on your findings, including your preferred two pro formas for both properties, but be sure to identify key risks and note how they might influence returns.

V. Isaac's Notes for Les Fontaines

Les Fontaines—Gurnee, Illinois

Le Fontaines (the "Property"), a 425-unit, 373,670 sf property in Chicago's suburban Lake County. The Property sits on over 15 acres with a desirable mix of one, two and three-bedroom apartments. Built 55 years ago, the Property is a 425-unit community of three California-style buildings. Approximately, 75% of the units have been recently renovated with updated bathrooms, new flooring and renovated kitchens (cabinets, countertops, appliances and tile). The complex includes such amenities as a clubhouse, pool, tennis and basketball courts, and multiple children's recreation areas.

The Property offers ample resident parking and on-site management and maintenance staff.

Being in a stable suburb of Chicago, located equidistant from Milwaukee (50 miles away) and downtown Chicago (40 miles away), has ensured a historically high occupancy rates for the Property, currently close to 100%. Additionally, the high level of maintenance and consistent capital improvements (interior and exterior) have kept the properties in demand, despite their over half-century age. There are several large newer properties in the area, many built within the last 20 years. However, their age has had negligible impact on rent levels, as both properties rent at or above market.

Additionally, the Property is just 5 miles from Gurnee Mills Shopping Center, Illinois' largest outlet and value shopping destination, with over 200 shops within the mall and countless other retailers, restaurants and entertainment options surrounding it. Across the highway from Gurnee Mills is also Six Flags Great America, a regional destination theme park which attracts millions of visitors each year.

Gurnee area demographics are strong for this product type, as 47% of the local population (108,291 people) rent and 88.1% are employed. With a media age of 33 years old and average income of $61,000, the area presents and upwardly mobile population able to afford market level returns (and potentially higher should the market trend upward.

While the Property has maintained a historically strong performance, its continued success is dependent on several variables. Should new product come online, the Property, even with its good upkeep and condition, may start to show signs of obsolesce and absent modern amenities. As many residents' economic health is directly tied to that of the local economy of two major metro areas, an economic downturn will impact the affordability of the rents, which has, in recent years, benefited from the continued uptick the in the national economy. Finally, with over 50 years of age per community, the Property may experience the need for significant capital improvements as major systems and infrastructure begin to breakdown.

In short, the Les Fontaines has performed quite well in recent years, but can this success be maintained, and for how long?

Les Fontaines trailing/pro forma cash flows.

Trailing/pro forma cash flows			
Operating revenue	Annualized Trailing 12 Mo	Annualized Trailing 3 Mo	Pro forma Year 1
Gross potential revenue	3,792,106	3,971,771	4,161,889
Vacancy	–	–	(208,094)
Nonrevenue units	–	–	(23,903)
Base rental revenue	3,792,106	3,971,771	3,929,892
Other income	114,792	97,283	113,666
Effective gross revenue	3,906,898	4,069,054	4,043,558
Operating expenses			
Repair & maintenance	403,906	416,146	368,475
Landscaping/ grounds	4,517	4,562	10,519
Staffing	361,607	350,867	390,150
Marketing	16,568	17,244	21,038
Administrative expenses	134,032	134,032	127,883
Utilities	507,054	507,054	497,327

Trailing/pro forma cash flows

Operating revenue	Annualized Trailing 12 Mo	Annualized Trailing 3 Mo	Pro forma Year 1
Insurance	118,647	118,647	94,669
Real estate taxes	766,526	736,466	758,560
Management fee	157,875	151,684	121,961
Total operating expenses	2,470,733	2,436,702	2,390,581
Net operating income	1,436,165	1,632,352	1,652,978
Replacement reserves	(130,050)	(124,950)	(124,950)
Net operating income after reserves	1,306,115	1,507,402	1,528,028

Broker Assumptions

Income Growth Rate	3.5%	per year
Annual Interest Rate	5.0%	per year
Term (Years)	3.0%	per year

Broker's pro forma cash flows

Operating revenue	Year 1	Year 2	Year 3	Year 4	Year 5	Year 6	Year 7	Year 8	Year 9	Year 10	Year 11
Gross potential revenue	4,161,889	4,307,555	4,458,320	4,614,361	4,775,863	4,943,019	5,116,024	5,295,085	5,480,413	5,672,228	5,870,756
Vacancy	(208,094)	(215,378)	(222,916)	(230,718)	(238,793)	(247,151)	(255,801)	(264,754)	(274,021)	(283,611)	(293,538)
Nonrevenue units	(23,903)	(24,739)	(25,605)	(26,501)	(27,429)	(28,389)	(29,383)	(30,411)	(31,475)	(32,577)	(33,717)
Base rental revenue	3,929,892	4,067,438	4,209,798	4,357,141	4,509,641	4,667,479	4,830,841	4,999,920	5,174,917	5,356,039	5,543,501
Other income	113,666	117,645	121,762	126,024	130,435	135,000	139,725	144,615	149,677	154,916	160,338
Effective gross revenue	4,043,558	4,185,083	4,331,561	4,483,165	4,640,076	4,802,479	4,970,566	5,144,535	5,324,594	5,510,955	5,703,838
Operating expenses											
Repair & maintenance	368,475	379,529	390,915	402,643	414,722	427,164	439,978	453,178	466,773	480,776	495,200
Landscaping/ grounds	10,519	10,834	11,159	11,494	11,839	12,194	12,560	12,937	13,325	13,725	14,136
Staffing	390,150	401,855	413,910	426,327	439,117	452,291	465,860	479,835	494,230	509,057	524,329
Marketing	21,038	21,669	22,319	22,988	23,678	24,388	25,120	25,873	26,650	27,449	28,273

Continued

Broker's pro forma cash flows

Operating revenue	Year 1	Year 2	Year 3	Year 4	Year 5	Year 6	Year 7	Year 8	Year 9	Year 10	Year 11
Administrative expenses	127,883	131,719	135,671	139,741	143,933	148,251	152,698	157,279	161,998	166,858	171,863
Utilities	497,327	512,246	527,614	543,442	559,745	576,538	593,834	611,649	629,998	648,898	668,365
Insurance	94,669	97,509	100,434	103,447	106,551	109,747	113,039	116,431	119,924	123,521	127,227
Real estate taxes	758,560	781,317	804,757	828,899	853,766	879,379	905,761	932,934	960,922	989,749	1,019,442
Management fee	121,961	125,620	129,389	133,270	137,269	141,387	145,628	149,997	154,497	159,132	163,906
Total operating expenses	2,390,581	2,462,298	2,536,167	2,612,252	2,690,620	2,771,338	2,854,478	2,940,113	3,028,316	3,119,166	3,212,741
Net operating income	1,652,978	1,722,785	1,795,394	1,870,913	1,949,457	2,031,141	2,116,087	2,204,423	2,296,278	2,391,789	2,491,098
Replacement reserves	(124,950)	(128,699)	(132,559)	(136,536)	(140,632)	(144,851)	(149,197)	(153,673)	(158,283)	(163,031)	
Net operating income after reserves	1,528,028	1,594,086	1,662,834	1,734,377	1,808,824	1,886,289	1,966,890	2,050,750	2,137,995	2,228,758	

Les Fontaines 1st Mortgage Options	Loan 1	Loan 2
LTV	55%	65%
Annual Interest Rate	4.50%	5.25%
Term (Years)	10	5
Amortization Period	30	30
Origination Fee	0.75%	1.00%

Les Fontaines Mezzanine Debt Option	Loan Terms
Mezzanine LTV	15%
Annual Interest Rate	9.00%
Term (Years)	Up to 10
Amortization Period	Interest Only
Origination Fee	1.25%

VI.   Isaac's Abstracts/Notes/Exhibit for Block Seven

Block Seven Apartments—Denver, Colorado

Block Seven Apartments (the "Property") is a 6.68-acre, 260-unit, 234,520 sf, luxury multifamily property located in Denver, Colorado. Just built, the Property offers residents a host of modern amenities, including a heated year-round pool, 50-chaise lounge courtyard with eight private cabanas and daily towel service, clubroom with coffee-bar and business center, 24.7 fitness center with top-of-the-line equipment, dog-wash and bike-wash rooms, BBQ grills, picnic areas, and courtesy bicycles.

The unit mix of the 260-unit, garden-style property consists of studio, one-bedroom and two-bedroom units, averaging 825 sf each. The 10-ft ceilings and 7-ft windows in every apartment home create a very open and large environment which is accented by wood-finished vinyl plank flooring, espresso cabinets, built-in wine racks, quartz countertops, and undermount sinks in both the kitchen and the bathrooms. Twenty-nine apartment homes have attached garages with direct unit access, and every apartment home offers an oversized patio or balcony.

The Block Seven community at large is a 200-acre, entertainment-anchored, multiuse community in the heart of the Denver-Boulder U.S. 36 Corridor. With street-level retail, commercial space (100% leased) and six parks, the community provides a live-work environment for those residents who desire it. Those residents who commute will benefit from the transit-oriented planning and proximity to Boulder and within Denver. The Highway 36 Corridor is often referred to as the "Rocky Mountain Silicon Valley" due to the increasing number of start-ups and high-tech firms in the area, including Oracle, Level 3 Communications and Ball Aerospace.

The Property's residents also receive first row access to the nearby 1STBANK Center, a 180,000, 6500-seat performance center. Hosting 100+ events per year. The center is estimated to attract 350,000 guests annually.

The Property's 97% occupancy is on par with nearby comparable properties built in recent years. However, its units average 150 sf below that of comparable properties and, while its gross rents remain competitive, its rent per square foot are at a 10%+ premium. Additionally, in recent years, several comparable properties have traded at strong valuations, averaging sales at $400 psf.

From a quantitative standpoint, the newly built property with its ample amenities has performed above expectations. From more subjective point of view, it is yet to be seen whether the glow of high-style and luxury living will fade. The market, in reaction to a young, hip start-up culture, has been supplied a steady flow of new, shiny properties, each boasting a better life-style than the next. The question remains, has market saturation been reached or will it soon? And, will the mercurial nature of millennial population, a one geographically mobile one, impact access to the desired demographic.

Block Seven Assumptions

REVENUE	Broker's Pro Forma	Annual Growth
Market Rent ($/unit/month)	$1,350	4.50%
Concessions (% of PGR)	0.00%	
Non-Revenue Units	2 units	
Loss (Gain) to Lease (% of PGR)	3.00%	
Other Income ($/unit/month)	$58.50	3.00%
Utility Income ($/unit/month)	$90.00	3.00%
Covered Parking Income ($/stall/month)	$99.00	3.00%
Covered Parking Stalls	127 spaces	
Vacancy	5.00%	

OPERATING EXPENSES		
Repairs & Maintenance ($/unit/year)	$175	3.00%
Contract Services ($/unit/year)	$150	3.00%
Turnover Costs ($/unit/year)	$100	3.00%
Payroll ($/year)	$347,625	3.00%
Administrative ($/unit/year)	$175	3.00%
Marketing ($/unit/year)	$200	3.00%
Utilities ($/year)	$297,354	3.00%
Taxes (% of Purchase Price)	1.00%	3.00%
Insurance ($/unit/year)	$130	3.00%
Management Fee (% of EGI)	2.50%	
Capital Reserves ($/unit/year)	$200	3.00%
Costs of Sales (% of Sale Price)	3.00%	

Block Seven Debt Options	Loan 1	Loan 2
LTV	60%	68%
Annual Interest Rate	4.75%	5.75%
Term (Years)	10	7
Amortization Period	30	30
Origination Fee	0.75%	1.00%

Block Seven Private Equity Option	
PE Contribution up to % of Price	85%
PE Share of Capital Stack	25%
Preferred Return	8.00%
Split of Remaining Cash Flow	40%

Case 4

Motor City Madness? The Search for Yield Takes Isaac to Detroit

So why not just buy ten houses in Detroit? It's not clear you can even buy one house in Los Angeles. And what happens to that one house when the sewer breaks? Your razor thin margin is gone. Buying in LA is madness.

I. Escape From Los Angeles

After almost 2 years of consulting work, Isaac Gilliland had saved what he hoped would be enough to become an owner of a real estate investment property. He had been careful to put away as much of each paycheck as he could. Consulting had been irregular, but a relatively good way for Isaac to begin his real estate career. He had been an architect, but returned to school to learn more about the rest of the real estate business because he wanted to be a developer and an owner. Architecture had been a terrific way to enter the business but a tough way create wealth or retain control of his ideas. Isaac wanted to be an entrepreneur and thought there were so many ways he could add value in real estate. Consulting allowed him to take on numerous roles while continuing to look for the deal that would finally be his own.

Isaac saw real estate as a competitive business, but also as messy and often inefficient. He had watched carefully for investment opportunities during the early parts of the recovery, and there were many. But until recently Isaac simply didn't have enough capital for any of them. By 2014, Isaac was growing worried that he would miss this cycle. He was well aware that for developers, most profits were made in a short window of time. Clearly, the bottom of a real estate cycle is a bad time for development—too much supply relative to demand. Typically, as a recovery occurs, demand picks up and vacancies begin to fall. At some point, some combination of new needs and overall demand drives prices to the point that developers can start construction with an expectation of a profit. While there are all sorts of risk associated with development, missing the cycle was the one that Isaac feared most. No matter how good his design or how well executed his plan, if the market slowed he would likely lose his equity and maybe control of the property. He knew it was possible to work through weak periods, but Isaac hoped to avoid that kind of headwind.

Underwriting Commercial Real Estate in a Dynamic Market. https://doi.org/10.1016/B978-0-12-815989-7.00004-5

By late 2014, many of his clients had already been investing aggressively in properties in major metropolitan areas all over the West. The recovery had shown itself to be durable, and after a slow start the sense of optimism in metropolitan areas throughout the region stayed high despite the first big deliveries of new apartment units. Isaac was looking hard for a way to find a deal and finally enter the market, but Los Angeles, San Francisco, Seattle, and Portland had been so thoroughly picked over that it was hard to think he would ever find a bargain there. He began looking to the emerging second-tier cities like Salt Lake City, Las Vegas, San Diego, Denver, and even Boise. There he found lower prices there that would allow him to stretch his savings further, but his enthusiasm was more than matched by that of other investors. Indeed, he found that supply and demand in these markets was perhaps even further out of balance relative to the primary markets in the West. Certainly, cap rates were higher in the secondary markets than in the primary markets, but the risk seemed significantly higher as well. How would Boise do when the economy slowed? Would he be happy buying a small apartment building there at a cap rate below 5%?

With the recovery well underway, Isaac felt the need to buy something soon or resign himself to another cycle of consulting. That would not be a bad outcome, but it wasn't what he wanted and it was a risk to his bigger plans. It could be another 5 or even 10 years before the market cycled again to the point that bargains appeared. By then, he might have a third kid, they might have to pay for their schools, there could be a larger house and a larger mortgage, and he might not be able to become the entrepreneur he had always planned to be. So while it was feeling a bit late to enter, his personal window was as open as it would ever be. After some thought and conversations with his wife and a new business partner, Isaac decided it was time to leave Los Angeles.

II.   Local Cycles and Discovering Detroit

Isaac's family was fully embedded in Los Angeles, so he wouldn't be packing them up and leaving entirely—but he could still go find deals elsewhere. What he learned in looking through the primary and secondary markets in the West Coast was that while real estate markets share some common elements, they are far from synchronous. The recovery seemed to be apparent first in San Francisco and Seattle, where a vibrant technology sector pushed prices right back up after an initial downturn. In Los Angeles, it was interesting to watch the recovery occur within the metropolitan area. Clearly submarkets in the Westside of Los Angeles like Santa Monica and Culver City recovered well before the submarkets at the eastern end of the metropolitan area. In places like Indio and Beaumont, house prices fell astonishingly far and had only recently hit something that resembled a firm bottom. The fact that these submarkets were connected within the same metropolitan area meant that they would be end up being correlated in the long run, but in the short term they could behave quite differently from one another.

While Isaac had been focused on properties closer to home, he decided to look for housing submarkets that have experienced pronounced price declines and at the same time had lower average prices. He first looked at suburban Phoenix and suburban Las Vegas. Two of these so-called "sand state" cities had been poster children for the mania that occurred during the housing bubble. Both of these markets experienced significant foreclosure activity and large falls in house prices from peak. In either one of these markets Isaac could have purchased numerous homes because prices had fallen so far. But by 2014 the real estate industry had seen the development of a new asset class: single-family residential (SFR) for rental. While household balance sheets were impaired, investors had discovered that these households wanted to stay in detached housing even if they couldn't own it. Indeed, this niche began to mature rapidly; several large firms amassed holdings in excess of 20,000 housing SFR rental units. And beyond these large players, an entire class of investors pursued a similar strategy at a smaller scale. A lot of capital had been invested in Phoenix and Las Vegas. Isaac was surprised to find that despite the severity of the decline in Phoenix, house price appreciation there from the beginning of 2012 to 2014 was higher than in the premier and expensive housing markets of San Francisco and Los Angeles. Of course, going forward that appreciation might make future gains lower.

While it was interesting to learn about these price dynamics, it meant that Isaac was probably too late to enter these markets and still expect a healthy return. So he searched further afield. In order to make his search more efficient, instead of working his way down from the most expensive markets, he went right to the bottom, opting to fly to Detroit and to spend several days driving around to try to understand its housing markets. Isaac understood that Detroit had experienced its glory days some six decades before. The peak population just before 1950 was over 2 million people. At that point, the car industry was so concentrated in Detroit that 65% of all the cars manufactured in the world were built there. Detroit was the most productive city in the world. But since then, Detroit had experienced a slow decline, with its population fleeing to the suburbs and its jobs heading out of the state and out of the country. The population in 2014 was less than 700,000; the housing stock built to accommodate 2 million people was much too large. In recent years, there were an estimated 30,000 vacant houses and 90,000 vacant buildings in Detroit. To make things worse, the subprime crisis had an outsized impact on the city. Fully one in three of the properties in Detroit had been foreclosed on. There were some success stories among a few of the cities around Detroit, but most had shared an analogous set of shocks from the decline of manufacturing and the rise and fall of subprime lending. When Isaac went to Detroit he knew he would find a housing market that met both his criteria: it would be both inexpensive and still reeling from the downturn. He didn't really need to fly there to know this. What he went there to see was whether or not he could find a good investment.

III. Rolling Up a Portfolio

Like many investments, Isaac's foray into southeast Michigan was a mix of purpose and happenstance. While visiting a friend, who was originally from Michigan, Isaac struck up a conversation with his friend's father Tom, a realtor focusing on the Detroit metro area. Tom specialized in single family homes, mostly for families, and told Isaac how inexpensive homes in the area had become as a result of the Great Recession. He was a local who never quite understood investing in Los Angeles: "So why not just buy ten houses here? For that amount, it's not clear you can even buy one house in Los Angeles. And what happens to that one house when the sewer breaks? Your razor thin margin is gone. Buying in LA is madness." After looking for homes in Los Angeles and then seeing some numbers for Detroit, Isaac was incredulous. "You can buy a decent house for $35,000 dollars? The tenant will pay around $700 a month in rent?" Half joking, half seriously, Isaac made an offer to Tom: "Find me a deal and if I get it under contract, I will come to the area and look for more." A few weeks later, Tom had found a property, had a handshake deal with the owner, and Isaac was on his way to Detroit. He drove from the airport directly to the house. It was exactly what he'd asked for: the price was low, the location seems reasonable, the condition was good, and the rent was quite attractive relative to the price.

Over his 5 days stay, he realized that there were many homes like this in the area. Isaac found himself thinking that while every property was unique in some ways, these homes seemed to be as close to commodities as possible in real estate. Moreover, the houses could be acquired quickly using a standard set of metrics. One he found a good candidate neighborhood, he would try to use his metrics to quickly identify and visit the properties. The challenge would be how much to adjust his bid for various items like condition, rent, location, etc. and figure out how he would manage multiple properties from thousands of miles away.

The first step was deciding where to look. In terms of selecting neighborhoods, Isaac looked for lower middle-class areas—ones that were safe, clean and full of employed working class people. This demographic was hit hard by the recession and could not (or chose not) to be homeowners, even though, by his calculation, rent was twice what a mortgage would be. The areas would also need to be within 45 min of each other maximum to allow for efficient management.

During his many property tours, Isaac starting asking brokers about his plans. From those conversations and after a bit of vetting, Isaac was able to assemble a team. By staying curious and asking questions, he identified a property manager and home inspector as the acquisitions and property management teams. Then Isaac was off and running. He put together a list of criteria and contacted several local realtors. He asked them for homes in Oakland or Macomb Counties, on the market for approximately $50,000 and able to generate a monthly rent of around

$800, with two or three bedrooms, and in good enough repair that a reasonable handyman could bring them to rentable condition.

For initial purchases, Isaac made several trips, looking at 20 or more properties each trip. Soon, however, he developed trust with realtors and could underwrite from afar, utilizing independent reviews from his property manager and home inspector. Isaac found many homes that met his criteria, and found reasons not to buy some of them. Mostly it was when the price and rent were off, but he also rejected several because of worries about surprises with capital expenses. He found bad sewer lines, potential foundation work, and a host of houses that he referred to as "functionally obsolescent" but that his inspector called "worse than a bad leisure suit." They were, as he said: "kidding themselves when they thought they were good looking back then; today all we see are regrets." After approximately 6 months, Isaac had made his first real estate deal by building a portfolio: 16 homes and 1 duplex.

IV. Raising Capital

Isaac funded the first two acquisitions personally with no concrete plans for further capital partners. However, after testing his concept on a microlevel for a few months, he was confident that his plan could work well as a fund model. In short order, he crafted a fund model with a noncompounding cumulative preferred return (a "pref") and simple split after return of equity and the owed pref. He then hired an attorney to draft the appropriate investor documentation. Since the investment was rather modest, Isaac held off on contracting friends and family investors until it was "turnkey"—when he was had the other 15 properties under contract and with his business plan and legal paperwork sorted out.

He proposed a $25,000 minimum investment and estimated a 5-year total investment timeline, which could be shorter or longer at his sole discretion. He contributed his first two properties as his personal equity to run *pari passu* with investor's cash, and the fund was off and running. What would determine how long the investment lasted? As he described to his investors, it would all be about operations and eventual sales: every time a renter vacated, Isaac would run an NPV calculation of projected rents and future sales value and compare against current market price. The market would determine when a house left the portfolio. This approach would be unemotional and provide some transparency to his choices.

V. Operating the Portfolio

Just like that, Isaac and his partner were the sponsors of portfolio. It had sounded impressive when he described it at first, until he completed the description: "...a portfolio in Detroit." Isaac grew to appreciate the range of responses that followed. Sometimes his pitch was met with silence and a sputtered "Oh, really. Detroit?" The stigma of an economy in decline for so many years made it seem that Detroit was an obvious place to avoid as an investment. But others responded differently. Isaac started to feel smart when other single-family renter entrepreneurs smiled and said, "You timed that one right. How many did you buy?" This sort of comment was rare, but frequent enough to help make Isaac sleep better.

Detroit had been in decline since the 1960s. Despite the pervasive weakness, the housing bubble actually caused a rise in house prices in Detroit in the early aughts. When the bubble burst, what had been a less than ideal situation for decades became dramatically worse: Detroit might be considered the classic example of what too much capital and too much optimism can do. But the correction—and perhaps an overcorrection in some places—was an essential part of Isaac's strategic plan. He thought two things would hold true. First, while Detroit was down, prices more than reflected this. His yield would be much greater than in Los Angeles or any of the other submarkets he had looked at. Second, Isaac tried to buy homes with existing tenants who had paid rent throughout the downturn. Things were not great, but there was a recovery underway. Isaac saw his primary risks as vacancy and capital expenditures. Choosing long-term residents might help with reduce turnover. And while Isaac did what he could to assess the quality of the structures, he thought the portfolio would help smooth his cash flow: while any one house might get a shock in the form of a sewer line break, expenses would be spread out over the 17 properties. And in fact, Isaac found over time that there were some headaches, but only idiosyncratic problems that the cash flow covered relatively easily.

VI. What Next?

In 2017, Isaac had his first instance of a tenant vacating and his team reporting that there was no ready replacement. It was his decision as to what do next. His investors had been apprised of his original plan to sell as soon there was turnover, but they had done well since the start of the fund. It had paid the quarterly preferred return on time and watched house prices rise in Detroit. Recalling those who had been supportive of his bet on Detroit, Isaac could report to his investors that house prices in the metropolitan area were up by almost 80% since the bottom of the market and up by almost 30% since Isaac started looking in Detroit. Isaac had learned quite a bit about Detroit and about managing real estate from afar. He thought he could hold the 17 properties for a while with little major effort, but retenanting would require more capital expenditures to freshen up the property, leasing commissions if he wanted to try and create a worthy pool of tenants, and an inevitable hit to the cash flow that had been so pleasant to receive and so gratifying to send along to investors.

What should Issac do?

VII. Deliverables

For this case, take on the role of Isaac. You are in a position to make a decision about the Detroit portfolio, and your job is to outline a strategy going forward.

Provide a memo to your partner that identifies the range of options you should consider, the strengths and weaknesses of each, and the impacts your choices have for you and your investors under the various options.

Some questions and issues may help you organize your memo.

a. Recall the original business plan. What is clearly articulated? What do you make of the "unemotional" rule Isaac suggested for when to sell a house? Do you understand his logic or how his math works?

b. How has the portfolio performed since inception? To investigate this question, assume that all of the values of the houses in the portfolio have appreciated at the same rate as the metropolitan area as a whole from October 2014 until July of 2018. Aggregate house price indexes showed a total 26% increase during this period. Rents for the same houses have increased, too, but not at the same rate. Assume that annual rents increases have been 2.5% less per year than house price appreciation during the hold. While these increases reflect changing demand for both rental and owned housing, operating expenses have followed general inflation and have grown only at about 2% per year. Build a portfolio level cash flow analysis for the 17 properties from acquisition to the beginning of July 2018. What would the unlevered IRR and equity multiple be if the portfolio were sold now? Assume costs of closing and brokerage of 3% of the house price.

c. If Isaac decided to hold the full portfolio for another 4 years, what would have to happen to rents and house prices to make the next 4 years as profitable as the holding period to date?

d. In light of the market in Detroit, do you think there's a reasonable expectation of meeting a combination of rent and house price increases such that holding the portfolio another 4 years would match the investment's history to date?

e. Do you think the buy/sell calculus has changed over this holding period? What were the economics of renting versus buying in 2014? Why was it so apparently imbalanced? And why were there so many renters? What is the balance now between renting and owning? Do the houses in the portfolio continue to suggest renting or owning as a better option?

f. Would it be beneficial to hold the full portfolio if Isaac was able to put a portfolio loan on them? That is, he could pull a lot of capital out and return it to investors and instead use the portfolio loan. The question would be what terms would make it beneficial. If a 4-year interest-only loan were structured to be equal to 50% of the total house values, what interest rate would yield the same return to equity? Isaac spoke with some hard money lenders about this structure, and he thought he could obtain such a loan at 10% per year. Would this loan help? If so, who would it help and how much?

g. What other options could Isaac explore? He started out looking to examine the PV for each property as it became vacant. Is this the right way to think about selling? What would a sale imply for the performance of the remaining properties and team? What about the investors?

Houses Purchased (Page 1)

Street		Bayne	Cushing	Hanson	Hillview	Leach	Oneil	Parklawn	Piper 1	Piper 2	Subtotal
City		Roseville	Eastpointe	St. Clair Shores	Roseville	Roseville	Roseville	Oak Park	Eastpointe	Eastpointe	9
Purchase price		35,400	54,200	45,400	28,250	45,300	50,500	45,300	50,240	47,290	401,880
Rehab		3195	5000	4100	1275	4000	1500	12,500	1500	4000	37,070
Total cost		**38,595**	**59,200**	**49,500**	**29,525**	**49,300**	**52,000**	**57,800**	**51,740**	**51,290**	**438,950**
Rent/month		725	925	825	695	825	925	800	1000	950	7670
Income											
PGI	8.00%	8700	11,100	9900	8340	9900	11,100	9600	12,000	11,400	92,040
Vacancy		(696)	(888)	(792)	(667)	(792)	(888)	(768)	(960)	(912)	(7363)
EGI		8004	10,212	9108	7673	9108	10,212	8832	11,040	10,488	84,677
Operating expenses											
Management fee	10.00%	800	1021	911	767	911	1021	883	1104	1049	8468
Insurance		418	504	500	440	556	500	500	500	470	4388
Property taxes		1250	2700	1500	1100	1200	1500	1950	2000	2200	15,400
Repairs and maintenance		1000	1000	1000	1000	1000	1000	1000	1000	1000	9000
Utilities (when vacant)		100	100	100	100	100	100	100	100	100	900
Total OpEX		3568	5325	4011	3407	3767	4121	4433	4704	4819	38,156
Expense load		44.6%	52.1%	44.0%	44.4%	41.4%	40.4%	50.2%	42.6%	45.9%	45.1%
NOI		**4436**	**4887**	**5097**	**4266**	**5341**	**6091**	**4399**	**6336**	**5669**	**46,521**
Going-in cap (all costs)		*11.5%*	*8.3%*	*10.3%*	*14.4%*	*10.8%*	*11.7%*	*7.6%*	*12.2%*	*11.1%*	*10.6%*
Leasing commissions	1 month/year	725	925	825	695	825	925	800	1000	950	7670
Net income		**3711**	**3962**	**4272**	**3571**	**4516**	**5166**	**3599**	**5336**	**4719**	**38,851**
Unlevered cash-on-cash		*9.61%*	*6.69%*	*8.63%*	*12.09%*	*9.16%*	*9.93%*	*6.23%*	*10.31%*	*9.20%*	*8.85%*

Houses Purchased (Page 2)

		Roseville	Standard 1	Standard 2	Stewart	Tallman	Timken	Virginia Park	Wallace	Subtotal	Total
Street											
City		Roseville	Center Line	Center Line	Warren	Warren	Warren	Center Line	Roseville	8	17
Purchase price		51,800	36,200	43,200	51,200	50,000	52,300	93,290	55,365	433,355	835,235
Rehab		1600	2500	2800	2500	2500	500	5000	9000	26,400	63,470
Total cost		**53,400**	**38,700**	**46,000**	**53,700**	**52,500**	**52,800**	**98,290**	**64,365**	**459,755**	**898,705**
Rent/month		1000	775	850	1100	900	925	1500	1000	8050	15,720
Income											
PGI		12,000	9300	10,200	13,200	10,800	11,100	18,000	12,000	96,600	188,640
Vacancy	8.00%	(960)	(744)	(816)	(1056)	(864)	(888)	(1440)	(960)	(7728)	(15,091)
EGI		11,040	8556	9384	12,144	9936	10,212	16,560	11,040	88,872	173,549
Operating expenses											
Management fee	10.00%	1104	856	938	1214	994	1021	1656	1104	8887	17,355
Insurance		515	500	500	500	600	525	950	700	4790	9178
Property taxes		1850	1815	1850	1715	1700	1400	3000	2200	15,530	30,930
Repairs and maintenance		1000	1000	1000	1000	1000	1000	2000	1000	9000	18,000
Utilities (when vacant)		100	100	100	100	100	100	100	100	800	1700
Total OpEX		4569	4271	4388	4529	4394	4046	7706	5104	39,007	77,163
Expense load		41.4%	49.9%	46.8%	37.3%	44.2%	39.6%	46.5%	46.2%	43.9%	44.5%
NOI		**6471**	**4285**	**4996**	**7615**	**5542**	**6166**	**8854**	**5936**	**49,865**	**96,386**
Going-in cap (all costs)		*12.1%*	*11.1%*	*10.9%*	*14.2%*	*10.6%*	*11.7%*	*9.0%*	*9.2%*	*10.8%*	*10.7%*
Leasing commissions	1 month/year	1000	775	850	1100	900	925	1500	1000	8050	15,720
Net income		**5471**	**3510**	**4146**	**6515**	**4642**	**5241**	**7354**	**4936**	**41,815**	**80,666**
Unlevered cash-on-cash		*10.25%*	*9.07%*	*9.01%*	*12.13%*	*8.84%*	*9.93%*	*7.48%*	*7.67%*	*9.10%*	*8.98%*

Houses Considered But Not Purchased

Street		Coleman	Webster	Continental	Curtis	Powell	Clovelawn	E 10 Mile
City		Clinton	Clinton	Warren	Roseville	Hazel Park	Oak Park	Ferndale
Purchase price		65,000	35,000	70,000	50,000	36,500	51,200	65,200
Rehab		500	20,000	1000	7500	5000	1600	4000
Total cost		**65,500**	**55,000**	**71,000**	**57,500**	**41,500**	**52,800**	**69,200**
Rent/month		950	800	800	875	700	800	800
Income								
PGI	8.00%	11,400	9600	9600	10,500	8400	9600	9600
Vacancy		(912)	(768)	(768)	(840)	(672)	(768)	(768)
EGI		10,488	8832	8832	9660	7728	8832	8832
Operating expenses								
Management fee	10.00%	1049	883	883	966	773	883	883
Insurance		600	700	650	600	450	625	500
Property taxes		2000	1400	2100	2200	1400	1800	1750
Repairs and maintenance		1000	1000	1000	1000	1000	1000	1000
Utilities (when vacant)		100	100	100	100	100	100	100
Total OpEX		4749	4083	4733	4866	3723	4408	4233
Expense load		*45.3%*	*46.2%*	*53.6%*	*50.4%*	*48.2%*	*49.9%*	*47.9%*
NOI		**5739**	**4749**	**4099**	**4794**	**4005**	**4424**	**4599**
Going-in cap (all costs)		*8.8%*	*8.6%*	*5.8%*	*8.3%*	*9.7%*	*8.4%*	*6.6%*
Reason for passing:		*Price*	*Sewer*	*Rent*	*Rebah*	*Location*	*Obsolete*	*Price*

Case 5

Forensic Underwriting or: What's the Opposite of Big Data?

I can see most of the outcomes, but where can I find the inputs?

I. "Big Data"

Rose spent the morning online looking for answers. She found mountains of economic and demographic data, she found sales data, and she found lots of generic opinions about the state of real estate. So why was she frustrated? Because despite all this readily accessible and free information, what she really wanted to know was nowhere to be found. While the era of "Big Data" appears to be well underway, Rose was really looking forward to the next era—the era of "Big Understanding." As much as she appreciated all the new ways she could get data, she wasn't sure that the same old junk-in/junk-out truism had changed that much. Instead, the same problems still seemed to exist but on a larger scale. Back in the old days—way back in 2000 when she started working—so much of the way she had gathered her information was from talking to brokers and going to conferences. It was there that she could learn about how others were running their businesses. Of course, no one would give out all their numbers, but she could get a general sense of how her business stacked up.

Another reason Rose had been a regular on the conference circuit was because she could get perspectives on the bigger picture and hear an academic's novel take on real estate. The subtext for all the sessions was always "taking a pulse"—everyone wanted to figure out where pricing was and would be, where leasing activity was and would be, and what returns sponsors were promising to investors. The scale and diversity of firms, product types, and submarkets meant that it would be rare to find any one speaker who would directly address the challenges she faced, but by being a regular attendee and by paying attention, Rose could construct a reasonable narrative about the economy and about the state of real estate. It helped her gain some confidence that she was seeing the market the right way.

While it wasn't as frequent as it once was, Rose still went to a handful of conferences every year—but now only when they were convenient or when she knew a good number of friends and colleagues would be there. Technically, the Internet could provide a connection to almost anyone, but it was still nice

Underwriting Commercial Real Estate in a Dynamic Market. https://doi.org/10.1016/B978-0-12-815989-7.00005-7

to see people in person. Once there she still enjoyed benchmarking her theses about real estate and the larger economy against other smart professionals. And when there was a good speaker, it was terrific to see someone who had done the hard work of synthesizing and interpreting broader trends that Rose couldn't see from talking with her local broker, banker, and contractor contacts. But really good presentations were rare today and it was easy to find general analyses from home: 10,000- to 30,000-ft level analyses on leasing, sales, and development at the submarket level were a dime a dozen. With so many different types of firms publishing these sorts of reports, the bigger challenge was figuring out which to trust. So there was more data, but that did not necessarily translate into more understanding.

This wasn't how it was supposed to be, Rose found herself thinking. Big Data was to be about clarity and finding the key information that would allow for better decision making. Big Data was supposed to be about bringing different data sources to bear and to making use of them to discover valuable patterns embedded in them. But Rose was getting jaded watching data scientists present fancy graphics. They were a huge step forward relative to the monotonous, bullet-pointed presentations she had sat through for years, but she still was not convinced the data folks were really thinking about the underlying real estate fundamentals that produced the data. Rose saw one presentation on single-family house prices that suggested that the housing bust had in fact been grossly overstated. The authors argued that with so many housing markets slowing during the downturn, it was only the worst houses (in terms of price declines) that were sold, and it was these sales and their unusually large price declines that comprised the data used in the commonly reported price indexes. Their novel approach was to correct for this sample selection. It was an interesting thesis, but what data did they use? Evidently they estimated the value of every house in the country and then simply aggregated these estimated price *even when there hadn't been any sales in some submarkets*. In trying to solve one sample selection problem, they had created another. Interesting? Yes. But, Rose was not ready to turn to that sort of "cutting-edge" technology to make her investment choices.

II. "Little Data"

Rose had attended that particular panel because she had hoped for guidance on a pattern every real estate professional would like to anticipate: turning points in the local cycle. Traditionally, it is here that the majority of the big returns and big losses in real estate occur. Many firms have sprung up to bring high-end analytics to bear on single-family housing prices and this is spreading to commercial real estate, but Rose gathered that even with more data and more sophisticated algorithms, predicting turning points remained difficult.

So while there may be a bright future for these new methods for crunching data, the things that Rose wants to know just aren't readily found online.

What was more frustrating was that the kind of fancy market analysis she could buy wasn't going to tell here whether she should try and flip an 8-plex two streets behind Lincoln Boulevard in Altadena, a 16-unit apartment building off Del Mar near Cal Tech, or even try the 27-unit apartment building just north of the 210 Freeway in Pasadena. The 10,000 ft level analysis she found for the San Gabriel Valley showed strong fundamentals and average rent trends that suggested all three would the same good investment. She joked to herself "I guess I can just pick one at random, they're all the same according this report." Rose was suspicious of aggregate data: "It's not that the report is wrong, it's just that you have to be careful using aggregate data to underwrite specific properties."

Rose would make use of all that Big Data offered her, but would stay focused on learning how best to use what she called "Little Data" by being smart and trying to tease out useful information about very local trends from a handful of good data points. At her fingertips were property dimensions, tax records, and sales histories for both a particular subject property as well as its comparables nearby. But she couldn't readily know how much money was spent on renovations, on marketing, or on maintenance. She couldn't figure out how a deal's capital stack had been assembled. Rose had been renovating apartments for more than a decade and she wanted to understand if she could make a profit doing so in Pasadena. Her experience in real estate would count for a lot, but she thought that much of generated over the past 15 years would just not helpful for looking ahead. Much of what Big Data did was churn through past data, but how exactly was today like the tech bubble in 2000? The years during the "Great Moderation"? The housing bubble? The housing bust? The Great Recession? There simply was no point in recent history that was replicated in today's economy. General patterns? Sure, but that would still leave her uninformed about specific decisions. She could find some other local developers and just ask them, but why bother? They would likely be pleasant, but they weren't going to give her their trade secrets. She wanted to local data on recent trades. What could she learn from the data she could find?

III.   Rose and Her Partners

Rose was one of five partners who had found themselves trying to squeeze in between "mom-and-pop" and "institutional" multifamily buyers. They had avoided mom-and-pop deals because they were hard to underwrite, idiosyncratic, and often too small to turn a profit. If it basically took the same amount of time and brain damage to see a larger deal through, why look at the small ones? Neither Rose nor her partners were excited by anything less than an eight-plex, and, importantly, neither were her team of subcontractors, lenders, and investors. At the other end of the spectrum, institutional capital investors applied the same thought process on a larger scale. Rose thought she'd heard at a recent conference that the minimum threshold for an institutional deal these days was $15 million. It had drifted lower over time as the market got more competitive and it was harder to find larger deals with good returns. Somewhere in between the cost of a mom-and-pop duplex or 4-plex and an institutional buyer of a 40-unit or larger apartment building was the market segment that was just right for Rose and her firm.

Fortunately for her, there were many of these in the greater Los Angeles area. So many neighborhoods went through a growth spurt from the 1950s through the 1970s. Many thousands of the units built in those days were aging badly, in no small part because regional supply had never caught up with the demand to live in the region. Landlords were free to raise rents while doing very little to maintain or improve units. More than a dozen California cities had forms of rent control, making buying and repositioning buildings difficult. A third contribution to the aging stock was Proposition 13. Passed in an era when inflation was high, Prop 13 had been a means to prevent runaway taxes, especially for households on fixed incomes. But it had a side-effect of removing an incentive for owners to invest in their own property. Rather than having high land prices result in high taxes, which would in turn lead to higher levels of reinvestment to mirror land prices, investors could be passive—content with a decent return without the complications and headache of undertaking renovations.

According to one commentator, "70% of Los Angeles needs to be renovated. It wasn't great quality to start with. It wasn't very then attractive and hasn't aged particularly well. And none of it is dense enough now." Rose lived in one of these homes and found the 70% percent estimate too high. Still, there were more than enough apartment buildings to renovate and reposition to keep her busy for some time. The key elements of a successful renovation were (1) finding a willing seller at a good price, (2) being diligent about renovation costs, (3) being brutally honest about the time it would take to complete the renovations, (4) being good at anticipating the updated rents and occupancy, and importantly (5) earning a decent return in the process. It was here that Rose become frustrated with Big Data: Google couldn't tell her whether or not a given building would meet these criteria. Rose would have to do her own sleuthing and use "little data" to learn what she needed to know.

IV. Reverse Engineering

Pasadena's housing market has done well and should continue to do well. It's well located within the vibrant Los Angeles metropolitan area. Pasadena is one of the many significant nodes of employment within its polycentric region. It has CalTech and the Jet Propulsion Laboratories to go with other strong employers. It has a rich history and many neighborhoods developed before WWII that have retained their charm. Pasadena is well connected to the larger region with many freeways and the Gold Line Metro extension that runs through downtown to Long Beach, Hollywood, and Santa Monica—and eventually LAX. Pasadena's position in the regional hierarchy should only rise in the years ahead. That said, Pasadena also shares the region's development history from the 1950s to the 1970s: it has many tired apartments that seem worthy of renovation.

Rose had successfully renovated units in nearby Eagle Rock and Highland Park, to the west and south of Pasadena. But these were different because they were within the City of Los Angeles. Pasadena is relatively well known as a more difficult place to develop—not impossible like some of the beach communities, but at best she could expect a host of new fees and procedures. Rose wanted to figure out how much costs were likely to be, but she had no direct contacts with local developers who would walk her though it. Perhaps more importantly, Rose wasn't sure how investors were pricing Pasadena. Her other deals were a bit more adventurous in north Los Angeles. Pasadena might be viewed as safer; maybe she could get larger loans at lower rates, and maybe her equity partners would require less compensation for risk if, in fact, it was safer here. She could find some contacts in Pasadena through her networks, but wanted to see what she could infer from the data she had at her fingertips.

She pulled out a perfect candidate for her and her partners: the Oakland Apartments. It had been on the market in late 2016, had been sold in June of 2017, and renovated since. By the fall of 2018, the renovated units now are occupied. What could Rose learn from a sale price and sale date and current rents? Between the time of the sale to the new owner who undertook the renovation and today, he must have done his market analysis, hired an architect, found a general contractor (GC), and gone through several iterations with the City to arrive at permits and construction.

Rose found bits of the offering memorandum on the internet. She found County parcel data and tax records that would indicate how much he paid for the Oakland Apartments. There must be a permit out there that had an estimate of the value of the renovation, but it wasn't online. She thought this would be a good number to know and made a note to see if she could find it later. Rose also found some other apartment sales nearby and found a host of for-rent sites that could give her a sense of what revenue would come from the renovated units.

It wasn't much to go on, but how far could she push it? She knew a lot about renovating apartments, so she could provide some assumptions…or at least some reasonable range of assumptions. Combined with the data she found, could she learn something useful about whether Pasadena was a market she should spend more time on finding more deals there? More generally, could this approach help her with deals throughout the region? Could she reverse engineer others' deals so that she could be more efficient about her own development plans?

V.   Playing With Little Data

The Oakland Apartments were built in 1957. The single two-story structure consists of 14,824 sq. ft over 25 units. The units were mostly one-bedroom/one-bath, but there were two studios, and three two-bedroom units. Each unit had one parking stall with some tucked under the units and some in a surface parking lot. At the center of the structure was an open-air pool with surrounding hardscape. At the time of the marketing of this sale, all of the apartments had been vacated and the property was being marketed as an obvious value-add investment. Core assets in Pasadena were trading at just below a 4% cap rate and turning this old, tired, and empty building into a four-cap asset was the broker's big pitch. The broker was right about it being a value-add deal. The exterior of the building had all the hallmarks of years of inadequate investment: cracked pavement, faded and crumbling stucco, low-quality single-pane windows, parking stalls from an era when cars were smaller. The interiors hid some of the 1950s by covering it with an assortment of design choices in the 1970s: multigeneration gray carpet, linoleum floors and Formica counter tops in the kitchen, and antiquated in-wall heating and A/C units. Rose guessed that it wasn't anywhere close to well-insulated, that the building was likely not be to code, and might need seismic work. These deficiencies didn't discourage Rose; this was her kind of property. She knew how to fix these things.

Rose heard that the owner who was selling in 2017 was a family trust, formed to benefit the grandchildren of an earlier owner. It had not been professionally managed for years, but had provided a check to the trust every month with essentially no effort. There had been no strong incentive to maximize the property because the eight grandchildren were spread out across the country and had somewhat divergent views of what to do with it over the years. A broker had contacted them with news about rising values and the demand for value-add investments, arguing that this would be right time for them to sell. They agreed and put it on the market.

Purchase Price Economics

Rose started with thinking about the last purchase price of the Oakland Apartments, in the spring of 2017 when it was marketed as a vacant, value-add investment. She found online that the purchase price was $6.1 million and it closed on June 2, 2017. She heard a broker's estimate for the average rent at the Oakland Apartments: $1350/month. She never really expected to find actual operating expense data on line, so she had to assume a number. She chose an operating expense load of 35% of effective gross rent. Given the condition of the building, it might have been lower if the previous owner was putting less into the property or higher if the older property was costing more to maintain and operate. She would have to think about this later.

What could she learn starting with the data she had now? She used a typical static analysis to take a first look at the going-in cap rate. See Exhibit 1 below for her first static analysis.

This put the going-in cap rate right at where she expected for Pasadena for higher quality apartments, but this was not "higher quality" yet. She wanted to see how other older properties that might be viewed as comparable value-add deals had been priced. She was able to find a handful of deals nearby that preceded the sale of the Oakland Apartments. See Exhibit 2 below for the sales comps and her notes.

Rose found these cap rates to be lower—some significantly lower. This was curious: what were the unit rents implied by the cap rates? Again, no data was available for the vacancy or operating expenses, so she began by assuming the same 5% vacancy and 35% operating expense load. The table generated by these assumptions made clear how much variation there was across the buildings and units with regard to size. She wondered if the per square foot rents from the data matched the broker's estimate of the average month rent of $1350 per month.

Question 1: Given the data from the sales comparables, is $1350 a month reasonable rent prior to renovation?

a. Exhibit 2 provides enough data to make some calculations, but the data are rough—maybe not all of them should be included in the comparisons. To start the analysis, use all the data, but if you feel that some of the comps are not, in fact, comparable, then exclude them. Using Rose's assumption of 35% operating expense load and a 5% vacancy, what are the implied rents per square foot among the apartments in Exhibit 2?

b. Repeat this exercise, but use the reported gross rent multiples in Exhibit 2 to calculate another estimate of rents per square foot for the properties in Exhibit 2. Do they correspond to the rent calculations using Rose's assumptions about vacancy and operating expense loads? Some assume that GRM is a better metric than using cap rates for projects like these because the operating expenses and vacancy can vary widely given the informal ownership. Which method (GRM or cap rates) were higher? Should they agree? If you adjusted Rose's assumptions about vacancy and OpEx load would you get more agreement? Vacancy in Pasadena was very tight; maybe her assumption of 5% was too high. And she was not sure about whether 35% was a good guess. Which assumptions about vacancy and operating expense load make the GRM and cap rate approaches more similar?

c. After tweaking Rose's assumptions, can you find consistency in terms of per square foot rents? The market analysis reports you find for current multifamily properties for Pasadena and the San Gabriel Valley report monthly unit rents at close to $2000. Is this close to what you find? Is there one rent for apartments in this submarkets? Are these aggregate reports helpful?

d. As for the local data you have, are they close in terms of per square foot rents? Which ones are outliers? Can you justify why you might want to exclude them?

e. What do you make of this exercise? Especially in light of the aggregate data, which data points do you find useful? Why?

Question 2: What's the current value of the newly renovated Oakland Apartments?

a. Turning to the current valuation: The Oakland Apartments appear to be a successful renovation. But how much so? And how much did the renovations cost? You can turn to the internet for help on this one. Rose found a recent ad for a unit in the Oakland Apartments for rent at $1800 a month, but it was taken and now the building is fully occupied. While Rose is maybe now less sure of using 35% as the right operating expense load, she's happier using it now that the units have been fully renovated. Vacancy is tricky in a tight market. The building is 100% full, but over the long term there must be some frictional vacancy. She decided to use 3%. Using these assumptions and the market cap rate of about 4% for the valuation cap rate, what is the current market value of Oakland Apartments?

b. What has the gross appreciation been since the last sale in June of 2017?

c. If it cost $35,000 a unit to renovate the apartments, what was the total profit? What's the gross profit margin? Does it look like the developer (now owner) would be happy with the outcome? What if the cost were closer to $100,000 per unit?

d. If the developer was expecting to hit a 30% profit margin, approximately what were the renovation costs? Do you need to make any additional assumptions to calculate this number?

Question 3: Does time matter?

a. What about returns? What about leverage? These are often better explored using discounted cash flow analysis rather than the static analyses used above. Assume that the renovation required 12 months. Further assume that redevelopment costs can be spread uniformly over the 12 months. At the end of the year-long renovation, lease up commences and it 3 months to lease up. Indeed one website suggested that the last unit was rented for $1800 a month at the end of September.

b. To keep the analysis relatively simple, assume that the holding costs during renovation are included in the redevelopment budget, so that it is only after the end of the 12th month that you must account for operating expenses. There are numerous ways to approximate these during lease up, but since lease up was very short because of the tightness in the housing market in Pasadena, it might be fair and easiest to use full operating expenses from day 1.

c. You know the purchase price in June of 2017 and you know the market value today from your static analysis above. Build out a monthly discounted cash flow to estimate the annualized unlevered IRR if the property were to be sold at the end of December 2018. What is it? And what is the unlevered equity multiple?

d. To explore leverage, assume a 70% acquisition loan that is used only to acquire the Oakland Apartments. The remaining 30% of the purchase price and the renovation costs are to be funded from equity. The loan terms is 19 months (12 months of development and 7 months of lease up and seasoning), the annual interest rate is 6.0% and the loan requires a 1% origination fee that is to be paid at close. Assume that the loan proceeds are available at close of the acquisition, that it accrues interest during the 12-month development period, and then rolls into an interest-only loan until the property is sold or refinanced at the end of December 2018. What is the levered IRR and the levered equity multiple? Make sure to be clear about your assumptions about rent growth, vacancy, and operating expense loads.

e. It is here that Rose may be able to learn something about the inner-workings of another developer. If Rose were to hear that the developer in fact could sell it today at market prices and earn a 22% levered IRR, what set of assumptions could produce this? That is, Rose will not likely hear more about any operational numbers, but can test a number of simultaneous assumptions that yield the assumed 22% levered IRR. Provide Rose with some ranges of renovation costs, rents, vacancy, and operating expenses that produce the 22% levered IRR.

f. Stepping back from these sets of assumptions and rethinking the market valuation, do you think Rose can reverse engineer any of the inner workings of another redevelopment and be right about it?

Rose would appreciate a short "white paper" on reverse engineering key assumptions about renovating apartment buildings using readily available data from online. Please advise her on the strengths and weaknesses of taking this approach. Also, advise her on what numbers you are most concerned about. It may be that this "little data" approach could be made significantly more accurate with some key data. It might be worth finding out which data could help and how she might go about finding it.

Finally, add to your white paper, a response to tension about Big Data in the case above: In light of all of this, do you think that "Big Data" will help Rose in the near term? Long term? If yes, how so? If not, why not?

VI. Exhibits

Exhibit 1—Static valuation/broker rent		
Purchase Price		6,100,000
Units		25
Unit Rent ($/mo)		1,350
Potential Gross Income		405,000
Vacancy	5% of PGI	(20,250)
EGI		384,750
OpEx	35% of EGI	(134,663)
NOI		250,088
Implied Cap Rate		4.10%
Implied Gross Rent Multiple		15.1

Exhibit 2—Sales comparables

	City	Year Built	Distance	Price	Sale Date	# Units	Avg Sf/ Unit	Cap Rate	GRM	Value-Add?
Subject	*Pasadena*	*1957*		*6,200,000*	*6/2/2017*	*25*	*593*	*3.92%*	*15.6*	*HVA*
1	Pasadena	1955	0.12	23,550,000	11/14/2017	93	596	2.50%		HVA
2	Pasadena	2004	0.24	14,000,000	10/24/2017	28	1253	4.25%		AsIs
3	Pasadena	2005	0.36	154,001,000	11/2/2016	99	3500	4.50%		AsIs
4	Pasadena	1929	0.63	2,600,000	2/17/2016	12	813	2.89%	17.5	VA
5	Pasadena	1961	0.82	4,300,000	8/31/2016	16	662	2.75%	19.9	LVA
6	Pasadena	1916	0.86	2,150,000	1/22/2016	7	598	2.50%		Bungalows
7	Pasadena	1950/2003	1.22	2,700,000	12/1/2016	10	565	3.50%		Renovated/ AsIs
8	Pasadena	1953	1.89	1,600,000	3/11/2016	6	867	3.35%	17.0	LVA
9	South Pasadena	1928	2.37	5,410,000	5/31/2016	24	600	2.27%	23.0	VA
10	South Pasadena	1966	3.27	9,500,000	1/26/2017	32	912	2.68%	21.3	VA

Notes: The "value-add" column reflects Rose's quick read on each property with regard to their quality and the scope for a value-add deal. "HVA" is a rough estimate that the property would be a "heavy value-add," i.e., the property is great need of reinvestment to bring it to current standard. "VA" is a typical value-add for her firm. This would typically involve a number of property systems in addition to the renovation of the units—carpet removal, new white goods and new countertops in the kitchen, updated bathroom, etc. "LVA" is light value-add. While "AsIs" means the property is sufficiently close to current standard that it wouldn't be worth investing additional capital at this point. Finally, "bungalows" were a note from Rose to explain that property six was not a traditional apartment building.

Part II

Extending the Framework: Commercial Leases

To begin extending our underwriting in different contexts, we continue with several cases that share one obvious characteristic: vacancy. We know that the value of real estate comes from a property's future cash flows, so on the face of it, vacancy would seem to impair a property's value: holding everything else constant, higher vacancy should reduce a property value. But an important point in these cases is that everything else is never constant. The perception of vacancy can vary markedly over the real estate cycle, across submarkets, and by rent roll. During periods of falling demand for office space, vacancy can be viewed as highly problematic because rents will generally have to fall to refill the building. But vacancy can also be seen as valuable in a tight market, or when a property can be recast as a "value-add" opportunity. The cases here focus on filling vacancy and on the many implications of commercial real estate leasing.

In this section we introduce longer-term commercial real estate leases and try to build on the framework we began developing in Section A. These longer-term commitments to exchange property rights for rent can have profound effects on real estate values and are a major source of noise when trying to interpret market data. But commercial leasing offers many opportunities to find value by thinking about the preferences of current and potential tenants, and also about those of lenders and future buyers. All three matter enormously for overall returns and it is best to underwrite their interactions rather than treat each as a distinct decision. In the last section, the emphasis was on local fundamentals at the time of sale, over the holding period, and at exit. The short term leases meant that the properties would be essentially be marked to market on an ongoing basis. In the cases included in this section, longer-term leases have the effect of transmitting fundamentals from one point in time to others. For example in the first case in this section, a Class A building in a great location is facing potentially large vacancy and will need to be retenanted. It may be desirable to find a long-term tenant take the space, but beyond all the usual lease terms to be considered, a long-term lease signed near the bottom of the cycle will cause the rents in the building to run below-market for some time. While there may be some urgency to generate immediate cash flow, it may be that doing so will impair the value of the property. This sort of tension is common in leasing. The landlord and the tenant are engaged in trading property rights and sharing risk, and there are numerous ways to structure a lease to accomplish this. But the trade-offs for the landlord are further complicated because other stakeholders will be influenced by the leasing choices the landlord makes. In particular, lenders will generally see stable and certain cash flows as lower risk investments. They are likely to lend more and at lower interest rates relative to properties with leases that are short and uncertain. Counterintuitively, it can be the case that offering lower rents to attract higher-quality tenants can actually enhance returns to equity when more lower-cost debt can be used. Whether and when this is true is a common question asked in this section of cases.

Case 6

Bayview Double Take

In 2006, the Bayview Corporate Center was a gem, located in Newport Beach—a top office submarket in Orange County, California. By 2008, Bayview had fallen out of escrow at a price that was well below its peak just two years earlier. It finally sold in 2009 for a price that suggested that Bayview was more a liability than a trophy property. During this time period, the perceived riskiness of the property changed and so, too, did the way risk was priced. Perceptions of risk and the cost of bearing it have continued to evolve since then and asset prices are once again back to historic highs. This case addresses two types of questions about underwriting commercial real estate. The first is a forensic analysis of the valuations in 2008 and the bidding for the Bayview Corporate Center in 2009; it asks "What was the 'right' way to underwrite an office building and which underwriting tools worked well?" Though we can now know the actual sale price in 2009, it is worth exploring the market's approach to underwriting at that time. Despite a general sense that the Newport Beach office market would eventually recover, it was not clear when it would or how a new owner would manage the property until then. This time period posed numerous challenges to standard underwriting tools; this case should build some intuition about their relative strengths and weaknesses. The second question posed in this case is, "Given our understanding of the underwriting in 2009, what can we say about the value of the Bayview Corporate Center today?" 100 Bayview, the "sister" building of the Bayview Corporate Center, has just been listed for sale. Will the sale of a "twin" give a solid valuation for Bayview? What more would one need to know to form a solid valuation and which underwriting tools are appropriate now?

I. Underwriting Under Duress

Your boss handed you the abstracted offering memorandum for the Bayview Corporate Center with only one piece of advice: "Be careful trying to catch a falling knife." According to the marketing material, the Bayview Corporate Center (BCC) is a "landmark, trophy office building in one of the most sought–after locations in the country." You had looked at BCC when it was marketed several years ago. Then it was too big a deal for you to pursue, but since the most recent sale had fallen through, maybe the price would fall low enough for you to find a way to own a good building with a Newport Beach address.

Much had changed since you last looked at it. The Bayview Corporate Center was still in Newport Beach, of course, and so it still had all the same

Underwriting Commercial Real Estate in a Dynamic Market. https://doi.org/10.1016/B978-0-12-815989-7.00006-9

extraordinary amenities that had been part of the earlier marketing materials. But the way you looked at it now was significantly different. The entire real estate world had started to slow in 2007, a decline that was punctuated by the failure of Bear Stearns and by the collapse of Lehman Brothers in 2008. By that point, investors were paying to avoid risk by accepting very low returns in assets that could at least preserve their principal. During this period, the 1-year US Treasury rate fell from just over 5% to less than 0.5% as investors sought a safe haven in government bonds. At the same time, the spread for office cap rates relative to Treasuries rose from almost 100 basis points to over 400 basis points. With treasury rates falling and office cap rates rising, it could be that office investments were being viewed as riskier, or it could be that the market had gotten less tolerant of the same risk—or both. Understanding this will matter for you because your firm is willing to bear volatility in the short run if the longer-term returns are high. If in fact there is too much office space and white-collar job losses persist, falling prices now could reflect this supply and demand imbalance. But if the market is simply overreacting and mispricing the same risk, then asset prices should rise. Right now it seems that the majority of real estate assets are being penalized simply for being in an impaired asset class. But you know that some submarkets and properties will do much better than others both through the downturn and beyond. These are the properties you are looking to acquire.

Your firm had been successful at raising its last fund through the end of 2006, but almost immediately after that your deal flow slowed. The fund had acquired a handful of deals since then that looked solid for now, but there remained a significant amount of capital at your disposal to pursue good office deals. But at a deal size rumored to be in a neighborhood of $100M or more, final bidding would likely have been too large for a single asset to fit the fund's investment criteria. Now with capital flowing out of real estate, it would be interesting to see how far pricing would fall. It was not an optimal time to sell an asset like this, but as the financial crisis ground on, it was becoming common to see even good assets up for sale. It could be that the current owners were hedging against further declines in asset prices, or it could be that some of the more of optimistic business plans from the late bubble years were simply proving flawed. In many of these cases, the owners had bet on NOI increasing, cap rates compressing, and had often levered up to make their deals work. It would be difficult for these owners to hold on through a slow recovery.

Given the drama in the larger economy, it is hard for you not to follow falling asset prices. You tracked prices on the way up and lost many deals at prices that, in hindsight, you were lucky to avoid. While this makes for interesting gossip around the office, you know it will be the nature of the recovery that determines whether any of this vintage of acquisitions will be profitable. If there's a traditional "V" shaped recession and a quick, robust recovery, then you might be very pleased you took the gamble on "catching the falling knife" now. But you read the paper every day and for every article mentioning "shoots of green" there are 10 more that document different manifestations of financial chaos. It is clear that the state of the market will not be settled soon. But by next week you would need to decide about acting on the BCC offering. Would BCC return to its previous status as a gem? Is this a chance to buy into a top-tier office market? Or is it a chance to take a ride down along with the rest of the owners who overpaid?

It's always easy in retrospect to see the bottom of a business cycle, but once you're sure the market has found its footing and started recovering, your chance to find a bargain may have gone. Certainly most owners who bought 2007 were feeling they overpaid, but so too were the first movers who had been confident that they had found a market bottom by mid-to-late 2008. Some of these early deals have already gone badly. A year into owning them, asset prices have fallen further and for many their NOI has continued to shrink. Looking around the local market, you see office vacancy climbing to more than 20%—and that doesn't include additional shadow vacancy. While job losses have slowed, there are still year-over-year losses in total employment. All of this is undermining your confidence about getting back into the market now. Plenty of broker packages come across your desk and with them are plenty of motivated sellers, something you haven't seen in years. Despite the marketing activity, you are not seeing many final sales. When will be the right time to get back in? Every real estate conference you've ever attended has at least one speaker who got the timing right and hit the "home run." It always sounds obvious as they narrate how they bought for "pennies on the dollar." But reading the government reports, the newspapers, the financial blogs, and the broker reports, nothing looks like an obvious "home run" now.

The fact is that it is very difficult to forecast anything given an unstable present and a highly uncertain future. In normal times, the longer term nature of office leases mean that there are some future cash flows you can estimate reasonably well. Given normal turnover, you might know something about where market pricing will be. The harder numbers to know—future leases and the exit cap rate—were somewhere out in the future where you might feel safe using long-term averages. But these were not normal times: current pricing is a total mystery, tenants—even good ones—are failing to make rent, and the standard rules of thumb about exit cap rates seem preposterous. In short, it seems unwise to make decisions based on textbook underwriting.

You know that the summary reports you read in the paper and from brokerages mask significant variation, so there is reason to look past the aggregates. The Newport Beach "micro-market"—where Bayview is located—has been one of the top performing submarkets of the Orange County office market for years. At one point, Orange County was considered a bedroom community for employees who worked in Los Angeles. Those days are long gone. The Orange County office market now exceeds 120 million sq. ft of office space, and more than 40 million of that is Class A. The Newport Beach submarket is the top of this now-mature urban area, and historically it has been a very expensive market to enter. At some point in the future, it seems likely that the Bayview Corporate Center will return to its former stature as a premier property in one of the best markets in the United States. The question you face in this underwriting is whether or not to acquire it now, at what price, and if you do, how to manage it through the recovery in order to realize any prospective gains.

Along with the warning about "catching falling knives," you have also been asked by your boss to start the underwriting anew. There are numerous ways to value an asset like BCC, you will have to engage in both static and dynamic underwriting. In the end you get to pick one value to bid. Arriving at that number will depend on which underwriting tools you use and how you choose to weigh them.

II. Static Valuation

Built in 1988, the BCC offers more than 337,000 sf of gross leasable area. This space does not include a well-appointed three-story concourse or other common areas. The property is now close to 99% occupied and generated an approximate annualized net operating income (NOI) of $8.37 million dollars. (See rent roll and annualized cash flows in the exhibits below.) The question you face is how to value the Bayview Corporate Center. Your broker contacts have provided you a well-argued narrative for why BCC is currently and will continue to be a gem. From them you gather some reasonable numbers. Then you call the sale broker, who suggests some "better" numbers, but prudently did not include a sale price. There are many reasons for this, but among them is a desire to have as many potential buyers as possible "see the dream"—to view the numbers favorably and grow attached to the idea of owning BCC. And though some of the data has changed, this abstract is telling essentially the same story as two years ago. It was clearly optimistic then and it may still be. Your task is to think hard about which numbers and what tools you should use for valuing BCC.

For example, the broker provided you with a careful analysis of what it would cost to replicate BCC. He also provided you with an annualized estimates of the trailing 3-month operating cash flows at BCC. From these you could calculate the net operating income and "cap it"—use direct capitalization to arrive a market value. But which NOI? Is this annualized NOI reflective of future cash flows? And which cap rate? Moreover, why not just use the replacement cost approach? It seems simpler.

Your boss likes to see robustness in your analysis. "No one number tells the story" she likes to say. So, you start with the simplest number and will add more sophistication if it can improve the quality of your underwriting. The broker's estimated cost of rebuilding BCC is $460 psf of gross leasable area. There is much to criticize about this approach, especially for a 20 year-old property in which functional obsolescence is hard to measure. But still, it is a commonly used valuation benchmark.

From there you have an assortment of cap rates you can use to apply to an NOI to obtain another set of estimates. Until recently, institutional cap rates for office were below 6%. Because of the location, assume that a fair valuation cap rate in late 2007 would have been 5.5%. With spreads widening, an average cap rate could be 7.75%. And yet, because of its location in the Newport Beach sub-market, maybe a more appropriate cap rate might be closer to 7.25%.

Questions About Static Analyses

a. Given the ease of the math behind the replacement cost approach, why not just use it? When would the replacement cost approach be useful? Accurate? When might it not help provide a good estimate of current value? Now in late 2009, is this a good time to use the replacement cost approach?

b. Estimate three values of the Bayview Corporate Center using the market comparable approach for each for the three different cap rate assumptions above using the broker's annualized estimate of NOI. The first, 5.50% is clearly too low, but it might be interesting to see how valuable BCC might have been considered recently. With that value in mind, what would explain the pricing today at a 7.75% cap rate for the broader Orange County office market? What would it imply for the value of the BCC? And, from these numbers, can you estimate how much the Newport Beach address is worth? Do any of these three valuations match the replacement cost approach? Can you reconcile these static estimates? Which one is "best" and make sure to define how you mean "best?"

c. It is typical for underwriters to use the prospective 12 months of operating cash flows to forecast a "pro forma NOI" when using the market compa-rable approach. Since the present is so uncertain, using long term averages might be best. The profession has long-used 3% as a safe annual growth rate to forecast. Inflate the lagging 12-month NOI you have in the exhibits to estimate a prospective "pro forma NOI" and revisit the current cap rate valuations for the broader Orange County office market and for the Newport Beach submarket. Do these numbers seem more appropriate to you? Why or why not?

d. Another approach to using market comparables is to use an "embedded NOI." Under this approach NOI is calculated as if rents were marked to market. We know there are leases in place at BCC, but much of the gross leasable area under lease will rollover soon and BCC has a weighted-rent that is below the current asking rents. Perhaps the market rent would be provide a better estimate of the market value of the property. The broker suggests $2.10 as a market rent for a NNN lease (with the Management Fee, Management Staff, and General and Administrative expenses not reim-bursed). Once more revisit the same static analysis from the previous steps and calculate new value estimates of the embedded NOI. And, again use the two valuation cap rates.

e. Finally, a lender friend made an off-hand comment to you about the way bank underwriting has become drastically more conservative. She said that her bank would give you no credit for leases less than 3 years of term or for any leases not signed by credit tenants. Looking over the rent roll, recalculate the value this bank might give BCC. That is, adjust the NOI to reflect the rent from tenants who had longer lease terms and were considered "credit" tenants, and then apply this new "lenders NOI" to the two valuation cap rates to determine how this lender might value BCC. If a typical commercial is sized using 60% loan-to-value, how much debt would a buyer be able to raise? How does this loan size compare to the some of the other valuations?

f. Using a minimal set of numbers, you've just produced a wide variety of property value estimates. How should you reconcile them? "The market" makes use of all of these approaches, but rarely uses all of them at once. Why do you think there is variation in their usage? Is any one of them preferable? Why?

g. If you had to pick one market valuation, which approach and which valuation would you choose? Why? In looking back at the assumptions, do you agree that there should be a significant premium (a lower cap rate) for properties in Newport Beach relative to rest of the Orange County market, or to the nearby airport submarket? Why should there be a spread between them? Do you think this spread is constant?

III. Valuation by Looking Forward

These quick snap shots of valuation for BCC may leave you ill at ease. You applied two "standard" underwriting tools and used typical slices of the data, and were left with a very wide range of property values. If you pick the highest, you might feel sure that you are likely to overpay. Alternatively, if you act like a lender in the middle of a downturn, you are likely to bid so low as to avoid ever becoming a property owner. Maybe it is time to try a different underwriting tool.

One problem with all of the market comparable approaches is that they are constrained by looking at cash flows at one point in time. The world is never a static place and it is decidedly not static today, so maybe this approach is not appropriate. The next set of valuation exercises you pursue includes making assumptions about the medium term cash flows for BCC using a discounted cash flow analysis (DCF). It is obvious to you that if you just plug generic numbers into your DCF, you'll get generic numbers out. But with some thought you feel you should be able to do better than "junk-in" so that you can avoid "junk-out."

Your boss will certainly want to see several different cash flow scenarios that can help reveal a range of plausible outcomes for the property. In light of your view of Newport Beach and its long-term strengths, you build an optimistic scenario for rent growth, occupancy, and exit cap rates that takes into account the current weakness, but also assumes that BCC returns to its status as a gem relatively quickly. This optimistic scenario is balanced by a more conservative set of assumptions that incorporate the extreme nature of the downturn so far and a growing sense that a full recovery is years into the future. Finally, you'd like to use your DCF to explore what to do with your largest tenant, a Savings and Loan (see the exhibits below). With over three quarters of the gross leasable area tied to the renewal of the Savings and Loan, it is essential for you to understand how you might approach lease negotiations.

Use the annualized cash flows as a starting point to build a 7-year holding period analysis using the following four scenarios.

a. Generic Optimistic Case: Strong recovery beginning in 2 years
  - Rent growth will be flat for 2 years, but then the recovery will take root and rent growth will rise to 5% through the end of the holding period.
  - Vacancy will remain low due to the existing leases and will remain tight as releasing begins to pick up. Use 5% vacancy throughout the holding period.
  - Exit cap rates will settle back to more normal levels. Use 6.25% as the exit cap rate. While higher than peak pricing in 2006, it is significantly lower than today's comparable sales.

b. Generic Pessimistic Case: Long downturn and slow recovery
  - Rent growth will stall, staying at 0% for 4 years before finally rising mildly to 1% per year throughout the remainder of the 7-year holding period.
  - Vacancy will follow a weak office market; use 25% vacancy for 2 years and then step the vacancy down by 5% per year until it reaches a long term level of 10%.
  - Assume exit cap rates reflect a permanent view of office investments as riskier—use an 8.0% exit cap rate.

c. Retaining both the corporate office and retail Savings and Loan tenants.
  - The Savings and Loan recognizes its leverage and bargains hard. It does not want to move, but also understands how many vacant buildings there are now with owners who are eager to fill them. Using the broker's market NNN rent of about $2.10/sf/month, assume that you can retain the S&L for a slight discount to market rent. Use $2.00/sf/month for a flat rent for a full 10-year lease. This low rent allows you to forego any new TIs or concessions.
  - Use a standard 10% vacancy on the balance of the space.
  - With the 10-year lease term signed, assume that the next owner will be able to pay more for BCC because it can retenant or release the space to an anticipated much-higher market rent in the third year of its hold. As a mild value-add deal, you assume that you can use a 5.75% exit cap rate at the end of your 7-year hold.

d. Losing both the corporate office and retail Savings and Loan tenants.
  - Assume the S&L does not want to renew. This means that their two leases will expire as scheduled and the space will return to inventory.
  - It is hard to nail down what it will take to fill the space again. The corporate office has been demised as a single tenant. And, it is tired space. To demise it for multiple tenants and bring the space to current standards could cost on the order of $150/sf, far in excess of the standard $50/sf tenant improvement package.

- Though waiting for a single tenant to take the space could be worth exploring, for now assume that you can get back to the background market vacancy rate in 2 years by charging market rent if you invest the $150/sf to update the space.

Around these key assumptions, also use a 3% growth rate in operating expenses. Assume other revenue sources grow along with rent growth. Because this is California, you will need to adjust the property taxes to 1.2% of whatever purchase price you use in your valuation, but be careful because property taxes grow by at most 2% per year due to Prop 13. Of course, brokers' fees and costs of sales are always going to be an issue, but they seem to be in flux like the rest of the market.

The four scenarios above are relatively crude, but span a range of plausible outcomes. Like the market comparable approaches above, your estimate will depend on your assumptions. Though there are plenty of assumptions provided to you above, you may need to make more. Think about them, note them, and move on. Given that you're explicitly building four scenarios with many different assumptions for each, how do you reconcile all the estimates you've created?

Questions:

a. Once you've translated the four scenarios into four different DCFs, you can assume a purchase price, from which you will be able to calculate an unlevered internal rate of return (IRR) and equity multiple (EM). Or you can work backwards, by selecting target investment thresholds and calculating the purchase price that generates them. Start with using some of the key valuation numbers from the first section as different purchase prices and calculate the returns for each: (1) Use the replacement costs as your purchase price and evaluate your returns under the different scenarios. (2) Use both the in-place NOI and "embedded NOI" with the submarket office cap rate of 7.25% and calculate the IRR and EM for each of the four scenarios.

b. Now work backwards. Using 9% unlevered IRR target, calculate the implied purchase price for each of the scenarios. Is it close to the replacement cost approach for valuation? Is it close to any of the static valuations from the first section?

c. While you've followed a different valuation approach in moving to a DCF from a static analysis, you've done something similar: you've made a host of reasonable assumptions and applied them to another standard valuation tool. Do you find similar outcomes? If there is consistency, can you explain it in light of the different assumptions you used? If there is divergence among the valuations, what do you do with it? That is, you can't give multiple bids that are conditional on different outcomes in the market; you can only make one offer. While choosing the lowest bid price will help protect you from downside risk, you're also not likely to end up owning the property. Given your understanding of the market behind the assumptions, what bid would you make? Why?

d. Feel free to extend the scenarios to incorporate your beliefs about the future cash flows. For example, rather than let the S&L leave, could you lower the rent to make sure they stay. What is the downside risk of owning a building with a long term tenant who is well below market rent? Is lowering the S&L rent a good idea?

e. Finally, do you think you learned anything from building these models and estimating many different returns? If the answer is no, when should you have stopped underwriting? That is, was there a point earlier at which you were sure of your bid? If no, would you want more time to explore more scenarios? Which ones and why? What is the return to you by running another scenario? Will the return decline with each additional scenario?

f. If you are really interested in pushing the analysis further, consider adding debt. Given the state of the banking industry, you are not likely to get a large loan or a cheap one, but debt can still enhance returns under some circumstances. To examine this dynamic, assume that you can obtain a 10-year loan from a life insurance company for 45% of the value of the property. This loan-to-value (LTV) is low, but banks are experiencing as much or more duress than real estate. The rate on the LifeCo loan would be 9.0% per year, amortizing over 30 years. The loan fee would be 1.5% of the loan amount at loan closing. This will be costly debt and offer little leverage, but will give you a long term capital source. You can also consider a local regional bank who will lend you a 65% LTV loan, but it will protect itself by offering only a short-term loan and require full recourse. It will offer you a 6.75% interest rate on a 4 years, interest-only loan. While this loan will come with full recourse, the life insurance company will not. Both loans will require BCC to generate enough income to maintain a debt-service coverage ratio (DCR) of at least 1.25. In both cases, the loan will be in default if this ratio is violated.

g. Is one of the two loans clearly better? If there are trade-offs, which ones do you focus on and why? How do you decide in light of the four DCF scenarios you explored above?

IV.   Iterating and Making Decisions

At this point you will have made extensive use of Excel and have created what feels like thousands of numbers across your pro formas. Is the goal of your job to produce more numbers or more useful insight? The nature of your job at your firm is varied. As one of a small team, you do a little bit of everything, but you are mainly responsible for modeling and starting the analysis. Your first assignment is to follow through on the various models you have outlined above. You should be able to write a short memo on both the static and dynamic cash flow analyses. Again, because you are with a small firm, add a section to the memo that supports your proposed bid, your proposed approach to renewing the S&L at below market rents, and the returns you expect your firm to earn. Be sure to address downside risk. If you pursue debt, argue for either of the two loans or argue that you should pay all cash, and explain why.

It is clear that there is more than one decision to make. While the number you are tasked with is a bid price, you understand right away that to find one you will have to make numerous other decisions. Do you try and keep the Savings and Loan as a tenant? Conditional on retaining them, what would you pay for BCC? What if you lose them? What would it cost to demise and retenant that large block of space? Given the location, someone who couldn't afford a Newport Beach address will take your vacant space, but how low should you go on the rent? Should you pursue a loan to help pay for the acquisition? Which loan is better? Does your answer depend on the Savings and Loan agreeing to a new long-term lease? It will take some iterations to arrive at these decisions.

Keep in mind that any of the analysts at the firm could get this assignment. And if they use the assumptions you use, the output of the scenarios should be the same as yours. But from that starting point, interpretations of the fundamentals at work both on the property and beyond the property lines can differ dramatically. For example, you may find that even the pessimistic scenario is too optimistic. That is, the assumptions above are general in the sense that they span one set of outcomes. Your job is to move from simply grinding the numbers to underwriting the property. What scenarios do you want to explore? Why? What do they imply for your plans with BCC? Once you have followed the assumptions and answered the questions above, articulate your own scenarios and execute them. Your final memo should address the tasks you've been assigned, but also address the ways you want to add value to the firm by informing the bidding process for the Bayview Corporate Center.

V.   Revisiting Bayview Today

This case was first written in 2009, when BCC was last on the market and so the memo you write about the Bayview Corporate Center is going to be dated by construction. Since 2009, this case has been used repeatedly because it helps students master the various ways to measure value and interpret differences across them. But having gone through the chaos of 2009, what can the case teach us about underwriting today? Were the strange numbers a function of the strange period in American economic history—and therefore something that may no longer be useful? Or are there general, durable insights that could help us underwriting BCC today?

One of great challenges of the case in 2009 was the lack of good comparables against which BCC could be compared. Today the adjacent property to BCC, 100 Bayview, is on the market and the offering memorandum is circulating. If you had this OM, would it help you arrive at a more accurate valuation of BCC than if you didn't?

Questions

a. Consider 100 Bayview as physically equivalent at the BCC—same location, same developer, built at the same time in the same style and materials. How relevant is 100 Bayview to our understanding of BCC?

b. If 100 Bayview sold for a 6.75% cap rate, would it be appropriate to use it at BCC?

c. To your memo, add several paragraphs about the various underwriting tools you have addressed above, commenting on how they should be viewed as more or less useful in light of the 100 Bayview abstract.

VI. Exhibits

Bayview rent roll				
Analysis date 10/1/2009				
Tenant name	End date	sf	Monthy rent/sf	Monthly rent
Leishman & Partners	Jan-2011	17,347	2.32	40,245
Island Inc.	Jan-2011	6298	2.90	18,264
Downey S&L Bank Branch	Dec-2013	9160	2.98	27,297
Downey S&L Office-HQ	Dec-2009	245,976	1.81	445,217
OC Brokers	Jul-2011	34,346	2.32	79,683
Amparo Salon	Mar-2012	3817	1.54	5878
Bayview Cafe	Apr-2013	1493	1.63	2434
Vacant		4319		–
Hunter Optical	Jan-2016	5066	2.90	14,691
Hunter Optical	Jan-2016	9562	2.93	28,017
Total leaseable area		*337,384*		*661,725*
Unweighted average rent			*2.37*	
Weighted average rent				*1.96*
If leases are shorter than		*2 Years*		*1.92*
Bayview—Current annualized cash flow				
Revenue				
Base rental revenue			8,063,534	
Vacancy and collection allowance	5%		(399,145)	
Expense reimbursement revenue			3,879,656	
Parking Inc. Excl. Downey			117,549	
Parking Inc.—Downey			941,313	

Continued

Bayview—Current annualized cash flow—cont'd		
Parking revenue		163,071
Effective gross revenue		12,765,977
Operating expenses		
Repairs		(131,274)
General building		(421,730)
HVAC		(70,142)
Electrical		(36,741)
Plumbing		(23,766)
Elevator		(60,729)
Cleaning		(507,972)
Landscaping		(137,340)
Garage expenses		(172,426)
Security		(175,440)
Utilities		(50,936)
Electricity		(1,159,132)
Property taxes		(775,477)
Insurance		(156,550)
Mgmt fee		(258,612)
Mgmt staff		(197,066)
G&A		(56,208)
Total operating expenses		(4,391,542)
NOI		8,374,436
Tenant improvements		(190,468)
Leasing commissions		(50,022)
Capital reserves		(50,608)
Total leasing and capital costs		(291,098)
Cash flow before debt service and taxes		8,083,338

Case 7

Excuse Me, Where's the Exit From Marina Bay?

"You make your money on the buy" was just the sort of thing that someone on the acquisition team would say.

I. Getting to Marina Bay

Lots in investors would like to own real estate in the San Francisco Bay Area, but wish they had acted on the impulse to buy two years ago. It felt expensive and risky then, but clearly "expensive" is a relative term. Current asset prices seem astonishingly high, perhaps suggesting that values must be near peak, but perhaps these recent trends suggest that the Bay Area's transition to becoming the new center of global capital is only now getting underway. At times it seemed that pricing was about which direction you faced: look backward and see that real estate prices now that are higher than ever before; look ahead and you can see scenarios in which there are still bargains to be had today. And if you look around at other office markets, higher prices can be found in Manhattan, and even higher prices and rents in Hong Kong.

While the question about whether San Francisco was overvalued or undervalued was on his mind pretty much every day, Erin Collins knew that the two office buildings she had just acquired for her firm, Willow Park Properties, were a bargain—at least relative to what she had been considered bidding on them last year. Then, the call for the "final and best" pricing had left her and his firm out of the running for 400 and 450 Marina Bay Boulevard in Brisbane, California. Erin had originally wanted to increase her firm's bid to make sure they would be in the final and best round of bidding for the two buildings, but in the end she just couldn't get comfortable at the pricing the broker suggested would be competitive. What kept her from getting comfortable with the higher pricing was the fact that both buildings were currently entirely vacant and had been so for five years—this despite an ever-tightening office market and views of the San Francisco Bay. Though Willow Park wanted to own more office space in the Bay Area, Erin actually dropped her original underwriting by almost 20% and submitted the offer price at well below what the seller broker had suggested. She was sure she would lose, but went ahead just because she had heard so often the adage that "you can't win if you don't play."

Underwriting Commercial Real Estate in a Dynamic Market. https://doi.org/10.1016/B978-0-12-815989-7.00007-0

Not surprisingly, Willow Park had been left out the final bidding, but three months later the sale broker at Marina Bay contacted Erin. He told her that the first two bidders fell out of contention for a number of reasons. After failing to close the sale with either of the other two higher bidders, the sale broker and the owner had jointly decided to prioritize certainty of close over top dollar and had picked Willow Park out of the other candidates to contact and try to work out an off-market deal. Willow Park had an excellent reputation for doing what it said it would and a long track record of being able to raise funds if needed. This was important: because the Marina Bay properties had been empty and lenders would not be keen to provide much debt. Willow Park would likely be able to pay cash in the event that no lender wanted to participate. Erin agreed that she would still buy the property at his original offer price, proposing some conditions, but otherwise agreeing to the seller's terms. And so began the process of thinking about how best to turn around the two buildings and maximize the returns on Willow Park's investment.

The question about whether the deal was a real bargain would depend on the larger Bay Area office market, the local submarket, and how well Erin would be able to execute his business plan. "You make your money on the buy" is an oft-repeated maxim in real estate, but always Erin thought it was the acquisition teams that repeated it the most. She was sure that execution would matter every bit as much. And as the owner of the property, Erin's specific decisions about how best to lease the space would be needed soon.

On the face of it, the Marina Bay buildings were full of potential. To begin with, the two buildings were exceptional in that they were in fact genuinely on the Bay. Unlike the thousands of properties that invoked water imagery in their marketing material but were far from any actual water, there were no other private properties between Marina Bay and the tide line. The land that separated the buildings form the water was the San Francisco Bay Trail, an obvious amenity. And from any floor on the northern and eastern sides of the buildings, one could gaze out at uninterrupted views of the Bay. These were substantially better views than Erin had seen at any other office buildings she had toured.

In other ways, the Marina Bay buildings were mostly unremarkable: both were slightly dated and inefficient. 400 Marina Bay was the larger of the two. It was a 78,000 sf, five-story building with an open atrium. On two sides, it had a unique window system that angled the panes into the building. The original window system was considered by some as innovative because the angled windows brought more natural light into the building. But in practice the window system didn't provide enough light to overcome the loss of useable space. The second building, 65,000 sf 450 Marina Bay, contained roughly three 22,000 sf floor plates and a translucent kalwall detail that blocked some light coming through on two of the floors.

Both of the buildings were built on a landfill. While each was on a structurally sound slab, there were issues with both entries to the property of both buildings. These problems could be solved, but it would take time to design solutions and funds to implement a fix. The first hurdle was to make changes to the window system at 400 Marina. While the atrium and four decks in the building created a collaborative and creative feel, the angled window system made it look bulky, did not allow for sufficient light, and hampered views of the bay.

The purchase-and-sale agreement was signed in January 2014, with an accompanying 3-month due diligence period before the 1% deposit became nonrefundable. Erin spent the next two months underwriting the deal and meeting with local constituents to work through the process of changing the shell. Changing the window system was essential to achieving the kind of returns Erin expected for Marina Bay. She envisioned attracting technology tenants from San Francisco, which would require updating the physical plants in both buildings and bringing them to current market standards.

Prior to having the deposit go nonrefundable, Erin attended a "float up" session at the Planning Commission to discuss their plans for the building. The planning commission appreciated how long the buildings had been vacant and the majority of the commissioners were generally in favor of the plan put forth by Willow Park. Though the new envelope of the property would be unchanged, the property had won an AAI Design Award a year after it was built in 1986. This award induced a long discussion about preserving it as a property of architectural significance. That discussion led to delays and costs, but was eventually followed by formal approval of the new designs. With this approval in hand, Willow Park closed on the acquisition in December 2014.

II.   Getting Marina Bay Leased Up

With the approval process completed, Erin started work renovating the shell on 400 Marina Bay and started the capital projects that would result in upgraded HVAC and other infrastructure. At the end of three months, both buildings could be ready to be leased. Both buildings would be built to an effective "cold shell" status. Erin's pressing need was to figure out the next dollar of investment. Would it be marketing to find a single tenant who could create a campus across the two buildings? Would it be to build out a suite to show potential tenants? Would it be for full floor tenants? Or would the space have to be demised and split for smaller tenants? The market for office space in the Bay Area was great if you were renting creative office space South of Market, but this was in far-flung Brisbane. The comparative set of rents and sales nearby were hard to read. Although Willow Park was not looking for a long hold, it was going to take time to assess Marina Bay's potential in order to put together a plan for its ultimate exit.

Leasing broker teams had started contacting her once Willow Park closed on the deal. At that point it had been premature to find a leasing partner. Even now, she saw the proposals and realized just how many ways she could take the leasing strategy. She also started fielding interest in specific space within the buildings. One of the prospects was a dentist who wanted space in the ground floor. It was an odd call to get, but it forced the question: would getting the leasing started by signing a dentist be a good thing? Or would it doom the rest of thousands of square feet to a generic multitenant future? She certainly wasn't ready to say yes. But if she said no, would that mean she was starting to hold out for larger tenants? Or even a single tenant to take all of the office space? That felt risky. Erin had been happy with the acquisition because she felt there were many ways to earn a good return given what she perceived as a low basis. But that instinct was not the same thing as a plan. The calls from tenant brokers were becoming specific requests about space availability, about operating costs, about load factors, and rents. It all meant that she needed a leasing strategy.

What should these two buildings become? What had they been? The Marina Bay buildings Willow Park now owned had been sitting empty for 5 years. As part of their underwriting, Willow Park management had decided to interpret the vacancy in part as a result of the economic downturn and the slow recovery in secondary submarkets. But those explanations were not enough to account for the vacancy in the Marina Bay buildings. The Bay Area was now long past the 2008 downturn, and many noncore submarkets were doing well. It was more likely that the reason that Marina Bay remained unleased was because the previous owner had been either unable to commit to a plan for them or because he was unable to fund those plans. In the end, the best way for him to capture the value he could was to find another buyer who could take the next steps.

The reason Willow Park had been looking at Marina Bay was because it was consistent with the firm's mission. According to its web site, Willow Park "sought out value-add properties with opportunities to earn exceptional capital appreciation in the short-term and excellent overall returns in the medium term." This fairly boilerplate marketing material was vague enough to reflect the sort of deals Erin had been tasked with finding. She interpreted this to mean that she should be targeting high teens to low-twenties percent IRRs to equity while making good risk-return trade-offs. The generic marketing language undersold Willow Park's willingness to stretch into deals others might avoid with regard to redevelopment risk. Indeed, they had a long track record of turning ugly, underutilized, and ill-positioned buildings into better properties. Their resume of successful turnarounds didn't happen by luck or magic; Willow Park earned it by retaining a staff that could understand the cost and time required to turn properties like the now-empty Marina Bay into cash-flowing assets.

Terms for an acquisition loan were not particularly helpful or cheap, so Willow Park paid all cash for the two buildings at close. They would seek a construction loan for the renovations and then rethink permanent debt and holding period plans after leasing was underway. With some leasing activity, Willow Park could then decide about holding the buildings or flipping the property. It was premature to think about these until there were some tenants paying rent. Even though it was a Saturday morning, Erin drove to the site to think about his options. As expected, she saw a crew prepping for the demolition of the angled windows. The clean-up would take a few months, but with it had now been started, and she could begin to market both buildings. The question she now faced was how best to do that.

While not in the primary office submarkets in San Francisco or Silicon Valley, the property had a great location, offering access to nodes of high-tech employment and amenities. To Erin, the biggest specific amenity, however, was the view. Both buildings were on the water and had full views of San Francisco and the Bay. Moreover, these views could not be blocked by future development. Though the area around Marina Bay lacked the density of San Francisco or the prestige of a Silicon Valley address, it still had a 415 area code and a great deal to offer.

III.   Leasing and Exiting Marina Bay

The obvious question for Erin was how to get out of the properties while creating the most value in the process. With two entirely vacant buildings, Erin would have a blank slate with regard to his leasing strategy. She now had some loose market data and some ideas, but not a well-defined strategy. This would not come in a single effort. Before meeting with the leasing teams that would start calling back next week, she thought best to develop a rough set of options and explore them with the data she had. She'd refine later with better data from the brokers.

She needed to develop a set of models for the cash flows associated with three generic options about how best to demise the space, if at all, and she needed to think about his exit from Marina Bay. After creating value by repositioning and leasing the buildings, when would be the right time to sell? She was sure that these two elements—leasing and exit—should be developed in conjunction with each other. This would make an already-complicated leasing situation that much more so, but Erin was sure that his leasing strategy would impact how future buyers would perceive and value Marina Bay.

The San Mateo County and Brisbane Class A office markets didn't look like the office markets in San Francisco or in Silicon Valley. For starters, the Brisbane Class A market was small—only 15 buildings and 1.89M sf of space. Occupancy for both San Mateo County and within Brisbane was around 75%, with rents slightly higher for the surrounding County areas than in the Brisbane market—on average $33.30 versus $31.41 annually psf on a full service gross (FSG) basis. Absorption for both was negative in 2013. The final results for absorption in 2014 were still to be calculated, but 2015 looked better than 2014.

Erin found rent comparables in this area difficult to interpret, but at least she had some comps. She found leases that ranged from the mid-$2.00 range per month for subleased full floors to $2.75–$3.75 psf full-service gross (FSG). The range gave her pause; more troubling still was the fact that these rent numbers were from different buildings using different leasing strategies—whole floor versus small tenants. In the case of Marina Bay, Erin could contemplate trying to find a single tenant to lease all of the space, creating a campus for one of the many maturing start-ups in the area—but there were no comps in the area for this approach. How should Erin underwrite these three different approaches? And how should tenant quality enter the conversation: should Erin try to find credit tenants? They might be more valuable for the next buyer; they would likely be able to bid more if they could borrow more given the safety of credit tenants. But credit tenants know they are valuable and would likely want discounts relative to market rents.

Erin simple started with some rough assumptions about the three strategies.

Prospective Numbers by Leasing Strategy

	Campus	Single floor tenants	Many tenants
Rent $ FSG psf/month	3.33	3.13	2.67
Rent $ FSG psf/year	40.00	37.50	32.00
OpEx $/year	10.00	10.00	10.00
TIs $ psf	30.00	25.00	15.00
Leasing commissions $ psf	20.00	12.50	7.50
Term in years	10	5	3
Rent commences (months)	6	3	–

Erin started with these ballpark numbers first, thinking it might reveal something useful and perhaps inform her ahead of the leasing pitches she would be hearing soon.

Having finally landing a well-priced office deal in the Bay Area, Erin was eager to work through the leasing. But she was also aware of the current price levels. They were high, and tech was not a stable industry: while the industry seemed to keep chugging along a rapid clip, any number of famous companies had failed in the past. Did she want that sort of risk? Given the good basis, maybe Willow Park had done enough to get some momentum at Marina Bay. Maybe they could flip the property after getting approvals and renovating. Recent nearby sale prices had been between $230 and $255 psf, but they had above average occupancy and she had an empty building.

These sales numbers made Erin relax a bit. Leasing would be a challenge, but at least she would have one key advantage: Willow Park's basis after acquisition and renovation would be between $200 and $220 psf. In 3 months, she would have two fully updated and "new" buildings, well-positioned to compete with the surrounding office space. With that thought in mind, she wondered if she should even engage in leasing risk. She got into the office market at a good price and the market was awash in capital looking for an investment with a Bay Area address. Given the state of the recovery and the amount of capital chasing deals, maybe someone was going to see the new buildings, the view of the Bay and start asking about Marina Bay. Maybe Willow Park should book the quick profit and let the next buyer run the leasing.

IV. Giving Directions

Your job is to help Erin think through his options. She knows the market well enough to start understanding qualitatively the strength and weaknesses of the different leasing strategies, but she needs to explore their quantitative implications. She got the property for far less than the initial bidding, but because those earlier bid prices did not result in a sale, she's not really sure about how much of a bargain she got. Regardless of what Willow Park paid for Marina Bay, she has to figure out how to make the best of it.

How would you advise Erin?

a. Can you build three discounted cash flows that reflect returns to each different leasing strategy? What numbers do you need to build them? Do you have enough information? What metrics would you use to evaluate the three options? What else could you add to the analysis?

b. If you feel that adding a construction loan would help you make a better recommendation to Erin, feel free make some simple assumptions about terms and note them in your analysis.

c. What are the returns? Are you confident in the returns? If not, how could you test them to see how robust your decisions about the three strategies would be? Given that Willow Park owns the property already, are returns important or is maximizing NPV more helpful? Or should it be the returns to the added investments associated with the three options? More generally, what's the best way for Erin to evaluate his options?

d. Obviously, Erin could fill the buildings by lowering rents. Would this make sense? What sort of fundamentals would make you recommend holding out for higher rents? How long should she be willing to hold out for a single tenant/campus build-out? Use the numbers in the table above to start the underwriting. Then test how they would change if you assumed that if you used the "Many tenant" lease strategy, you could lease up the space evenly over a 2-year period. Then assume using a "Single Floor Tenant" approach would take longer: 36 months to reach stabilization. Finally, assume that every year there is a 25% chance that you land the single tenant who could lease both of the buildings. These are arbitrary assumptions, but might reveal something useful about the relative merits of the three choices. Do they?

e. Are there really only three options? Or are there a lot more? Should you build pro formas for all of them? What dictates when you need a new model? What are the returns to your own time in exploring one more scenario? This is an important question. If you were being hired to work for Erin to help her underwrite the leasing options, could you justify asking for one more day of time to explore one more option?

f. Finally, how sensitive are your assumptions to the kind of tenants who lease at Marina Bay? Is this too fine a point to explore now, at these early stages of developing a leasing plan? Do your assumptions about the quality of your tenants inform your exit cap rate assumptions, or is this just an assumption one too many? That is, of course tenant quality matters at some level, but is it something you should help Erin with in this first pass, as being important enough to be included in the preliminary analysis? Some market analysis will be needed. But to start, assume that credit tenants will pay a 10% lower rent. In exchange for the lower rent, assume that the credit tenant will allow you to use a lower exit cap rate by 25 basis points.

Having thought through these issues, what are your recommendations for Erin? Include a specific plan and the arguments that support your recommendations over other options (and any exhibits you might find helpful in making the case). Your recommendation can be to use more resources to better understand the choices. But be mindful that Erin is asking for help reaching a decision. "It depends" is not the answer she needs now.

Case 8

Atwood Corporate Center

The only thing you know for sure is that your pro forma is going to be wrong.

I. Finalizing the Investment Memo

You are an associate with S&D Partners. You've inherited a tentative memo outlining an acquisition of the Atwood Corporate Center. A team at S&D had started the investment memo with a particular strategy in mind, but their plan was met with some resistence from the partners. Now that team has become buried in other projects and has had to put their memo—and the unanswered questions—aside. You've been assigned the task of picking up the unfinished memo, reviewing the existing work, underwriting the remaining issues, and making final recommendations.

II. Atwood—Property Description and History

S&D Partners is considering pursuing the acquisition of Atwood Corporate Center, La Palma Street #4, Placentia, CA ("the Project") at a purchase price of $9.85 million ($63.09/sf). The proposed capital budget is $7.08 million ($45.38/sf) which is required for additional capital costs associated with the tenant improvements, renovation and commissions of the Project for a total cost of $17.14 million ($109.75/sf). The Project will be acquired on an all-cash basis with financing considered either during or upon stabilization, subject to the decision of the joint venture.

The current owner of the Project, TPG (the "Seller"), is offering for sale fee title to the project through a leading regional brokerage. TPG foreclosed on the property in 2010 from the previous owner, CorePlus Investments.

The Project was developed as one of several structures for a build-to-suit for the Hughes Corporation in 1978. Building #4 was originally built as two separate industrial structures, but in 1983 they were attached to comprise one building ("the Project"). The Hughes Corporation moved out of the project in 1993 and the entire property was sold out of foreclosure by Prudential Insurance in 1994.

Sales Project History Since 1994

- 1994: Prudential sold the entire four building project to Carl Rogers for $8.5M ($21.47/sf)
- 1995: Carl Rogers sold the entire four building project to Magellan for $15.25M ($38.51/sf)

Underwriting Commercial Real Estate in a Dynamic Market. https://doi.org/10.1016/B978-0-12-815989-7.00008-2

- 1995: Micro Metal purchased La Palma Street #1 for $2.45M ($45/sf)
- 1997: Magellan sold last three buildings to Trinet for $29M ($84.81/sf) at a 9.22% cap rate
- 2001: Calvary Chapel purchased La Palma Street #2 for $4.5M ($85/sf)
- 2003: Birtcher Anderson purchased La Palma Street #3 for $10.6M ($80/sf)
- 2005: Wescom Credit Union purchased La Palma Street #3 for $17.4M ($131.07/sf) as an Owner-User
- 2006: CorePlus Investment purchased Building #4 for $34.5M ($221/sf) from iFinancial
- 2009: The tenant in Building #4 vacated the project and moved their operations to Texas
- 2010: CorePlus defaulted on their $24.6M ($157.56/sf) loan, and TPG foreclosed on the property

III. Proposed Acquisition Details

Capital Requirements

S&D has proposed a purchase price of $9.85 million, all-cash. Based on the underwriting, S&D is projecting a 4-year unlevered IRR of 11.96% and an equity multiple of 1.57 based on an equity investment of $17.14 million ($109.75/sf). At $17.14 million ($109.75/sf), the total purchase price and renovation is <60% of replacement cost. No acquisition loan is being considered because it is highly unlikely that a bank would lend without a long-term lease in place.

Timeline

Estimated due diligence start date:	11/11/2010
Contingency end date:	11/25/2010
Closing:	12/6/2010

Property

The Property is a two-story, Class "B," ±156,125 rentable sf office building situated on approximately ±8.51 acres in the Anaheim Hills submarket of North Orange County. The Property was originally developed as the corporate headquarters for Hughes Corporation in 1978 using tilt-up construction. The project is currently called the Atwood Corporate Center.

Positive attributes:

- The Property provides direct access to the 91 freeway allowing for easy access to all of Orange County and Southern California
- The Property is currently parked at 5.5/1000 parking spaces psf which is attractive to back office users most likely to lease the space

- The Property has very limited competition among existing properties in Orange County in terms of square footage and parking
- The Property has numerous amenities directly across the street offering access to retail, restaurants, and hotels.
- Total stabilized costs of $109.75/sf is significantly less than estimated replacement costs of $240–255/sf.
- Limited window line around rear of building
- Building best suited for a single tenant; challenging to multitenant the project

Property Condition/Capital Budget

Atwood Corporate Center's overall physical condition will be further vetted in due diligence, including obtaining a current property condition report, Phase I environmental assessment, and seismic analysis. S&D has completed the preliminary physical inspection, and based on the initial assessment from all its vendors, has underwritten $55K for HVAC work, $10K for electrical repairs, $131K to repair sections of the roof, $25K to repair the windows, and $5K to upgrade the fire life safety in the building. This totals $226K of work to be completed after purchasing the building.

Tenancy/Occupancy

The Project is currently 100% vacant.

Lease project history since 1996:

- 1996: LA Cellular (now AT&T) leased the project.
- 2009: AT&T vacated the project and moved their operations to Texas

S&D is currently negotiating with a tenant, Transit Technologies, to lease the entire project starting in October 2011 on a 10-year lease. The proposed terms from Transit Tech are below:

Lease abstract:

- Start date: 10/1/2011
- Size: 156,135 sf
- Term: 10 years
- Free rent: 12 months
- Rent: $0.75 NNN with 3% yearly increases
- TI's: $30 psf
- Termination option: At month 60 with 6 months' notice with termination fee. If option exercised, termination fee equal to last 12 months' rent

Though the suggested lease is a net lease, the previous team provided you with anticipated operating expenses for Year 1, assuming Transit Tech signs the lease—though most of the operating expenses will be valid even if they don't sign the lease.

Operating expense	Year 1
Property taxes	108,847
Repairs and maintenance	51,590
Electrical	24,782
FLS monitoring	5377
Elevator work	372
Insurance	83,638
Association	52,042
Utilities	443,358
Janitorial	282,136
Property management	120,000
General and administrative	25,814

All units are in $/year. Under the Transit Tech lease, all but the G&A expenses will be reimbursed.

IV. The Open Questions

This was the point at which you inherited the first investment memo. The materials in front of you suggest as to why they were not ready to make a decision—scribbled on the cover sheet are these notes: "(a) reject the TT lease (it's low)?, (b) sign the lease at low rent? we'd get NOI in place; (c) push back on the TT lease?" You decide to start your underwriting with these three options as a starting point. But you know that you will also have to think for yourself, there may be other options they did not consider. After talking with the first team, you get a little more information and formalize the framework for starting your underwriting.

The Basic Framework

- **Plan A**—The lease offered by Transit Technologies has a face rent that is low relative to market. If S&D chooses not to accept it, S&D will commence marketing the project for lease. Under this scenario, a 24-month marketing period to find a single tenant is anticipated. Marketing and subsequent capital costs required to sign the tenant are expected to be $7.08M ($45.38/sf).
- **Plan B**—Execute the lease with Transit Technologies prior to close of the acquisition of Atwood.
- **Plan C**—Counter the lease offer from Transit Technologies.

Market Overview

Orange County Office Market

The Orange County office market consists of approximately 99.9 million sf of office space located within five distinct markets: North Orange County, Central Orange County, West Orange County, Greater Airport Area and South Orange County. At the end of second Quarter 2010, North Orange County experienced the second highest total vacancy among the five submarkets in Orange County. Below is a breakdown of how the North Orange County has fared in comparison to other Orange County submarkets.

Exhibit 1: Broader market analysis

Market area	Building RBA	Total vacancy rate	Direct vacancy rate
Greater Airport Area	47,131,950	19.60%	17.60%
South Orange County	22,787,674	17.90%	16.70%
North Orange County	**8,596,656**	**15.00%**	**14.60%**
Central Orange County	16,635,737	18.40%	17.50%
West Orange County	4,789,857	11.10%	9.8.0%

North Orange County Market Overview

Within Orange County, North Orange County is the second smallest submarket totaling 8.59 million sf of office space. Tenants are drawn to the area for its central location and moderately priced housing alternatives, access to a large and highly skilled labor pool, an abundance of retail and entertainment amenities, access to major freeways and close proximity to many forms of transportation. In the second quarter of 2010, vacancy stood at 15% in North Orange County submarket.

Current Demand in the Marketplace

According to one of the top Colliers leasing teams for North/Central Orange County, more than 3 million sf of office requirements currently exist in the marketplace. The same leasing team provided their latest tenant prospect report for Central and North Orange County tenant requirements occurring through the end of 2013. The results are encouraging; a total of 17 leases above 50,000 sf are anticipated to roll in that time frame.

Below is a more detailed breakout of the rollover:

- 7 leases: >100,000 sf
- 10 leases: 50,000–99,999 sf

Exhibit 2: Direct competitive set

Property	Size (sf)	Occupied	Typical floor	Parking ratio	Asking rate ($/month)	Purchase price ($)	Purchase date
13,280 Chapman (Crystal Cathedral)	136,988	0.0%	27,393	8.00	2.25 NNN	N/A	N/A
505 City Parkway (Abbey/Baupost)	204,710	28.5%	20,471	4.00	1.95 FSG	14,872,181	May '09
1800 E. Imperial (LBA Realty)	145,501	29.7%	72,750	4.00	1.85 FSG	31,282,715	Aug '10
2727 E. Imperial (AEW)	104,662	0.0%	68,692	4.00	1.85 FSG	18,205,954	Feb '05
400 Metropolitan (Wells Fargo)	182,935	27.4%	45,734	5.50	2.20 FSG	38,000,000	Jul '06
Anaheim Concourse (Panattoni/ING)	851,726	0.0%	100,000	4.00	1.25 NNN	75,000,000	Feb '08
Total/wt. average	1,626,502	14.3%					

Exit Strategy

Upon stabilization, the Project will be suitable for acquisition by an institutional buyer, public or private REIT, or high net worth investor. During ownership, S&D would stabilize the asset by securing a tenant to lease the entire building on a long term basis. A stabilized capitalization rate for this type of asset would typically be in the 8% range. However, based on a number of factors, the first team used a capitalization rate of 7.5% in our model. Some of these factors include limited market rent growth utilized in the model, competitive project advantages—including location and higher parking ratio, a relative discount to replacement cost, and peak value market pricing.

V.   Key Decision Makers

S&D and Transit Tech

S&D Partners is a joint venture. It combines local expertise and capital with Wall Street capital with the goal of maximizing risk-adjusted return. The firm is run by real estate people who use their equity and their track record of finding good deals to get access to more capital from two equity funds. Both funds have backed S&D projects for a number of years. While there are loose investment criteria, the funds have developed enough trust in S&D that they are ready to turn over the underwriting decisions to S&D. To be clear, the funds will require a thorough review of all deals. But they trust that S&D will find the best use for their capital. This allows S&D great latitude to find the highest risk-adjusted returns and to pursue whatever strategy achieves them. S&D is not bound to particular hurdles, property classes, tenant types, etc. S&D is a young firm with ambitious long-term plans—they fully intend to be worthy stewards of their partner's capital.

With regards to the Atwood Corporate Center, S&D is pursuing this deal but has not yet determined if it will meet the asking price. Nor has S&D decided about its holding period, if it does acquire the property. Given S&D's mandate, it will look to ensure the best risk-return tradeoff. It is authorized to flip the asset, just as it is authorized to take on permanent debt and hold up to 10 years. S&D is generally rewarded as a function of IRR hurdles, with S&D earning a larger share of the cash flows as the returns to equity rise.

Transit Tech

Transit Tech is a developer of electric motors and vehicles for consumer markets. They view themselves as a manufacturer whose core asset is the creative engineering they bring to bear on the challenges inherent in the development and commercialization of new technology. They are users of flex-space, combining the need of office and lab spaces in close proximity. Currently Transit Tech is housed in three separate flex-space facilities. While the three facilities are not too far from one another, Transit Tech is keen to keep their people proximal to facilitate face-to-face communication. In fact, Transit Tech is atypical in their use of flex-tech space. Most flex-tech facilities are parked at a 3:1000 ratio—below the 4:1000 ratio of office buildings—due to lab space not generating as much parking as office space. Transit Tech, in contrast, is running into minor legal trouble in their current facilities because of the high number of employees they put into their office spaces. Their philosophy is to organize their employees into "creative teams" and operate them in close proximity. That is, rather than distinct offices, most of these teams will work in shared space known as "bull-pens." Only a few single-person offices would be built. This purposeful interaction of high human capital employees is credited with its productivity and with pushing the company as far as it has come as fast as it has. While the firm will use some lab space, they will use more office space and at greater intensity than typical office layouts.

Transit Tech has received $575M in venture capital recently and has just signed a contract with the Department of Energy of almost equal value. They have signed letters of intent to provide prototypes of final production vehicles over the next two years. The demands of these contracts will require more space and more efficiency. They are eager to consolidate and get on track to meet the contract deadlines. They are also aware of the state of the market and are looking to maximize the value of their next lease by achieving a long-term, low-cost lease.

VI. Deliverables

You are a junior member of the S&D team. With a vacancy rate above 15%, the area has plenty of supply. Moreover, this likely understates the competition for Atwood due to all the shadow space that is surely not accounted for. But with a tenant in tow, you are in a position to see the value of the building that has a long-term lease in place. The asking price is fixed, so there is no chance to bargain for a lower price. The current property owner was the lender to the previous owner. The bank had to take possession of the property when the previous owner (and borrower) made it clear that they had no prospective income that could service the loan they had taken out to acquire the Atwood property. Regulators are not pushing the current owner, TPG, to write down their bad assets yet, so TPG is not desperate to unload Atwood. They have set an aggressive price and will stand by it for the foreseeable future.

Given this price, you have to evaluate the three business plans and make a recommendation to your boss within a week. Your team is small and your boss has been in and out of this deal for weeks and knows the property well. He is a local real estate veteran and has carved out some great returns in a down market by being smart and by being willing to take good risks. Right now he is busy taking advantage of inefficiency in the market. He's sure that as long as markets are still trying to find a new equilibrium, they'll be deals but the window for these will be closing as people like him and others get back in to the market.

He assigned Atwood to you because he thought "something seemed right about this one." But given his own workload, he'll need you to decide whether he should spend more time on it or not. If no, tell him why not, but be clear why. He did not assign it to find a "no" but that may be the right choice. If you think there is a viable way to earn a good return, tell him how—give him a rough business plan. Remember that you asked for the majority of your compensation to be in the form of bonuses, with the idea that ultimately you would get to co-invest and participate in the firm's cash flows. Is Atwood worth pursuing for the firm? If so, should you push to have your bonus in this deal? How would you structure the business plan? Would you and and S&D share the same incentives?

As you begin underwriting, it might be useful to think through a number of relevant issues:

a. What is the market value of the Atwood Corporate Center? Is this easy or hard to determine? What sort of reasonable ranges could you estimate using the comps given to you? Are these close to the current asking price from the bank?

b. Is looking at comparables the right way to view the value of Atwood? Why or why not? Is the market as inefficient as your boss believes? What would that mean for real estate valuation? What sort of assumptions are implicit in market valuations? Does "the market" face the same assumptions S&D face?

c. Looking ahead, what set of reasonable assumptions could you make about your first two options: going to market with Atwood as a vacant building and finding tenants or going with the TransitTech lease? Which one is better? Why?

d. What are your assumptions about the exit from Atwood? Could you flip it? Could you put debt on and hold it for a longer term? Is S&D in a position to hold through a long recovery? To explore this, use a typical joint venture waterfall to test how sensitive the returns to a sponsor (S&D in this case) to longer holding periods.

e. With regard to the lease, what do you think you do to push back on the pre-liminary lease terms? Which ones will TransitTech require and which ones were likely simply starting points for negotiation? Which terms are more important for you to create value? How much does TransitTech want to be at Atwood? Are there reasons to believe that we would have a strong position as the owners of Atwood to push for a better lease?

f. What lease terms would help or hurt obtaining a good loan?

g. If this whole enterprise of buying a vacant building near the bottom of an uncertain future makes you too nervous, should you pass on it? That is, not only will S&D have capital at risk, but so too could you. And, if you opted not to push to have your bonus invested in Atwood, why would you recommend it for S&D? Furthermore, if you say no to this deal, do you think there are better deals out there? Remember as a deal's sponsor, S&D will make most of its money by outperforming some standard benchmarks. Getting an ordinary return is likely mean that you work hard on a deal and get little to show for it. As your boss says, "The deal has to be at least a double to make it worthwhile." Is Atwood a extra-base hit?

As ever, your boss is not interested in pretending that any one of your pro formas is going to be forecast what actually happens, indeed he's always reminding you not to get too hung up on any one discounted cash flow model: "The only thing you know for sure is that your pro forma is going to be wrong." But he is still eager to have you build them to test broad assumptions and he is very keen on exploring the these different business plans and identifying the big risks for each. He'll expect your memo shortly. He's sure the market is finding bottom now and it'll only be harder to find bargains later. If it's not going to be Atwood, it'll be time to move on.

Case 9

Lombard Street

Jack of all things, master of most.

I.   Running Lean

Since the downturn in 2008, real estate firms have been forced to run "lean"; real estate contributed to the worst downturn since the Great Depression and the industry was rewarded with several long years of waiting for a recovery. With only asset management keeping the lights on, many firms let go every nonessential employee. Others fought to keep their teams together because they wanted to have existing platforms to be ready to buy when the market turned. There were several types of firms that found themselves in 2009 with access to capital and a sense that the bottom was near. Some were those who saw trouble coming and had the fortitude to liquidate early—even as their colleagues couldn't believe they were passing on more deals in 2006 and 2007. Others raised opportunity funds once the defaults started mounting; they saw the emerging bank crisis as the chance of a career to replicate Tom Barrack and Sam Zell's success from the days of the Resolution Trust Corporation, when the RTC took over or resolved almost 750 thrifts and sold large pools of real estate assets. This process allowed some investors to find great deals on properties for "pennies on the dollar." But during the Great Recession of 2008–09, a fire sale of that size didn't happen. Instead, "pretend and extend" become a typical pattern; banks didn't write down and sell off their portfolios at large discounts in the way some had anticipated. This meant that rather than fresh ownership with a lower basis, many commercial properties were stuck with owners and tenants at odds about what to do next. Fixing these deals would be both capital and time intensive.

In a different downturn, these properties might have been taken back by a bank and auctioned, providing a new start. But in 2010 there were many of these complicated, "stuck" assets. For Green Bay Partners (GBP), this complexity—or "hair on the deal" as it's called—meant that there would be less competition and more opportunity to unlock the value that was stuck. And so while others waited for a fire sale, GBP stayed busy throughout the downturn. Green Bay Partners had built a business model around finding opportunities at every point in the real estate cycle. They had a reputation for being smart capital allocators when it was time to buy real estate. But when things turned down, Green Bay could turn to property and asset management. It could run any kind of property well. But more crucially, it would take on almost any real estate problem and help salvage broken real estate from which others fled. Indeed, GBP's work-out group was as important to the firm's success as any other group, earning a healthy return for fixing the problems that others created. And for years after 2008, the world was full of problem real estate.

After the bust, GBP found it relatively easy to raise capital because of its track record and willingness to co-invest. It got active with acquisitions even as demand for its workout services grew. In many cases, ownership or partial ownership was the result of a workout with the existing owners—who hadn't been forced out but who didn't have enough capital to retenant and refinance. It had a series of obvious wins to show for this approach through the downturn and early recovery. But while GBP was busy, its fees were thin and its capital was tied up in deals that would be profitable and provide free cash flow only at some point in the future. This meant that GBP was like lots of real estate firms at the time and "ran lean." Rather than hire new talent to help with these diverse set of projects, everyone just took on more roles. When this became simply too much, GBP finally had to hire someone. The first new hire since the downturn was Anthony Rogers.

During the bubble years, Anthony had been an analyst and then an associate at a boutique development and investment firm in Atlanta. There he worked on real estate over its full life-cycle—development, acquisition, leasing, operations, and disposition. When things slowed at the firm, he saw it was a great chance to head back to school. After graduation, he was hired at Green Bay Partners in 2010 because of his experience and because of his newly minted degree, which rounded out an already strong CV. Anthony was happy to land a position with GBP. He had a formal title, but it was clear his real job would be doing whatever GBP needed him to do. Given how busy GBP was, this meant doing a little of everything. Anthony would have to be a "jack of all trades, master of most."

II. Changing Hats

An example of this multiple-specialization approach is Anthony's experience with 214 Lombard Street, a 76,500 sf office building in Charlotte. Six months into GBP's ownership of 214 Lombard Street, Anthony was being asked to help think about leasing issues at the property. Anthony had been on the acquisition team that had found and structured the deal that put 214 Lombardi in GBP's portfolio, so he was familiar with the deal:

215 Lombard Street

- 76,500 sf Class A, four-story office building
- Constructed in 1993; full interior renovations on top two floors occurred in 2012
- Situated lakeside on 8.29 acres with 330 parking stalls

- Transaction closed on July 1st, 2014
- Green Bay acquired 100% of Lombard Street
- Purchase price was $9,800,000 ($128.10 psf)/estimated replacement cost at closing was $16.4 mm ($214.38 psf)
- Leverage at close: $6.65 mm (67.8% LTV) with a 25-year amortization period after 6-month I/O at 4.65% fixed for a term of 66 months

The building had been operating well, at 95% occupied, but there was some risk on the horizon. The top two floors were occupied by Starr Systems, a global provider of industrial infrastructure. The second floor tenant was Lofton Inc., a recently sold spin off of Starr Systems. Lofton headquarters would be consolidated elsewhere and they would begin marketing their space on a sublease at the beginning of 2015Q3. On the first floor there were two suites. One was vacant. The other suite held Hornung Valves. (See the rent roll and lease abstracts in the exhibits below.) During due diligence, it was discovered through a tenant interview that Hornung was being purchased by a local competitor. The acquiring firm is currently paying rent on the suite, but Hornung is not occupying the space and it is being marketed for sublease. Moreover, the Hornung management has contacted GBP to discuss a lease buy out.

In 2011, Starr hired a nationally recognized architectural firm to redesign a number of their offices around a cutting-edge hoteling design. The build-out has aged well and is viewed as successful. Starr's international reputation and balance sheet make them a clear credit tenant. Starr recently approached GBP with a request to help them reorganize their leasing at Lombard Street. Starr indicated it would be starting a new joint venture—called Starr/Madison—and it would need approximately 35,000 sf of space, including a requirement of ground access for noninvasive lab equipment. At the same time, Starr didn't need both of its full floors and proposed assigning the third floor space to the new Starr/Madison JV using the same lease terms except for a longer duration. Starr outlined its proposal as follows:

- Starr and Starr/Madison would sign new 8-year leases
- Starr would remain in the fourth floor and extend the existing lease for the new 8-year term
- Starr would assign third floor lease to Starr/Madison, and use the same lease terms, but with the updated 8-year extension
- Starr/Madison would sign a new lease on entire ground floor (including the 3,000 sf of vacant space), using the same lease terms on the third floor.
- GBP would take three months to renovate the first and third floor using a tenant improvement allowance of $5 psf over full useable areas of these floors.

Starr requested a letter of intent (LOI) from GBP so that it could begin its own internal deliberations about how best to organize and locate Starr/Madison, as well as rethink its own use of space. It would be Anthony's job to analyze and propose a draft LOI for the credit committee at GBP. While he had planned on pursuing more acquisition targets this week, running lean meant there was no leasing team to hand the Starr LOI request to. And because he had run the acquisition of Lombard Street, he probably was the best person to think through adjusting the leasing strategies, and perhaps the plan for holding it.

Anthony didn't think he'd be working on Lombard Street so soon. The building was close to full when he structured the acquisition. But the Starr proposal made this a much more complicated situation than just lease extensions. Anthony knew immediately that adding more Starr activities to the rent roll would likely increase the quality of the tenants. This could make GBP rethink its debt and holding period plans as well. At the same time, Starr knew that it brought something valuable to GBP, and this could be seen in its suggestion that the new space be rented at lease rates that were signed in the depths of the slowdown. And as much as it would nice to get the first floor with Starr/Madison, it was not his to offer: Hornung occupied suite #100 and still held control of the space through the end of its lease.

Anthony thought he'd made a great deal in buying Lombard Street. He had good tenants and a basis that was well under replacement costs. He'd heard a dozen times that "you make your money on the buy." Clichés often turn out to hold some truth, but they're not business plans. Clearly, the basis wouldn't hurt the returns, but the response to Starr's request would involve changing the business plan he laid out when he bought it. Now he had another chance to capture value. The question was how best to navigate the proposal from Starr. He had the original rent roll from his acquisition documents. Would this simply be about filling the vacant space and increasing NOI? Or was the longer term going to result in a more valuable asset? Market rents had been recovering, so maybe having more vacancy would be better.

Anthony received the email from the Starr folks at lunch while traveling looking for new deals. He scanned the outline of the proposal and saw that he would now have different priorities for his next week. He wrapped up his afternoon site visit and headed back to the airport. He knew Lombard Street well, but he would have to rethink it in light of the lease proposal from Starr.

III.   Deliverables

Anthony needs to prepare a letter of intent (LOI) in response to the Starr proposal. He will need to share it with his own internal credit committee at GBP before sending it to Starr. Please help Anthony prepare a draft LOI for the credit committee. Because this will be an internal document, be expansive. That is, the draft memo to Starr should be given to the credit committee with supporting documentation, describing the strengths and weaknesses of the LOI to Starr. Be aware that Starr is a major tenant and while GBP is eager to increase the NOI from Lombard and its value, Starr will be eager to see a fair proposal.

Questions:

a. Lombard Street is valuable because of the cash flow it can produce. Do you understand both the current tenants and how their leases will work over their terms?

b. Why is there a vacant suite in the building? Why isn't it full? If GBP just lowered the rent, couldn't it get something for the space instead of having it idle? On the other hand, is there a value to vacant space?

c. What is the present value of the current leases? What discount rate would apply to the future cash flows? Should you use the same discount rate to all of the tenants?

d. What is the value of the Lombard property if it were vacant and you were able to obtain market rents and experience market vacancy? It's now the first quarter in 2014, and office vacancy rates have been falling but are still at 11%. Average asking rents are $19.75/sf on a full-service gross basis. Lombard is in a very good suburban office submarket, so maybe asking rents are a little higher there. While the building is getting older, the competitors in the submarket were all built in the same era and a recent renovation at Lombard gives it a slight edge in terms of building performance and desirability.

e. Charlotte's growth in its CBD is becoming apparent. Like lots of other cities of this size, its downtown has been receiving more interest from Millennials and it is become more active and beginning to show a real advantage in amenities. Does this matter for the value of Lombard? Does it matter for the valuation of the leases and your memo to Anthony and the credit committee?

f. How does your leasing strategy influence your debt and holding decisions? If you were able to fill the building with credit-quality tenants, assume you could lower the existing interest rate by 50 basis points and obtain a new 7-year 65% LTV loan. If the origination fee was 1% on the loan amount, would this influence your proposal to Starr? Would it change your holding period?

You may need to make some assumptions in exploring these issues. Make sure to note them and support them as best you can. The credit committee likes to ask many follow up questions and will certainly ask you to test other assumptions as they vet your proposal.

Lombard Street rent roll at acquisition.

#	Tenant name type & suite number lease dates & term	Floor sf bldg share	Rate per year per month	Changes on	Changes to	Months to abate	Pcnt to abate	Operating expense reimb.	Gross up provision
1	Hornung Valves		$18.75	May-2015	$19.27		95%	See notes	
	Office, Suite: 100	15,241	$1.56	May-2016	$19.80				
	Apr-2013 to Nov-2018	19.90%		May-2017	$20.34				
	68 months			May-2018	$20.90				
2	VACANT (STATIC)		–	–	–	–	–	FSG	
	Office, Suite: 150	3208							
	Jan-2025 to Dec-2049	4.20%							
	300 months								
3	Lofton Inc.		$18.47	Aug-2014	$18.84	61–63	100%	See notes	95%
	Office, Suite: 200	19,125	$1.54	Aug-2015	$19.21				
	Aug-2011 to Jul-2018	25.00%		Aug-2016	$19.60				
	84 months			Aug-2017	$20.00				
4	Starr Systems		$18.47	Aug-2014	$18.84	61–63	100%	See notes	95%
	Office, Suite: 300/400	38,250	$1.54	Aug-2015	$19.21				
	Aug-2011 to Jul-2018	50.00%		Aug-2016	$19.60				
	84 months			Aug-2017	$20.00				

5	Building Misc (STATIC)				–	–	–	–	–	–	FSG
	Office, Suite: Misc	676									
	Jan-2025 to Dec-2049	0.90%									
	300 months										

Summary	SF	Share
Total occupied sf	72,616	94.9%
Total available sf	3884	5.1%
Total building sf	76,500	100%

Notes: Floors 3 and 4 are not reimbursed for HVAC outside normal hours. See OpEx Below.

Lombard operating expenses—Month 1.

Operating expenses

General and administrative	77
Utilities	11,244
Snow removal	57
Salary reimbursement PM	1524
Association fee	237
Repairs and maintenance	6668
Rubbish removal	305
Landscaping	3073
Fire and safety	395
Telephone	576
Elevator and generator	1382
HVAC	3272
Janitorial	4026
Management fee	3610
Insurance	2184
Real estate taxes	7449
Owner's expenses (NR)	25
Floors 3/4 overtime HVAC (NR)	3505
Total	49,609

Note: NR, not reimbursable.

Case 10

An Uncommon Option for Cloverfield Commons

I think you're making a mistake, one that's going to cost us dearly at some point. Maybe, maybe not. But all I know now is that if we offer a lower rent, with 100% probability it'll cost us something starting today and every month going forward.

I. What the Analyst Heard

After a couple of hours of brainstorming and some sharp words between the principals, the Cloverfield Commons working group has decided to call it a day. This isn't how you planned to spend your afternoon. Earlier this week, you'd been cc'd on the lease abstracts for the Cloverfield Commons property. The tone of the emails had suggested that the firm had reached an agreement with a tenant who would lease all of the property's space. What you've learned from the working group's argument this afternoon is that not only are the lease negotiations not done, but that your firm might not get the tenant after all. Once again it has become clear that leasing isn't really done until a tenant is signed, moved in, and paying rent.

As part of the team, you have been following the negotiations from the beginning. There had been a clear sense that both parties wanted to make a deal and the negotiations had been friendly, perhaps too much so. Rather than drive to a quick agreement, the principals had allowed the conversation to wander and stretch out, feeling they could get a great lease if they could just be patient. The tenant was not used to leasing nor lease negotiations, and their "team" seemed to have an ever-changing set of members and priorities. As a result, you had been tasked with preparing at least a dozen different lease packages for them to consider. Cloverfield Commons had been a tough deal from the beginning; principals had argued over its acquisition about as much as they argued this afternoon about lease terms. If the leasing could be finished, the firm could begin marketing Cloverfield Common as a core-plus office building in a great submarket. Instead, if we tried to keep to our plan of a short holding period, we would have to sell it as an empty building that might better be described as an opportunistic investment.

The truth was that Cloverfield Commons was not a great property. It was in Santa Monica, but not in a particularly desirable area. But with a long-term lease in place, Cloverfield Commons might suddenly look like a bargain: the

Underwriting Commercial Real Estate in a Dynamic Market. https://doi.org/10.1016/B978-0-12-815989-7.00010-0

market for a safe cash flow amid these fundamentals is strong. The next owner would be buying a long-term cash flow with very little risk, and would be acquiring real estate in a market that is almost certain to appreciate at a rate greater than inflation in the long-term. The debate about our acquisition of Cloverfield had now become a debate about signing the tenant. The only broad agreement in the room that afternoon was that if we didn't land the tenant, we would have to admit that we overpaid for Cloverfield in the first place. That would make one of the principals right, and both of them unhappy.

In fact, we had overpaid relative to other bidders, but that's the nature of an auction. We paid what we did for the property after running the numbers assuming a single tenant who would take the entire space. This would save demolition, renovation, marketing, leasing, the inefficiency of multiple tenants, and holding costs—expenses that others bidders had built into their pro formas. We estimated our initial expenses to include some tenant improvements and brokers' fees. If the tenant-in-tow assumption was right, then we had not overpaid. If it was wrong, there might be trouble ahead. And as of this afternoon, our assumption having an anchor tenant was now looking premature.

II. Working Harder to Get to Close

After the early casual back-and-forth lease negotiation, two other office building owners got wind of the tenant's search for office space and began trying to get the tenant to rent their properties. During the last several weeks of more urgent conversations, the new competition had forced us to trim some of the fat off the lease we had originally hoped to get signed. With the leaner lease package, the deal would not be a home run, but it was still worth pursuing because the alternative would be to begin bearing costs the firm had assumed it would avoid. This would almost certainly guarantee a very low return to the investment in Cloverfield.

The tenant continued to say they wanted to sign with us under the revised lease terms, but the new competitors are making it difficult to say yes and sign our revised lease. The tenant wrote earlier today: "You know we liked the last lease and this one is better. The building is perfect for us, and we really like the location. But we have the voters to answer to and we'll need to justify turning down the other two options." At this point, the question has become how to sweeten the lease deal just a bit to get the tenant to sign the lease at Cloverfield. For weeks the basic negotiations have been about making concessions to the face rent, the tenant improvement package, the escalations, the months of free rent, and the lease term. No one wants to completely reopen negotiations, so we have started talking about other lease terms that might interest the tenant. Now, after arguing about how best to reach one last proposal, we've just called it a day without reaching agreement on what to propose next.

It seems clear that even the leaner revised lease is not going to be enough to get the tenant to sign. The fight you'd been watching this afternoon was about the final deal sweeteners—that last set of terms to get the tenant in to Cloverfield Commons and us on to the next step of marketing a fully leased building. The conversation included a lot of novel ideas, but two took root. Based on what you heard, it is not clear to you that either of these proposed revisions would make the lease worth signing.

As the meeting wrapped up, you were tasked with underwriting the two general proposals that had divided the group into competing camps: "going green" and "selling the future." The first camp wants to offer some commitment to reach building performance goals—something about sustainability and efficiency. This would play on the tenant's desire to lower operating expenses and to be associated with environmental stewardship. This option would involve some additional capital expenditures to install new insulation and new windows (to "upgrade the building envelope" as the tenant wrote). This approach would cost us more up front and, because the lease is a net lease, would mean we would not receive any of the direct benefits from energy savings. Of course, we would own the improvements, which ought to prove valuable over time. The "going green" camp prefers this approach because it makes the underwriting straightforward—just a one-time lump sum investment and maybe some reduction in the exit cap rate in the future. The second camp ("selling the future") wants to give a lease option to the tenant that would allow the tenant to buy the building at some future date. The tenant expects to be in the community for a long time, and having some control over ownership rights might move the tenant toward signing the lease. The two competing camps share common ground in only one area: they both oppose giving up more rent. Each side of the argument sees its sweeteners as benign, appealing to the tenants but not costing much in returns to our firm.

It is not clear to you that either of the proposed revisions would make the lease worth signing. You wonder if a third option might be better: why we don't just lower the rent one last time? At least then we would have a lease that could be easily valued by prospective buyers to whom we will be marketing in the near term. You've been tasked with underwriting the three options and informing the working group about the strengths and weaknesses of each. Both "going green" and "selling the future" have their precedents. "Going green" is similar to a larger TI package, but perhaps these dollars might yield a higher and more durable return over time. "Selling the future" is fundamentally an option, something common in the commercial leasing world. But, valuing options is difficult and this one is quite novel. That alone might make this problematic. Finally, "cutting rent" is just plain routine lease negotiations. Simple or not, no one else on the lease team seemed enthusiastic about the idea of lowering rent, but the principals have allowed you to include it in your analysis. Your task if to review the property summary and current lease terms one more time, then build a set of valuation exhibits that will allow you to assess which of the three options is best: (1) going green, (2) selling the future, or (3) lowering the rent.

III. The Last Month and the Potential

The Cloverfield Commons property is a Class B office building not far from the intersection of Cloverfield and Colorado boulevards in Santa Monica. The building offers three stories of approximately 35,000 sf of office space. The structure was built in the late 1990s and is in good, but dated, condition. As such, Cloverfield's primary attraction is not its design and building amenities but rather those amenities that are outside the building: it is located in one of the best spots in the Los Angeles office market; it offers exceptional access to key highway arterials and easy access to high human capital; and other tenants in the submarket are world class. While they are not likely to take space at Cloverfield, they are a good indicator of the broader demand in Santa Monica. Indeed, the Westside has attracted some of the blue chip tech, entertainment and venture capital firms that signal that it will be significant node of white collar employment for years to come. That said, these star tenants have not found this particular block yet. Cloverfield came onto our radar from a motivated seller with whom we had an ongoing relationship. Evidently the seller felt he needed to push rents at Cloverfield and lost his last tenant, who comprised the entire rent roll. The seller was not interested in retenanting himself and decided to take advantage of the buzz in the submarket to sell the property. He accepted our bid, requiring only that the transaction close quickly and cleanly. Given our history and balance sheet, we could guarantee both. We agreed to the deal, believing we could negotiate a long-term lease with a quasigovernmental tenant who could take the entire building. This tenant had outgrown its space and wanted to remain in Santa Monica over the long term. It had pushed for at least a 15-year lease of the property.

IV. Discussions and Deadlines

Tomorrow would be our last day to argue about our options to sweeten the lease terms. After slow-playing the negotiations, the tenant has decided to make two days from today the day for choosing from among the final lease proposals for the three buildings. You felt uneasy with both "going green" and "selling the future" because you felt both involved guessing about futures that were hard to understand and underwrite well. Indeed, the principal who wanted to "go green" was blunt about how he felt about giving the tenant the right to buy the property: "I think you're making a mistake, one that's going to cost us dearly at some point." The other principal was equally blunt in her response: "Maybe, maybe not. But I know that investing in going green will cost money now and it's unclear if we earn a dime on those dollars." And then turning to you, she said "And I also know if we offer a lower rent, we'll lose income with 100% probability. It'll cost us something starting today and every month going forward."

With these comments fresh on your mind it was time to return to your desk and sort out how best to answer the question about how to proceed. Tomorrow morning, the team would head to the conference room to hammer out our sweeteners for the final lease proposal. You had some reasonable assumptions about the proposal to reduce the rent, but the other principals had little in the way of concrete numbers for their proposals. In fact, this lack of certainty may have made each more willing to argue in favor of his or her proposal; not knowing the costs made it possible to suggest that they might be minimal. You knew you would not be able to prove anything with certainty by tomorrow morning. The goal for evening would be to build a set of models that would illustrate the risks and opportunities with each lease option.

V. The Revised Offer

Provide an internal memo for the working group that will summarize your arguments. The group will not have a consensus about the right assumptions, so your memo should address a range of assumptions. But also make sure your model is flexible enough to allow the working group to explore your assumptions further. It will be very helpful to articulate the right way to make a decision about these three lease options. Returns could be one tool, but so too could be NPV or even an alternative like minimizing current investment. Again, this group has not settled on many things about the Cloverfield Commons and which decision metric or metrics will be another source of debate. Because you have been asked to lead this conversation, be clear to discuss which metrics are best and why.

In brief, your firm purchased the 35,000 sf Cloverfield Commons for $25,375,000 dollars, closing on the property 6 weeks ago. Now there are three basic options you are to explore. The numbers below are starting points. The basic agreed upon lease terms are:

- Triple net lease rate: $3.75/sf/month
- Lease term: 15 years
- Rent escalations: Annual 3.0% rent increases
- Tenant improvements: $35/sf

Option 1: "Go Green"
Invest an additional $1.75M budget to improve building performance. This could include replacing/upgrading insulation, installing new higher grade windows, modernizing the HVAC system, and installing kalwall, solar tube or other natural lighting systems. Assume that the work could be completed in 6 months, during which the tenant is not paying rent. Also assume that operating expenses are $18/sf whether or not the building is occupied.
Option 2: "Sell the Future"
Give the option to the tenant (only) the right to purchase Cloverfield Commons at the end of the 15-year term. The sale price will be determined by using the recent purchase price and inflating it at the national Consumer Price Index for All Urban Consumers as published by the US Bureau of Labor Statistics.

Option 3: Reduce the Rent

Propose any number of ways to reduce the rent. You could lower the face rent, lower the growth rate in rents, offer free rent up front, or some combination of these. As you consider each possibility, be thoughtful about how you will argue for which is "best" and why the other combinations you explore are not as good.

As you underwrite these options, make sure to consider the issues below.

a. Lowering rent is easy, but had a direct cost to the cash flows. What other costs might be associated with lowering the rent? What are the benefits? Do the timing of the rent reductions matter? How so? It is common to use an NPV calculation based on the lease terms alone. How does this miss relevant information about the property?

b. A 15 lease is a long lease for an office building. Why are most office lease terms shorter? Does the long lease mean more or less safety for an owner?

c. "Going green" is a common refrain in commercial real estate, but in particular in the City of Santa Monica. But "going green" is a moving target. The LEED standards have evolved significantly over the last 15 years. Does that matter to this option? Would you care about how these dollars are invested or would you be happy to just give the $1.75M green investment budget to the tenant as a larger TI package? If you do care, where would it show up in your underwriting? How would the numbers look differently if the dollars were invested in better furniture and a nicer reception area instead of "green" infrastructure? Would it matter if the "green" investment was cutting edge solar windows that are transparent but also generate some electricity, or if the "green" investment was simply a significant improvement in insulation and building efficiency?

d. How should you value the tenant's option to buy the building at the end of 15 years? What is the nominal value of the option to buy the building at the end of the lease? What is the present value of the option to buy the building at the end of the lease? Can you make a comparison between the value of the option and an equivalently reduced rent?

Knowing this will require a lot of assumptions. With that in mind, can you answer the big question: Are any of these options "big" give-aways? If not, would you care about any of them if they were all "small" impacts on the overall lease value? Thinking about these issues numerically should help you understand the qualitative nature of the lease options the working group is considering. Your goal is to write a memo that can fundamentally inform the working group about the strengths and weakness of each option.

Part III

Framework, Deal Structure, and Risk and Return

I initially labeled this section "Deal Structure," but abandoned that title because in fact all 20 cases in this book involve deal structure. What links the five cases in this section is their more narrow initial questions. They do focus heavily on deal structure, but more specific questions can cause students to lose focus on the larger contexts that remain in the background. In the first case, students are asked to value an investment in a distressed hotel and dig deeply into the stakeholders within the capital stack. The second case addresses the nuances of underwriting from the perspective of a fund or from one of the properties within it. They are not the same thing. In the third case, the underwriting for how to get into a deal is already complete and in the past. The case now asks the question of whether it is possible to exit the deal with an institutional JV partner. The last two cases are two distinctly different takes on a rapidly evolving retail market place. The first offers a kind of retail investment that is offered as a safe "bond-like" investment. In the other case the protagonist argues that property-level success may involve abandoning standard retail leases in favor of potentially riskier leases at stores within a regional retail center. The common theme among the 5 cases is that narrower questions are being asked relative to the previous 10 cases, which focused more on big picture valuations and some of the key features that influence them. In this section, students will have to decide if the larger context are of primary or secondary issues relative to the preliminary questions being asked. It is here that students might begin to see that underwriting is costly and that while it might otherwise be nice to undertake more due diligence, that time and effort might could be used on other deals.

Case 11

Making Sense of Eastgate

I. Background

It is February 2011, and the private equity real estate fund you work for has the opportunity to acquire the first mortgage of the 676-key Eastgate Hotel located in downtown Seattle. You are a Managing Director with the firm, and an associate who reports to you recently created the following investment memo, which you are expected to present to the investment committee tomorrow. You need to review the following memo. It is incomplete, requiring a suggested course of action. Think through the memo, make your own recommendation, and prepare for any issues/concerns that might be raised by members of the committee.

II. Traveler Group—The Investment Memo

To: Traveler Group Investment Committee
  RE: Eastgate Hotel Senior Mortgage Acquisition—Seattle, WA
  Date: February 9, 2011
  Our firm, Traveler Group (TG), is able to purchase the $150 million first mortgage, secured by the fee simple interest in the Eastgate Hotel in Seattle, for $146 million. In the event that TG is able to obtain title to the hotel, TG has agreed to pay an additional $3 million to the "B3" lender (see Exhibit A for more details).

The hotel has 676 rooms (almost all of which are King and Double/Double), approximately 23,000 RSF of meeting space, a full-service restaurant called Duchesne, a workout center powered by Reebok, and a full-service business center. The hotel's A+ location is withing the most desirable hotel submarket in Seattle. It is a short distance from the financial district, the ferry system, and several important transportation links. The surrounding area offers an excellent set of amenities, including access to top local businesses, as well as a dense and diverse collection of dining, entertainment, and shopping activities.

The current owner acquired the hotel in 2006 for $180 million. In 2008, the borrower completed a $28 million major renovation of rooms and common areas, as well as a repositioning of the premier restaurant of the property. Following the renovation, the owner entered into a franchise licensing agreement with Puget Sound Hotels (PSH) to place the Eastgate flag on the hotel. TG estimates that the borrower's all-in basis following the renovation is approximately $232 million. After its origination, the $150 million first mortgage that TG is interested in purchasing was split into four tranches and sold to three different parties (Exhibit A). The mortgage

Underwriting Commercial Real Estate in a Dynamic Market. https://doi.org/10.1016/B978-0-12-815989-7.00011-2
115

carries an interest rate of Libor + 2% and had an initial maturity of April 2008 along with three 1-year extension options. The mortgage currently is in maturity default due to a failure to meet a debt service coverage test in April 2010. For the past year the borrower has been in restructuring discussions with the loan servicer.

Exhibit A: Eastgate Hotel Capital Stack		
A Note	$88,000,000 ($130,178 per key)	Major Bank
B1 Note	$28,000,000 ($171,598 per key)	Life Co.
B2 Note	$17,000,000 ($196,746 per key)	Life Co.
B3 Note	$17,000,000 ($221,893 per key)	Credit Corp.
Senior Mezzanine Note	$22,000,000 ($254,438 per key)	Institutional Fund
Junior Mezzanine Note	$40,000,000 ($313,609 per key)	Private Equity Fund
Equity	$20,000,000 ($328,402 per key)	Operator

Counsel has advised TG that under the terms of the franchise license agreement with Puget Sound Hotels, TG could elect to change the asset's brand and management without payment of any termination fee to PSH. This ability provides substantial leverage to renegotiate more favorable contract terms with PSH, thereby immediately adding value to the hotel.

Alternative Scenarios

There are two ways in which TG can obtain title to the hotel: (1) complete a mortgage foreclosure, which is expected to take approximately 6 months; or (2) negotiate a deed-in-lieu (DIL) agreement with the borrower. The primary risk in either scenario lies in the fact that TG believes the fair market value of the hotel falls in the Institutional Fund's (Fund) Senior Mezzanine tranche. As the "fulcrum piece," this gives the fund significant rights and claims which need to be thoroughly examined before proceeding with this investment.

Scenario 1—Foreclosure

Should TG pursue a foreclosure, both the Institutional Fund and the Private Equity Fund will have the ability to exercise their par purchase options on the mortgage as provided for under the terms of the intercreditor agreement. The Institutional Fund has priority over the Private Equity Fund. Either Fund can exercise this option right up until the completion of TG's foreclosure process or receipt of a DIL of foreclosure. Either Fund can also elect to file for a UCC (Uniform Commercial Code) foreclosure at any time which typically takes up to 30–45 days to complete. In order to pursue a UCC foreclosure, Funds would first be required to cure any amounts payable to the mortgage lender other than principal, such as accrued interest, default interest, and late fees. Upon completion of the UCC foreclosure, Fund would then be required to repay the entire mortgage principal balance at par.

Scenario 2—Deed-in-Lieu

The other alternative would be for TG to negotiate a DIL agreement with the borrower. In this scenario, TG would be able to halt Fund's ability to complete a UCC foreclosure by simply acquiring fee title to the property in exchange for cancellation of the mortgage debt and repaying the Senior Mezzanine Note. Assuming a DIL can be arranged with the borrower, TG will be able to obtain title to the hotel at essentially a fixed price because the Junior Mezzanine Lender is not expected to exercise any rights or claims.

The Mortgage

Loan Amount

Initial funding:	$81,740,939
Renovation holdback:	$28,000,000
Future funding:	$40,259,061
Total loan amount:	$150,000,000

Interest Rate

Initial/future funding:	Libor+1.77%
Renovation holdback:	Libor+3.00%
Total blended rate:	Libor+2.00%
Default rate:	Lesser of (1) or (2): (1) Maximum legal rate or (2) 2% above the current rate

Maturity Date

April 9, 2008, subject to three successive 1-year extensions.

Tests per Extension

(a) no event of default may have occurred or be continuing
(b) borrower must provide notice between 1 and 6 months prior
(c) borrower will obtain replacement interest rate caps
(d) borrower will pay a fee of 0.125% of the outstanding principal balance

Cash Sweep

The hotel enters into a cash sweep beginning at the start of the fourth year of the loan term, unless it generates $13,000,000 of net cash flow on a trailing twelve month (TTM) basis, or unless it generates $15,000,000 of net cash flow on a TTM basis in year 5 of the loan term. TG has been advised that the asset is currently under a cash sweep, the excess proceeds of which would benefit the lender upon foreclosure. The loan servicer currently releases cash to the borrower to pay necessary operating expenses under a protective advance agreement.

Intercreditor Agreement

Purchase Rights

The senior mezzanine lender and the junior mezzanine lender each have the right to purchase the mortgage at par. Upon an event of default, this right is triggered after the mortgage lender sends a notice of sale to the senior mezzanine and junior mezzanine lenders. This notice has already been sent and neither of the mezzanine lenders exercised their purchase option. Although the purchase option triggering notice was sent in June 2010, both mezzanine lenders retain the right to exercise the purchase option until the mortgage is repaid or a foreclosure or DIL of foreclosure is completed. The junior mezzanine lender must also purchase the senior mezzanine loan as well as the mortgage at par plus accrued default interest and costs if it elects to exercise the purchase option.

Foreclosure

No junior lender may complete a foreclosure unless transferee:

(1) is a qualified transferee;
(2) provides a replacement guarantor;
(3) cures all senior debt;
(4) pays all expenses of the senior lenders.

Each junior lender agrees not to pursue claims against the guarantor if the mortgage lender is simultaneously exercising such claims or the pursuit of such claims would cause the guarantor to not satisfy liquidity or net worth tests.

Mortgage Transfer

Mortgage lender may transfer all or any portion of the mortgage without consent of any junior lender; provided that mortgage lender may not make any transfer to borrower or an affiliate of borrower.

Senior Mezzanine Loan Transfer

No junior lender shall transfer more than 49% of its beneficial interest unless: (1) a rating agency confirmation is received; (2) the transfer is to a qualified transferee; (3) it complies with all sections of the intercreditor agreement.

Junior Mezzanine Loan Transfer

The junior mezzanine lender may not transfer all or any portion of the junior mezzanine loan (other than to an affiliated entity) without the prior written consent of the mortgage lender and senior mezzanine lender, which consent may be withheld at their sole and absolute discretion.

Guarantees

The mortgage benefits from the following guarantees, which are triggered upon so-called "bad-boy" acts. TG had not been able to obtain any guarantor financials. In the event that any of the "bad boy" acts are triggered, TG may pursue these guarantors for actual losses:

- Borrower
- Junior mezzanine lender (Guaranty is capped at $22,500,000)
- An individual (sole owner of the borrowing entity)—guaranty is limited to bankruptcy related to "bad boy" acts

If the borrower believes that its equity position is "in the money," it may file for voluntary bankruptcy despite these guarantees. Should the borrower file for bankruptcy, this would stay any foreclosure proceedings initiated by TG until the bankruptcy is resolved. The borrower would then have to offer a reorganization plan for approval by the bankruptcy court and the creditors. During this process, TG would have the right to pursue the guarantors for all actual losses, including legal costs.

Foreclosure Process

Upon acquisition of the mortgage, TG would also be required to send a notice of default to all interested parties, as provided by the title company. If the borrower does not cure the default within 90 days, a notice of sale can then be recorded and published. The private foreclosure sale date is generally scheduled at least 30 days following recordation of the notice of sale. Absent contractual restrictions, litigation, or bankruptcy to restrain or delay a sale, TG has been advised by counsel that 5 months is a reasonable period of time to complete a private, nonjudicial foreclosure sale in California. At the foreclosure sale, the mortgage lender has the right to credit bid the full par amount of the mortgage plus accrued and unpaid interest, attorney's fees and other unpaid costs and expenses. All other bidders at the foreclosure sale are required to "cash" bid. Until the foreclosure sale is completed, the senior mezzanine lender and junior mezzanine lender have the right to purchase the mortgage at par plus accrued and unpaid default interest and other costs and expenses pursuant to the intercreditor agreement.

Hotel Operations

TG assumes that the hotel stabilizes at 88% occupancy with ADR growth of 7% for the 3 years following acquisition. In terms of operating leverage, TG has assumed that the asset stabilizes at an NOI margin of ~17%, which is ~3% less than its peak performance in 2008. The following is a brief summary of actual and expected operating performance.

Actual/Expected Hotel Operations

Year	2007A	2008A	2009A	2010A	2011E	2012E	2013E	2014E	2015E
Occupancy	72.3%	88.0%	91.4%	90.8%	90.3%	88.0%	88.0%	88.0%	88.0%
ADR	$186	$201	$167	$177	$192	$209	$223	$230	$237
RevPAR	$134	$177	$152	$161	$174	$184	$196	$202	$208
% Change		31.7%	(13.8%)	5.6%	7.8%	5.8%	7.0%	3.0%	3.0%
NOI ($Mil.)	$6.0	$11.8	$5.6	$4.7	$6.0	$7.8	$10.2	$10.9	$11.6

Investment Returns

Traveler Group has an opportunity to purchase the mortgage for an all-in basis of $146 million, representing a last-dollar basis of approximately $217,000 per key. TG assumes that it will successfully negotiate a DIL transaction with the borrower and will repay the senior mezzanine lender at 100% of par (while it is possible that TG receives a discount on the senior mezzanine debt, that scenario would be considered upside to the base case and was not explicitly modeled). The underwriting contemplates a scenario in which TG is paid off at par (senior mezzanine lender exercises its par purchase option) and a scenario in TG obtains title to the hotel through foreclosure.

Payoff Scenario

In the event TG is repaid at par by the senior mezzanine lender in June 2011 prior to completing a foreclosure or DIL, the returns to TG would be an 11% unlevered annual IRR. This scenario would yield profits of approximately $5 million on total equity of $146 million.

Obtain Title via DIL Scenario

In this scenario, TG obtains title to the hotel in June 2011 requiring total peak equity of $169 million ($149 million senior mortgage + $20 million senior mezzanine loan) prior to obtaining financing. TG anticipates financing the hotel shortly after obtaining title. TG has conservatively assumed that it is able to obtain $69 million of financing proceeds at an all-in interest rate of 7%. The financing adjusted peak equity is $100 million. Assuming TG sells the hotel at the end of 2013 for $325,000 per key (total proceeds of ~$220 million; predicated on a 5% cap rate), this yields a 17.2% IRR and a 1.6x financing adjusted equity multiple. Below is a sensitivity analysis of the levered returns based upon the percent of par paid to the Senior Mezzanine Lender.

Returns and % of Par Paid to Senior Mezzanine Lender						
	50%	60%	70%	80%	90%	100%
IRR	20.6%	19.9%	19.2%	18.5%	17.8%	17.2%
EM	1.8x	1.7x	1.7x	1.7x	1.6x	1.6x

III. Completing the Memo

How should TG proceed? What should you suggest to your firm's partners? The following are several questions to think about and prepare for prior to your presentation to the investment committee tomorrow.

a. What is the significance of owning a hotel property that has no contractual obligation to any specific brand or management chain? How much value does such flexibility add to the asset?

b. Analyze historical Libor rates and calculate the approximate interest payment owned annually by the borrower. Why did the asset fail its loan extension test?

c. What are the primary drivers of possible downside risks to this investment? Are the returns worth the risks?

d. How concerned should you be that probable fair market value of the asset lies within the Senior Mezzanine Tranche?

e. Traveler Group already owns the Seattle Adelphi Hotel and the mezzanine loan on the Terrace Hotel, both of which are approximately one block from the Eastgate Hotel. Will this concern the investment committee? Should it cause diversification concerns or will the increase in market share allow for positive pricing pressures?

f. There are six parties to this transaction, each of which has legal counsel and possibly external financial advisors. What are the logistical/timing concerns of successfully executing a transaction with so many parties involved?

g. How important is it to the success of this investment that TG receives a discount on the Senior Mezzanine loan?

h. What are some strategies that could help TG ensure the current borrower's cooperation and that prevent him/her from delaying foreclosure by filing for bankruptcy? What are the implications for TG and Eastgate if the owner declares bankruptcy? How could TG incentivize him/her to pursue a DIL course of action?

Ahead of your presentation, please prepare a short memo on your suggested course of action. Include specifically what actions you want the credit committee to approve, the returns you expect over what horizon, as well as a section on key risks and mitigants.

Case 12

Exiting Fund IV

I. The Email From Your Boss

Good morning team,

  We finally have a broker's opinion of value (BOV) on 257 Main Street. As expected, it's not a firm sale price. Instead, it's a range from $73M to $82M. The range is not wholly unexpected because we are not done leasing and we don't have any proven cash flow history. But, this raises the issue I'd like you to address. If we were able to get a pre-sale agreement with the broker's client, should we accept it? Crucially, what would the right sale price be? What assumptions did you use to get to that number?

  As you know 257 Main Street is the final asset from Fund IV. It was the first deal in and will be the last one out. We were not alone in missing the underwriting in 2006 when the fund started. Indeed if you recall, we thought we were getting the deal at below "market." While that may have felt good at the time, it was a bargain only relative to the frothy bidding at the time. We found out quickly after our acquisition that "the market" was way ahead of itself – so much so that no well-struck deals bought in 2006 looked good by the end of 2007.

  We were fortunate to be able to hold off on development until the market recovered. I'm grateful for the leadership the team showed in changing the original development plans. It was proactive on our part to acquire the adjacent site and design a more efficient and larger scale project that could prove that we made the most of a bad situation. We now have an asset that looks better that it has in almost a decade.

  We will meet with the broker and the potential buyer in two weeks' time and I need you to develop a "breakeven" or "indifference" number – the price at which we would not care if the buyer agreed to terms or walked away. My notes are abstracted below, including both the proposed sale terms and some of the fund and deal history.

  In our meeting next week, we will have to develop that indifference number and be confident in it. I will be talking with the seller next week ahead of our meeting to learn more. But he and I have already held a calendar date for an "LOI Lunch" in two weeks. If we're going to go with this seller, we'll need to focus on this asset now. If we don't pursue this option, we will move on to the next set of steps – leasing up and seasoning the rent roll, discovering if the rents and concessions we underwrote are solid, and see how the property and its cash flows are priced when we are ready to sell. Clearly,

Underwriting Commercial Real Estate in a Dynamic Market. https://doi.org/10.1016/B978-0-12-815989-7.00012-4

there are risks with a presale, but there is a whole new world of potential risks if we do not accept the presale terms.

Please prepare your thoughts for our strategy session week. Let me stress that selling 257 Main will have implications for Fund IV beyond simply booking the proceeds. Our underwriting session next week will have to consider both the nuts and bolts of the terms of the sale on its own merits, and also how the sale impacts the overall fund economics/returns.

Thanks. Have a great weekend, dns. -- Director, West Region Acquisitions

II. MetroVantage Advisors

Founded in 2001, MetroVantage Advisors is a premier investment management and development firm focused on urban residential real estate in the Western United States. At the center of the firm's success is its strong professional team which possesses deep expertise in real estate, (including development, entitlement, design, and construction) operations, finance and asset management.

MetroVantage Advisors targets complex multifamily housing opportunities in urban markets which are overlooked by others due to transaction and development challenges such as entitlement or environmental issues, political hurdles or community relations. The majority of MetroVantage Advisors' projects are within walking distance of transportation hubs, job centers, schools, retail services, healthcare facilities and cultural amenities. For each transaction, the firm's goal is to generate top-quartile returns for its limited partners while striving to measurably improve the surrounding community.

MetroVantage Advisors' investors include some of the largest and most sophisticated public pension plans and financial institutions, including: several states' Public Employees' Retirement System (PERS), several states' Teacher Retirement System (STERS), three County Employees Retirement Associations (CERAs), several major Fire and Police Plans (FPPs), and a handful of private equity firms who don't have their own real estate departments.

MetroVantage Advisors currently manages a combination of eight funds and separately managed accounts. Collectively, the firm's funds have invested in more than 80 projects and have generated more than $3.0 billion in urban investment. The firm is headquartered in Los Angeles and has regional offices in San Francisco, Seattle, and Dallas.

III. Investment Philosophy

MetroVantage Advisors targets urban areas it believes will continue to grow and thrive due to demographic and cultural changes which are attracting people to the nation's city centers. In response, cities are looking to improve their overall infrastructure and other amenities to satisfy this demand. This shift is fueling demand for housing in dense, high-cost markets such as the San Francisco Bay area and coastal Southern California, where the housing supply is constrained and barriers to entry are high. These market conditions are ideal for MetroVantage Advisors' brand of investing which combines deep local real estate knowledge with experienced investment, development and asset management capabilities.

In addition, the ability to provide stable cash flows from rental incomes and consistent demand means that multifamily housing has traditionally performed well throughout various market cycles and provided investors with superior risk-adjusted returns. This makes it an ideal asset class for institutional investors looking to diversify their portfolios through allocations to real estate.

IV. Fund Timeline and Sale Terms

MetroVantage Advisors (MVA) raised the $200M Fund IV in 2006 to focus on multifamily development. The fund's strategic approach was to find development opportunities ahead of where others would be later. MVA found good locations in Oakland, when returns in San Francisco were too thin. The same approach yielded developments in secondary neighborhoods that offered significantly better yields with only marginally great risk. While MVA's track record with investors gave it some latitude in picking properties, the returns that MVA promised to investors imply that candidate sites are not in core submarkets.

Fund IV was structured as an 8-year life with two 1-year optional extensions. The Fund began with a 3-year commitment period, but you were able to negotiate with the investors for a 2-year extension given the unprecedented downturn and the significant amount of uncommitted capital at the end of the first 3 years. At the end of the holding period, MVA would be required to undergo an "Orderly Liquidation Period" (OLP). This OLP would not be a fire sale; rather it requires that MVA sell off all remaining assets with the goal of maximizing value and mitigating marginal risks to investors.

MVA's track record has afforded it greater control over selecting properties and developing business plans for them, and the same record has made possible a unique joint venture structure for the Fund. The investors (limited partners or LPs) put up 100% of the equity capital needed for acquisition and redevelopment. On that investment, the waterfall is as follows:

- Tier 1 (preferred return): 100% of the available cash flow after debt service flows to the LPs, earning a 9% preferred return (compounded quarterly) on their investments.
- Tier 2 (return of capital): 100% of available cash flow after Tier 1 goes to the LPs until their capital investments are returned in full.
- Tier 3 (catch up): After Tier 2, remaining cash flows are to be distributed 50% LP/50% GP until cumulative distributions yield 80% to LP/20% to GP.
- Tier 4 (promote): Any remaining cash flows after Tier 3 will be distributed 80% LP/20% GP.

Although the investment window spanned the Great Recession, the Fund is projected to be profitable. Over the extended 5-year acquisition window MVA acquired or developed 15 assets. 14 of these have been sold. The net cash flows from the Fund to date are reported in the exhibits below. These encompass the capital contributions (recorded as positive cash flows) and distributions (as negative cash flows) through the 14 sales to date.

Notes From MVA's Director of Acquisitions

257 Main Street Property and Development Description

- Location: Torrance, CA
- Units: 250
- Avg. size: 900 sf
- 30% leased to date
- 1/2 month—Upfront Concessions to date
- $2.35 avg. psf
- Operating expense projections
- Current Cost Basis is $60M
- Absorption schedule: 25 units/month (since opening)

The property is now complete. There are finish issues to work through including a number of units that needs white goods, countertops, fixtures, and paint. But, the project is on budget and can consider development over. We currently have a $40M construction loan on the project that is fully prepayable but not due for 1 year. We will be able to finish this work ahead of the absorption schedule.

Proposed Sale Terms for 257 Main Street

The structured sale for the final asset is outlined in bullet form based on numbers from the broker and MVA's director of acquisitions. They should be seen as preliminary. MVA would issue a short term loan to the buyer to give him/her time to arrange for permanent financing. More will be clarified later, but to begin the analysis, use the following assumptions:

- Purchase Price: TBD (BOV range $73M–$82M)
- Timing: MVA must complete leasing, reaching 90% occupancy at market rents within 1-year. But the buyer will have the option of closing on the sale before then.
- Carry-Back Financing:
  - $50M Loan
  - 5% Interest Rate
  - 12 month term
  - Fully prepayable

The structured sale will cause the construction loan to require accelerated repayment. So, in order to complete the presale transaction you have to get a refinance bridge loan on the project, you have the following term sheet information:

- Proceeds: $40M
- 12 month term
- Interest Rate: 4%
- Fully prepayable

The bridge loan interest will accrue and be paid out of the interest from the carry-back financing. For the purposes of the Fund analysis, these two loan cash flows can be considered as zero net cash flow.

V. Deliverables

MVA has a relatively standard set of metrics it considers in making these sorts of decisions. Use the stabilized cash flow assumptions below to arrive at a proposed sale price. Be sure to explain how you went about arriving at this number. And, at the proposed purchase price, provide the following metrics:

- Fund IV Profit
- Fund IV Internal Rate of Return (IRR)
- Fund IV Multiple on Invested Capital (MOIC)
- Limited Partner (LP) Profit
- LP IRR
- LP MOIC
- General Partner (GP/MVA) Promote
- GP % of Total Profit (including Preferred Return)
- Aggregate Promote paid to the LP

Provide a summary of your thoughts about the "indifference" price and the assumptions needed to arrive at it. Include in your summary an analysis of the risks and opportunities associated with the presale and with going to market next year when leasing is done. The memo should incorporate the impacts to MVA, but also to the LPs in Fund IV. It should address the presale deal structure as well as key development and operating decisions. Key assumptions and your rationale should be clear. Identifying risks and opportunity is of paramount importance.

You will lead a discussion of your investment memo. The director of the Fund will join the usual credit committee in vetting your proposals. The goal will be to ready to decide on how best to proceed with selling 257 Main Street and exit from Fund IV.

Questions:

a. It is always essential to understand the timing of the fund activities. Given the unusual extension during the acquisition window, the two optional 1-year extensions at the end of the fund, and the "orderly liquidation period," can you diagram the time line for MVA's Fund IV? Do you understand why extensions were negotiated during the original Fund operating agreement? Do you understand why the additional extension was given during acquisitions? Who benefits from these? Why did both parties agree to them? Who would not want to allow an extension and why?

b. Do you understand the equity waterfall that details how cash flows from the Fund are to be distributed? Qualitatively, does MVA more or less than the LPs? How does this depend on the sale at 257 Main? Given the time line and cash flows to and from Fund IV to date, can you provide a rough estimate of the basic return to it? The credit committee has asked for numerous metrics, can you define these? Do you understand what they represent and how well they measure performance?

c. Repeat the step above by including two final sale values, one at the high point of the sale range, one at the low end. How do the metrics you've just calculated in the previous step change with the addition of the final sale from the assets in Fund IV? How much difference do these sale price ranges influence these metrics?

d. Who are the stakeholders in the current negotiations about 257 Main? What are their incentives? What control do they have? Are these short term or long term in nature? Do their perspectives on time horizon influence the way they underwrite this potential deal?

e. Because you are sitting at MVA, what do you want to happen with regard to this deal? The case is not clear about how you are compensated, but would your answer change if your bonus were paid out of the Fund's return? To MVA's share of the Fund return? Or, what if you your career path depended on MVA's long-term performance?

f. Having wrestled with these steps, do you need to examine the real estate numbers in the static valuation? That is, the broker has offered a range of values, what range do you think is right? How would you determine what ranges you think you would experience if you didn't accept a presale and took it to market when it was seasoned?

g. In short, what risks do you face if you accept an offer and if you don't? It may be useful to stress test a number of key variables to explore these outcomes.

In light of all of the above, what do you include in memo recommending what's best for MVA with regard to 257 Main? Because this is an internal document, be blunt about the risks and returns for the various options you considered. If you do not consider an option deeply, explain why you can dismiss it out of hand. If you do pursue the presale, please address why the seller will agree to the price.

Preliminary Static Underwriting.

Stabilized value analysis	Total
Scheduled rent	6,345,000
Loss to lease	–
Gross potential rent	**6,345,000**
Vacancy	(317,250)
Bad debt	(31,725)
Rental concessions	–
Nonrevenue units	(25,380)
Gross rental income	**5,970,645**
Other income	135,000
Utility RUBS	225,000
Effective gross income	**6,330,645**
Fixed expenses	
Property taxes	750,000
Insurance	62,500
Utilities	37,500
Reserves	62,500
Subtotal	**912,500**
Variable expenses	
R&M	100,000
Unit turnover	62,500
Building services	150,000
Management fee	189,919
Payroll	437,500
G&A	68,750
Marketing	65,000
Subtotal	**1,073,669**
Total expenses	**1,986,169**
NOI	**4,344,476**

Fund IV—Cash flows (not including final sale)	
Date	Fund cash flows
3/31/2006	15.0
6/30/2006	15.0
6/30/2007	30.0
12/31/2008	−10.0
3/31/2009	37.5
6/30/2009	37.5
9/30/2009	02.5
12/31/2009	02.5
3/31/2010	35.0
6/30/2010	17.5
9/30/2010	−50.0
12/31/2010	17.5
3/31/2011	−05.0
6/30/2011	05.0
9/30/2011	−05.0
12/31/2011	−05.0
6/30/2012	−40.0
12/31/2012	50.0
3/31/2013	−20.0
12/31/2013	−80.0
3/31/2014	−50.0
6/30/2014	−20.0
9/30/2014	−20.0
12/31/2014	−20.0
3/31/2015	−20.0
6/30/2015	−20.0
9/30/2015	−20.0

Note: all cash flows in $ millions.

Case 13

A Changing Retail Landscape and a Lease to Match

I think the real analysis needs to reflect that you can destroy value by doing the right thing defined narrowly as opposed to doing the right thing for your overall goal.

I. Muddled Metaphors

Jim loved his job, but there were times he wasn't sure if he was a real estate professional or someone working at a sports bar. He blamed it on the rise of ESPN and the need to fill content. While he still found sports as compelling as ever, he wished that its tired idioms had stayed out of real estate. He might ask "Where are we in the cycle," but more often than not the industry would ask, "What inning are we in?" They might complain about someone "moving the goal posts" or "dropping the ball." But the worst for Jim was the motivational language; he hated "Just win baby!" just as much as "Winning isn't everything, it's the only thing!" Jim had discovered that it wasn't just coliseum-sports that made it into daily life. One of his co-workers had been a climber but now has turned to cycling, and so he will alternatively use "drop the hammer" or "go hard or go home" when he was trying to get himself or his team motivated. Jim had been a competitive athlete and understood how challenging real estate was, but the suggestion that the business was a zero-sum game struck him as simple-minded. Jim knew that reality was more complicated than the tired catchphrases allowed. He had read Vince Lombardi's speech a long time ago, and the "Winning" quote that so many repeated was just wrong. Lombardi had actually said: "Winning is not a sometime thing; it's an all-time thing. You don't win once in a while, you don't do things right once in a while, you do them right all the time. Winning is not everything, but wanting to win is." This was a quote that Jim could live with and that roughly captured his approach to real estate.

Jim had just wrapped up a long day of sessions at the International Council of Shopping Centers (ICSC) annual meetings in Las Vegas and had headed to the cocktail hour. It was full of retail brokers and the air was full of sports jargon, but Jim couldn't quite tell if it was sports references or actual sports. "… right down the fairway" was either about a firm sticking to its proven business plan, or about an actual round of golf that morning. Jim settled into a table with some business contacts, met some new ones, and then started talking to a

Underwriting Commercial Real Estate in a Dynamic Market. https://doi.org/10.1016/B978-0-12-815989-7.00013-6

tenant rep for a strong regional brand who was on Jim's short list to fill a space at his center. The conversation was fine, but it wasn't feeling promising when his phone rang. As he left the table, excusing himself to take the call, Jim had heard the rep yell after him, "Call me. Let's do this!" Of course, there was nothing wrong with showing commitment to getting things done, but what was the "this" he was talking about? For Jim, "this" should always be about making the best decision for his property, but he wasn't sure the broker would interpret it that way. Jim was also aware that his own sentiment could be equally murky: after all, what did it mean to say "the best decision for this property"?

The property in question was a retail center in one of key submarkets in the San Francisco Bay area. Jim's grumpiness at the ICSC meetings was that "best" seemed to mean something different to him than for many of his colleagues. The whole feel of the place was fundamentally confrontational: the owner would take on the tenant rep, the two of them would size up who had leverage, and they would play an elaborate game of chicken. The owner would judge his location and its desirability; while the tenant rep would be aware of the hole in the owner's rent roll that was not paying rent or covering any of the fixed costs. The lease would lock them in a legal relationship and the two would manage rights and responsibilities accordingly. It struck Jim that according to this view of things, being happy about a lease would have to mean taking more from a deal than perhaps your leverage deserved.

It was obvious to him that the best retail centers were those where all the parts were working well collectively, when all were contributing to each other's success. As the owner, he had a long list of things he needed to do to provide the right environment, but it was the tenants—the retailers themselves—doing their part that was most critical. If they weren't producing the best possible utilization of the space, experience, connection with the customer, and of course sales, then they weren't generating foot traffic that would help the rest of the tenants and the center. In Jim's view, being happy with tenants who were simply paying rent was setting his bar way too low.

The last tenant rep he had spoken with at ICSC had kept starting his sentences with "Here's what I want…" because he wanted to jam Jim with a lease that was good for his tenant but also very good for him. The conversation had gone badly because while Jim could concede favorable rents, a long lease term, and a rich TI package, it would only happen if he was just as confident that the tenant could guarantee gross sales and foot traffic for the full 10-year lease— and the tenant rep wasn't interested in offering these sorts of guarantees. The number of tenants he'd bet on being around for 10 years—and being just as profitable for each of those 10 years—could be counted on one hand. This retailer had a business concept that was hot now, but was far from a sure thing. Jim wanted more performance criteria as part of the lease and he and the tenant rep had talked past each other until Jim had excused himself to take his phone call. Certainly, Jim thought it was telling that the tenant rep had yelled out "Let's do this" as Jim stepped away and started to find a quiet spot to talk on the phone. Maybe the rep had revealed that he really did want to find a way to close this deal in particular.

After his phone call Jim thought over the last conversation with the tenant rep. Jim wanted to find a way to get the rep and the retailer to buy into the success of the whole property, not just that of retailer he represented. But after mocking the others here for leaning on so much sports imagery, he cringed as he caught himself thinking: "There is no 'I' in team." He got back to the notion that there must be a way to structure a lease that could help him make his a great retail center and make the retailer happy, too. He returned to the happy hour and found the tenant rep again. "Oh sure" remembered the tenant rep, "You have the mall with the great location that somehow has vacant space." Jim immediately regretted walking back again, but persisted: "Did you just call my property a mall? You can call my kids ugly, but you can't call my property a mall." Jim then reminded the rep that the whole notion of the traditional mall was what got retail into so much trouble. He reintroduced his vision for his center and pitched again the idea of a different lease that would serve them all. The tenant rep did not agree on the spot, but saw there might be room for some more discussion. That's all Jim wanted. They agreed to meet back in San Francisco later next week. In the meantime, Jim would send him a couple of different lease abstracts with notes. Jim had a preference among them, but wanted to make sure he sent the message the he could be open-minded as well.

Whatever he came up with, Jim would need to run the deal by his own firm. The property was one of many that Jim was responsible for, but if he was going to start changing the company's standard lease, he'd need to get it approved by the CFO and a couple of other key people in senior management. He'd need to argue strengths and weaknesses, and he didn't have a lot of time to do that if he was going to present legitimate options for the tenant rep next week. He laughed again as he heard himself think: "Game time" and headed to the airport.

II. Lease Agreements

Jim was sure that he'd have to rethink the boilerplate language that his firm and many others used as the starting point for most lease negotiations. The retail industry had arrived at a standard lease over many years; along with that evolution went the received wisdom that it was the "right" way to structure a lease. If Jim was going to argue for a departure from that starting point, he'd have to both show why the current lease was inadequate and that his alternative was a substantial improvement. Crucially, Jim knew that he would have to argue that enough tenants would actually want to sign it as well. It was easy to draw up a lease that was favorable to an owner, but it would not be as easy to get retailers to agree to it.

The standard retail lease is a nuanced version of a standard commercial lease in which an owner sells some of his or her property rights to a tenant.

That simple construct gets messy almost immediately when the details are introduced. While there was a lot of variation, Jim's typical retail lease terms these days included:

i. Term: An initial primary term is typically 5–10 years depending on the size of the deal, and the amount of capital that goes in to the lease.

ii. Options to extend: Clauses that give the Tenant the right to extend the lease, after the expiration of the primary term, for a specified length of time and on specified terms. The most common option is a 5-year option. Terms can range from Fair Market Value to fixed rents. Options clearly favor the Tenant and limit Landlord control.

iii. Base rent: TBD/Market, with annual increases of 3%—this despite a CPI that's been below 2% for a decade.

iv. Percentage rent: 6% of Gross Sales Revenue above a natural breakpoint. Jim spent a lot of time negotiating with retailers over both the "natural breakpoint" and the percentage rent itself. But while it was fun to think about how much income this would mean if the retailer was successful, in his experience, the percentage of tenants that actually ever hit their breakpoint was very small.

v. Tenant improvement allowance (TIs): A cash contribution given to the Tenant by the Landlord to offset Tenant's cost of installing leasehold improvements. Typically both parties will amortize/depreciate these costs over the primary term of the lease so the allowance and term are often linked in negotiations.

vi. Go dark clause: This clause that allows or prohibits a Tenant from simply closing up shop (going dark) during their term. Tenants will of course ask for the right to go dark and Landlords will typically want explicit language in the lease that will not give that right to a Tenant. Practically speaking, if a Tenant goes out, there is not much you can do about it. This is why Jim spent so much time vetting tenants and looking for tenants who could (and would) weather inevitable economic downturns.

vii. Deposit: This was another necessity that was exceptionally hard to define. Of course, Jim would like to be able to demand an escrow account in the full amount of the future lease commitments, but the retailer would like zero deposit. The truth was that Jim felt that if they were negotiating hard over the deposit, maybe the retailer didn't belong at his center. This was one of the typical negotiations that led him to contemplate a different sort of lease.

viii. Kickout clause: A lease clause that allows a tenant the unilateral option to close the store and terminate the lease at a specific date if the sales of that store are below a prenegotiated number, during a measuring period. This concept protects the tenant from carrying an underperforming store for a significant term and allows the tenant to reassess the initial occupancy decision with specific operating knowledge. There are often penalties imposed on tenant for exercising such rights, including the repayment of the unamortized tenant improvement allowances, unamortized leasing commission and possibly even a penalty of several months of gross rent.

ix. Co-tenancy clause: A provision of typical retail leases that allows a tenant to reduce its rent or terminate the lease if other named tenants or a percentage of the overall project are not leased. There is quite a bit of nuance in this concept that makes every lease unique, but the general ramification is that it is possible for a landlord to lose a performing tenant simply because a different underperforming tenant somewhere else in the center closes and cannot be replaced.

Typically, these terms were part of every preliminary lease meeting. There were many more details to be worked out, but these were the key elements that he and his potential tenants focused on. Again, what would happen to a tenant who just didn't work out, but didn't quit? They would probably understaff and undermarket the store. The store might become an eyesore and a potential cancer at the center: who would want to be located next to the underperformer? Would the adjacent retailer keep his or her efforts and investments as high if they felt this was not a great location for them? Would star retailers come to a center after they saw obvious signs of weakness on the property? In this sense, the sports metaphors about winners really did resonate. Knute Rockne may have gotten this one right: "Show me a gracious loser and I'll show you a failure."

Retailing is a tough industry and it is not possible to assume all of the tenants are going to succeed. Changes in retail trends can be sudden and severe, with whole categories of retailers wiped out almost overnight. Jim wanted weak tenants out whether it was from bad execution or bad luck in shifting consumer preferences. Jim thought of two lease approaches that might help.

The first was to keep the conversation as it has been but be more forceful about elements that would give Jim more chances to keep him actively managing the rent roll. This would mean more performance thresholds, especially gross sales. He could push for higher and escalating thresholds, below which the tenant would be in default—this could induce financial penalties or even allow him to kick them out of his center. Alternatively, Jim could push for short leases, maybe holding them to no more than five years. In this way, he would have a chance to change tenants at most every five years. It seemed like a lifetime in his business, but it was better than many of the 10-year and longer leases that were norms in the retail world.

Jim's second lease approach was a bit more radical. It involved short term leases with fewer and shorter options to extend the lease, with each of the options being contingent on minimum gross sale thresholds. They would not offer co-tenancy clauses. After all, big boxes were no longer a sure way to create foot traffic. Perhaps most radical was the mutual nature terminations: the landlord or the tenant exercise an option to terminate early if things weren't working out in terms of sales, not just the tenant as has traditionally been the case.

The trade-off would be economic but not in terms of rents, but rather in terms of overall flexibility. Fundamentally, the retail industry has changed significantly. The days of "set it and forget it" are over. The shelf lives of brands are shorter and the consumer is conditioned to embrace change—quickly. With shorter term leases, you are able to remove underperforming tenants sooner, refresh more often, distinguish between core tenants that should be long term, and ancillary tenants that can be changed more frequently. Jim's pitch as to what the tenants would get would be about an active management that would make sure the center as the major draw in the first place and stayed as vibrant and attractive as possible.

As Jim argued "As is often the case, change begets change. Changing out underperformers is as critical as rent is a function of sales and low sales performers make it hard to justify higher rents. As to the economics, some of the shorter term leases have percentage rent-only concepts. These are less about the length of the terms, and more about where the retailer is in their growth. The new, digitally native brands are not sure they will be around in two years, let alone ten, and have no historic benchmark for what rent they can pay since they have never done a brick and mortar sale in their lives. At the same time, some of the younger companies that do have stores, will pay a very real rent, just not on a ten-year term."

Jim sketched a rough table that might try allow comparisons to be made.

Lease term	Traditional lease	Creative lease
Length of term	10 years	2–5 years
Options to extend	2–5-year options	1–5-year option with a minimum threshold of $650 psf to exercise
Base rent	$75 psf per annum	Year 1—12.5% of sales Year 2—$75 psf per annum 3% annual increases thereafter
Percentage rent	6% over a natural breakpoint	6% over a natural breakpoint calculated based on 8%.
Tenant improvement allowance	$50 psf	None, but Landlord will white box the space in generic fashion.
Go dark right	Tenant shall have the right to go dark at any time during the lease term.	Tenant shall not have the right to go dark at any time during the lease term.
Kickout	Tenant shall have the one time right at the end of the fifth lease year to terminate the lease if sales for the fifth lease year are less than $500.00 psf. Should tenant elect to terminate, Tenant shall reimburse Landlord for the unamortized tenant improvement allowance, Commission and 6 months of gross rent.	No kickout right as the lease term is shorter and thus this concession is not necessary.

Lease term	Traditional lease	Creative lease
Co-tenancy	Should the occupancy of the center fall below 85%, or should the named anchor tenants (names to be added) fail to be open at the project, Tenant may pay, in lied of the minimum rent in the lease, the lesser of 5% of gross sales or the contract rent. Should the co-tenancy failure continue for 12 months, Tenant shall be granted the one time right to terminate the lease on 90 days' notice. Should tenant elect not to terminate the lease, Tenant shall revert to the minimum rent pursuant to the lease agreement.	No co-tenancy provision as the lease term is shorter and thus this concession is not necessary.

Jim knew that a standard approach to lease evaluation is a traditional present value calculation. But in his experience, the straight PV analysis almost always proves that the long term lease is the way to go. That is really a big part of the problem. A lot of real estate in the last 20 years had crafted its direction from a spreadsheet. The issue here really is survivability. "Take for example a current brand name and credit tenant at my center. They will pay me anything I want, 'Name my price' effectively. I could create a deal that would be so good on a PV basis there is nothing I could create that would compare. But in doing so, I close the door on my next 15 up-and-coming retailers because they do not want to be near this same retailer. So I go with the merchandising over the immediate rent. I don't see how to prove that my way will net out better over the long haul financially. I can tell you that – with where retail is going – I think I'm giving myself the best chance of success. I think the real analysis needs to reflect that you can destroy value by doing the easy thing as opposed to the right thing."

Your job is to provide guidance to Jim. By all means, help him support his argument that his new lease options are better than the traditional lease. But if you cannot make this case, help Jim avoid embarrassing himself with his senior management and with the broker community. Jim has a good enough reputation at his firm that he could survive a goofy idea or two, but his ability to attract good retailers is essential to his success. If he develops a reputation as somewhat of a "man without a plan," he can hurt the center in two significant ways. First, retailers may lose confidence in him as the person most responsible for creating the best environment for them to be successful. If retailers become concerned about his strategy and his ability to execute, they'll become concerned about the center and hesitate to commit fully to their stores within the center. Doubt can create negative feedback, and make concern self-fulling—"A death spiral," as Jim acknowledges. But the second risk is potentially more problematic. If Jim is seen simply as someone who is paying smaller broker's fees, then the tenant reps will not bring him the retailers in the first place. ("Game over," laughed Jim.) Brokers make their income from fees that are based on the present value of the lease. Basically, if it's high rent and long term, brokers make a lot of money. If the lease is short and performance-based, then the traditional fees will be small. All the logic about cooperation between a center's owner and a retailer will be beside the point if they never meet because brokers don't connect them. Jim will have to think about both of them.

Jim returned to his office and started assembling numbers on his white board. This was reflexive. He did this every time some material issue came up. On top of the board he wrote: "WHY? Why is this center here? Why is this tenant here? Why does the customer care?" According to Jim, "development (especially retail) without a plan is insanity these days. People are scrambling to fill a center without ever asking these simple questions. If you cannot answer them, then there is no thesis for the decisions you make." With these central questions on the white board, he then started adding key numbers.

Jim wanted to anticipate the tenant rep's responses to the new leases. So he began by comparing lease terms between his center and the larger superregional mall nearby. Jim would try to and argue that the rep would want to bring his client to Jim's center. The issue of inducing the rep to do this would come next. First Jim put a table up on the white board of lease term ranges by tenant type. These were representative numbers he could use to engage the tenant rep with some alternative approaches to leasing.

Lifestyle center

Tenant type	Size	Rent psf	Sales psf	% Rent paid psf
Anchor	20,000 sf and up	$30–$45	$400–$500	$0
Junior anchor	6,000–20,000	$45–$65	$500–$800	$0
Small shop	1000–5000	$65–$90	$800–$1200	$10
Small restaurant	1000–3000	$75–$90	$1200–$1800	$20
Large restaurant	4000 and up	$50–$60	$800–$1200	$30

Mall

Tenant type	Size	Rent psf	Sales psf	% Rent paid psf
Department store	100,000 and up	$0–$20	$100–$300	$0
Anchor	20,000–40,000	$50–$60	$200–$400	$0
Junior anchor	6000–20,0000	$100–$200	$400–$600	$0

Mall

Tenant type	Size	Rent psf	Sales psf	% Rent paid psf
Small shop	1000–5000	$200–$300	$800–$1200	$0
Small restaurant	1000–3000	$250–$350	$800–$1500	$20
Large restaurant	4000 and up	$100–$150	$700–$800	$0

III. Deliverables

Jim had to think about how quickly this had changed since he started 20 years earlier. The superregional mall nearby had its start in the 1950, but had been remade several times. In the 1990s, it was the unmatched retail center in the region, attracting a roster of premier anchor and inline tenants. While still a powerhouse, the mall had been forced to reckon challenges both big and small. Several large national retailers had left, while others were able to obtain rent reductions to stay. Inline tenants were a larger mix of quality. The mall appeared to be readying another expansion, under the theses that it would concentration that would save it from Amazon. After the expansion, it looked to be more than 2 million sf of retail space. They evidently felt that with the range of choices under one—large—roof, consumers would still make the trip.

Jim's center offered a third of that retail space but was more mixed-use, making it a more holistic urban center than the mall label Jim was quick to reject. To him, change in retail was inevitable, and this time around it would be active management and a smaller, curated center that would be the best defense. He though he needed a new lease to help him do exactly this. Jim's table of leasing terms started to tell a story but it would take a bit more thought to assemble a tight argument for why the tenant rep he would be meeting next week should bring his client to Jim's center. And, it would certainly take more analysis to pass any new changes in leasing standard by his credit committee. Jim knew there would be no single item or fact that would prove his case, but it was not enough to have a hunch.

Your job is read through the discussion above and consider the data you have. What Jim needs more than "an answer" is a clean, defensible narrative. His track record will allow him to get a crack at something novel if he can just argue well that changing a standard lease is warranted. After again considering his internal and external conversations, respond with your own advice for Jim. You do not have to agree with Jim. Indeed, if you disagree it is your job to point out the weaknesses of his assumptions and conclusions from them. If you agree with Jim, help him frame a more rigorous argument to take to his credit committee and to the tenant rep.

Questions/Issues

a. Is it right to think of retail as a single category within real estate? If retail is "getting hammered by Amazon" why should Jim be thinking this hard about his center? More to the point of this case, are Jim's center and the superregional mall competitors or not? Is Amazon a competitor? Are these three entities completely interchangeable because they are all "retail"? What do your observations complements and substitutes tell you about the larger forces at work in retail?

b. The case presents leasing as a tension between owner and tenant. Who loses from more softness in retail, the landlord or the tenant? What about who wins? Does this suggest who best to bear the risk of retail? Or is it more nuanced than that?

c. As a thought exercise consider the tenant rep who has played a significant role in the narrative above. Does he care about where his client ends up? What if the retailer—the tenant's rep client—ends up in a bad mall, a main street on a dying exurban submarket, or a tries turning itself into an online platform? What are the implications for the retailer, for the rep?

d. Now consider the alternative, what if the retailer ends up in a vibrant location and succeeds? Now what are the implications for the retailer and the tenant rep?

e. Relatively speaking how important is a retailer's base rent to the retailer?

f. How are tenant reps compensated?

g. What are the socio-economic factors that influence spending on retail? Are these uniformly felt within the country? Within the state or metropolitan area? Across retailers?

h. Returning to the lease details, what is "the" standard retail lease? Is there really a standard? Or are there a number of standard versions? Why do the standard lease(s) exist? Markets have a way of culling bad ideas over time; if Jim thinks current leasing is wrong, why are there standard leases?

i. Does the evolution of retail require new standard leases? Who bears the risk of these new structures? Will they sign? Do they have the leverage to say no? Does Jim have the leverage to impose his leases?

j. How will traditional retail lenders view Jim's new lease? Bankers are notoriously conservative, but how much leverage to they have if they want to stink with the traditional approaches to leasing? Should Jim worry about lenders as his puts together his proposal?

k. Jim made several strong claims about a commonly used tool for lease analysis. Consider using numerical examples of different lease types to examine how the cash flows for tenants and Jim's center under different leases. That is, use the table above to calculate the present value of different leases under different assumptions about lease terms. Under good and bad outcomes, who wins from Jim's lease? Who loses? Would they be better off under more traditional leases? You might start with the tenant rep again. In his case, he represents an inline tenant looking at a 10-year lease at the superregional mall. The table above provides some important difference across Jim's lifestyle center and the mall down the street from him. Explore these numbers to test Jim's claim that PV math doesn't help him.

l. Keep in mind that these are typical ranges given the current economics in his submarket. But, what if there's a downturn? If sales fall do you think retailers want to stay open? If the sales double, do you think they want to stay in the same store format? How do the different lease structures help or hurt her under these scenarios?

m. Finally, Jim is fairly excited about his new lease options. You can imagine arguing with him might be tough. Why is he asking for help?

Case 14

Finding a Safe Way to Park: Investing in NNN Lease Properties

"Really? Enid, Oklahoma and a 4 cap? I've got some Lehman bonds for you to look at."
"There's nothing quite like a covered land play to help you sleep well at night."

I. Blurring Asset Classes

Real estate has appropriated a number of English words and reassigned them other uses. "Brain damage" is the cost of complexity; "pencil" is used in real estate as a verb, as in "the deal didn't pencil at that price, so we walked away." Internally, real estate divides itself into four main primary categories, often referred to as "food groups." These include office, industrial, multifamily, and retail. This arrangement actually sits within a more formal division of investment into stocks, bonds, commodities, and real estate. These taxonomies of investment and real estate obscure some shared elements that blur the lines between categories. Bonds are a kind of fixed income securities, those that generate a somewhat predictable income at regular intervals. In real estate, mortgages behave this way: they are debt contracts that typically require regular and predictable payments. Another form of real estate equity is also marketed as "bond-like."

These triple-net leases—often referred to as "net lease properties"—are typically single-tenant buildings. They are common in quick-service restaurants (QSR), but many different types of retail tenants use this lease structure. Firms like Starbucks, Jack in the Box, CVS, Walgreens, and Chase Bank want to establish and hold good locations for long terms, but they don't want their capital tied up in the land or their structures. As a result, these firms turn to net lease properties in which net lease investors and developers build the structures or ground lease the land, while the tenants are wholly responsible for operation and management. In the case of a ground lease, the tenant is even responsible for the construction of the building. The owners then need only accept the rent payments. The regular payments, the net nature of the lease, and relative security of a credit tenant makes net lease investors begin to look like bond investors despite the important difference that one is equity while the other is debt.

Underwriting Commercial Real Estate in a Dynamic Market. https://doi.org/10.1016/B978-0-12-815989-7.00014-8
143

While both debt and equity can experience volatility, real estate debt is considered safer than equity because it is typically collateralized and receives priority payment relative to equity. It is usually equity that first bears the brunt of changes in rents, vacancy, utility costs, insurance rates, etc. And it is usually equity who is responsible for managing the property itself. In the net lease world, all these risks and responsibilities fall to the tenant. The owner simply collects rent checks and when the lease is over, the owner still owns the land and its improvements. It is in this way that equity investment in real estate is bond-like. And, like a bond, the value of a net-lease property is a function of the regular rent payments, the value of the improvements when the owner gains control at the end of the lease, and the risk associated with both.

The net lease market is a niche in which developers are constantly looking for good locations that can attract high-credit tenants who will sign leases that will generate long-term and predictable cash flows. The cash flow from these leases is presumed (1) safe because of the tenant quality; (2) predictable because all the variation has been "netted" out; and generally (3) long-term, because these tenants choose locations with the purpose of making a long term commitment to establishing a brand there. Indeed, once a Starbucks is located, an entire network of people will begin to adjust their routines to arrive there in the morning or after lunch. This habit formation is part of what allows Starbucks to remain so profitable.

Net lease tenants do move, usually in one of two ways. The first is when they find a new format that is significantly more profitable. Currently, Starbucks is actively trying to move their stores to parcels that allow drive-thrus, because they are significantly more productive than equivalent locations without them. The second way tenants leave is when they find a location is no longer profitable. In this case, tenants may decline their option to extend their lease or they may default on the lease. This is the central reason that so much emphasis is placed on the quality of the tenant. The reason Starbucks and tenants like them are so valued is that they are unlikely to fail to make lease payments, even if a store is no longer operating. But certainly defaults can occur with either credit or noncredit tenants.

Ultimately, the risk a landlord faces depends on demand for the parcel. Having a credit tenant like Starbucks greatly reduces risk relative to noncredit tenants, but even Starbucks may choose to exit rather than extend their lease, as they are now doing when they can find nearby drive-thru stores. The big question for a net lease property owner is if he/she can replace the lost income, and at what cost. If the structure is sufficiently obsolete, it may require significant additional capital to renovate or even tear down and rebuild to current standards. In the case of Starbucks's new drive-thrus, many are on very small parcels that have no inside seating. If Starbucks left, who would want such a facility? If the answer is "no one," what alternative use could be put on such a small parcel? Maybe another drive-thru coffee retailer, but what are the chances that it'll pay more in rent than Starbucks? The economics of net leases, then, involves both the lease and the location.

A developer who has purchased a site and built a structure that perfectly suits a high-credit net lease tenant has created a "bond-like" asset that markets crave. While not as safe as a US Treasury bond, leases signed by firms like Starbucks are pretty close. The income from the net rent is priced accordingly and has among the lowest cap rates in all of real estate. The developer who can find good sites, execute on construction, and successfully find a net-lease tenant is in a great position to sell a very safe asset in a world that is always looking for them. The question then becomes: is it easy to find sites that are reasonably priced and attractive to A-list tenants? Is it really easy to create a safe asset through an instrument like a net lease? Like all markets, success breeds competitors and prices soon reflect fundamentals. But market efficiency is a function of information, and information in real estate is never complete. Cities change, neighborhoods evolve, demographics shift, and preferences change. Over time, what was a modern and durable facility can become obsolete. Finding real estate that isn't priced at its highest and best use is tough when it's hard to determine exactly what that is.

II. RSNet and Its Perspective on Risk

Ryan is director at RSNet, a boutique real estate development firm that develops and redevelops high-end food retail. RSNet covers a wide variety of retail, but is particularly strong at QSR single-tenant development and redevelopment. While everyone at RSNet focuses on retail, Ryan has led a recent effort to raise capital around net-lease property development. It has gone well. RSNet has a good track record, but perhaps more importantly, US Treasuries and high-quality bond rates are earning so little that conservative investors are feeling pinched and looking for more yield, but only if the risk is quite low. RSNet's pitch to investors is fundamentally about safety and the marginal gain in yield over other safe assets. RSNet also emphasizes that they focus on locations that will further reduce risk. As part of the effort to market RSNet and its net-lease program, Ryan has agreed to be on numerous real estate conference panels. As usual, his fellow panelists are colleagues and competitors. The net-lease segment is a small world in which Ryan is well-known as friendly and competent, but also not universally agreed with. Of course, this might describe most every panelist at a real estate conference.

The difference at his last panel turned on location and risk. At issue was the question of long term leases and whether they minimize location risk. The thought process for one of the other panelists was simple: "If Starbucks has signed a 15- or 20-year lease, they're going to pay the rent for every single one of those years. 20 years from now, who cares what the residual land value is? The lease is the value." Ryan was willing to push back: "In 20 years, my Starbucks in Culver City will be worth a mint. With population growth over that horizon, I'll probably be able to sell it to an apartment developer who will put the Starbucks on the ground floor. I'll get the new Starbucks lease and all the land value from the apartments. I'll sell that pad for multiples of what I paid for it. I fully agree with you that the lease is essential, but it is not the only thing that matters. Moreover, I bet you can't get a 20-year lease everywhere. More often than not you get a 10-year lease with the tenant's option to stay. You'll only get 20 years if the market is working in your favor. And that's not a sure thing, especially outside the gateway cities." With that exchange, the crowd and the moderator pushed for more. The debate took most of the session with Ryan's closing comment to his colleague: "So you'll buy pads and put in the capital to build a Starbucks anywhere because you think there's a buyer somewhere who wants it at a 4 percent cap rate. Really? Enid, Oklahoma and a 4 cap? Okay then, let's talk after this session; I've got some Lehman bonds I'd like you to look at."

This argument was at the heart of RSNet's approach to finding sites and investing. It was also common to have partners and investors who felt that "the lease is the value" push RSNet to do more deals. One potential investor who had watched Ryan talk on the panel approached him afterward and posed an interesting challenge to him. "I buy your basic thesis that net-leasing is an attractive investment. Right now I'm looking to find a partner to roll out a significant program of my own. Your opinions on the panel suggest that you and RSNet might be a good partner, but I'd like you to demonstrate first that the difference between an urban site like Culver City and a small city like Enid really could have different risk and return characteristics. I am skeptical that they do. Markets are too efficient to allow a big difference to persist, and certainly not big enough for me to get a systematically better return across all the capital I'm planning on putting into net-lease properties. Second, I'd like you rank a set of potential sites I've been looking at. Some are raw land, others are redevelopment options, and several include ground leases. But, as I understand it, your claim isn't about the specific structure I use, it's about the submarket and long-term fundamentals." He paused and then asked "Would you do this? I like what I heard on the panel, and I'd like to see how the numbers work and if there really is a difference in risk and return that would make me want to have you as my partner."

Ryan was eager to raise capital. The potential investor suggested that he was ready to put together his "own program." There would be issues to negotiate about fees and about the co-invest. RSNet would have to think about if and how much capital of its own it would invest and keep with the JV. Maybe it would be zero and RSNet would simply book the fees and move on. This would require no capital and potentially significant fees. But those issues would have to wait. The first step was testing the theory that the lease is something, but not everything.

III. NNN Investment

Ryan took the potential investor's card and went back to the office. His challenge now was to provide some solid evidence of his hypothesis, so he had to refine it. Ryan knew he had been reacting to the other panelist who was selling the triple-net model. Ryan agreed with the basic premise: net-leasing could be a great investment for many types of investors. But the sweeping generalization that "the lease is the value" just struck him as overly simply. As he did for every investment, he knew he would have think through the possible cash flows for a net-lease investment under a number of different locations and scenarios, being thoughtful about the diversity of net leases typical in the current market.

Net leases are like many other commercial leases in terms of structure. They fundamentally involve an owner selling rights to a tenant for a fixed term in exchange for some responsibilities. What makes net leases unique is the degree of responsibilities: essentially all the roles a landlord typically plays are handled by the tenant. In most cases, the landlord will retain responsibility for environmental issues related to the land itself and may be required to rebuild the structure in the event of significant damage. In the case of a ground lease, even the structure is actually owned by the ground lessee. So there is some risk to the owner, but all the usual operating risks—utility costs, operating, landscaping, insurance, taxes, etc. are typically turned over to the tenant. Net leases are usually longer term and have options for extension at the tenant's choice. It is not uncommon to have a 10-year lease with four 5-year extensions—allowing a possible tenure of 30 years. The details of rent bumps vary widely from deal to deal. At some point, either the tenant opts not to exercise an option to extend or all the extensions have been taken. At this point, the owner has a parcel with a structure that is likely quite dated. Some hold up better than others, but it is not uncommon to have very little value left in the structure itself. As for the value of the underlying land, that is an issue of local fundamentals at the time the lease is up. A colleague of Ryan summed the net lease up thusly: "When I buy NNN deals for me or my family we are fixated on replacement rents and land basis, because that's the only way to recycle the real estate down the road. There's nothing quite like a covered land play to help you sleep well at night."

Recalling his conversation at the conference with the potential investor, Ryan needed to think through how best to test and (if he was right) demonstrate his claim that it's not just the lease itself that generates the value. Once back in the office, he pulled a bunch of comps from Southern California and further afield. He would scan them and try to find a way to test his thesis. How would he think about replacement risk?

IV.   Deliverables

Ryan asked for data from two different analysts at RSNet. In the first, he asked for "noncore" net lease comparables; in the second, he asked for "core" net lease comparables. Interestingly, the reports reflected some differences of opinions as to what "core" and "noncore" real estate is. But both reports also show a great deal of variation in pricing, in lease term remaining, in options, and in tenants. They varied in their retail segments and in their guarantees, but mostly they varied in location. And both analysts said, "This is the best I can do without spending a lot more time calling brokers and doing trip counts." Trip counts and a dozen other key variables would be needed to underwrite each property rigorously, but that was not the exercise Ryan had in mind. Did the data he was already holding offer enough to start testing his hypothesis?

Your first step is to read through the lease terms and understand the mechanics of the leases. Then you should build the associated cash flows for each, being mindful about what sources of uncertainty exist in the cash flows. It may be necessary to build multiple scenarios to assess what different eventualities an owner could experience—in different submarkets at different points in the business cycle and with different types of tenants. To be clear, there is a lot of information that you would need to underwrite any one of these properties in detail, but Ryan's charge is to demonstrate a larger thesis. At this point, use the data here to explore his question and demonstrate something about it. He will be able to revisit specific properties later if you can show some reason to keep looking. For now, there must be something he can learn using this representative sample of net lease deals. Here are some questions/issues to consider as you prepare your memo to Ryan.

Questions/Issues

a. What is the present value of $1000 dollars at the end of 30 years if you use a 10% discount rate? What is the present value of $1M dollars at the end of 10 years if you use a 5% discount rate? What determines if a parcel is worth $1000 or $1M? What determines if you get control of your parcel at the end of 10 years or 30 years? What determines if you choose a 5% discount rate or a 10% rate?

b. What determines if a tenant decides to take an extension, to renew, or to stop rent payment? If they do fail to pay rent, what are the owner's options?

c. Assume that all of the leases were signed at market. What factors can change both parties' decision to sign the lease as time passes? Are the leases static? Is the market static? Clearly, the landlord and tenant agreed at the outset, but would they continue to agree to the same terms? What would change for each over the holding period?

d. Several of the net lease properties are on ground leases. Do you understand how a ground lease differences from the other net leases? Can you say anything about the pricing between the two types of lease structures?

e. Ryan went out of his way to impugn his fellow panelist by telling him he "had Lehman bonds" he would be willing to sell him. What did that mean? What point was Ryan making by tying the failure of an enormous and long-lived investment bank to rather ordinary and relatively small scale real estate investments?

f. Did Ryan find a "4 cap" deal in Enid? Something similar? Are there deals in tertiary markets that look like core deals and vice versa? Can you make sense of the pricing across the two samples?

g. Looking across both sets of net lease comparables, does the pricing look fair? What factors do you see as risks being priced into the cap rates? Are there any systematic patterns in the data? Are there exceptions?

h. Is there any way to try and isolate categories of risk? Are some tenants priced differently? Regions? Is there an obvious difference between the "core" and "noncore" properties?

i. While specific addresses aren't given, can you find other historical data around the comparables by looking on line? Can you assemble investment narratives that make sense using these?

j. What was the potential investor arguing when he said: "Markets are too efficient to allow a big difference to persist, and certainly not big enough for me to get a systematically better return across all the capital I'm planning on putting into net-lease properties"? What difference was he referring to? Do you think real estate is generally priced efficiently? Or can Ryan and RSNet outperform the competitors? Is it their thesis that makes this possible? Do you agree with it?

Ryan made a claim that the value of a net lease property was more than just the lease. The variation in the comparables seems to make this clear, but the question he wants to know is more subtle than that. Are investors putting too much weight on the tenant and lease terms relative to the changing demand for the land underneath the properties? If you need to make some assumptions to help answer Ryan's questions, do so, but annotate and defend them. Write a memo to Ryan—whether or not your research supports his claim. The goal is not proof—there are many details that are missing from the data, but rather a rigorous qualitative demonstration exercise that he might be able to use to attract the potential investor from the conference.

NNN Lease Property Comparables

"Noncore" Properties

Quick Casual Restaurant #1, National Chain—Raleigh, NC
- $2,059,200 (8.25% cap rate)
- 5 years remaining on NNN lease
- 10% increases every 5 years
- One, 5-year option
- 12-unit franchisee guarantee

Automotive Retailer/Repair, National Chain—Gardner, KS
- $1,960,000 (5.76% cap rate)
- 10 years remaining on NNN lease
- 10% increases in each option
- Four, 5-year options
- Corporate guarantee

QSR Burger #1—Lincoln, NE
- $1,985,000 (6.35% cap rate)
- 6 years remaining on NNN lease

- 5% increases every 5 years
- Five, 5-year options
- Large franchisee guarantee

Daycare, Regional Chain—Bakersfield, CA
- $2,020,000 (7.85% cap rate)
- 5 years remaining on NNN lease
- 10% increases every 5 years
- Two, 5-year options
- Corporate guarantee

Coffee Retailer #1, National Chain—Montebello, CA (Ground Lease)
- $3,000,000 (3.83% cap rate)
- 20 years remaining on NNN ground lease
- Kick-out clause in year 10
- 10% increases every 5 years
- Three, 5-year options
- Corporate guarantee

QSR Burger #1, National Chain—Northwood, OH
- $1,500,000 (8.25% cap rate)
- 5 years remaining on NNN lease
- 1% annual increases
- Two, 5-year options
- Corporate guarantee

QSR Burger #1, National Chain—Plainwell, MI
- $1,580,000 (6.96% cap rate)
- 6 years remaining on NNN lease
- $10,000 rent increase every 5 years
- Three, 5-year options
- Corporate guarantee

QSR #1, National Chain—Portland, OR (Owner User Deal)
- $1,835,000 (6.81% cap rate)
- Represented tenant in their right of first refusal
- Franchisee guarantee

Quick Casual Restaurant #2—Apopka, FL
- $2,000,000 (6.65% cap rate)
- 6 years remaining on NNN lease
- Landlord collects base rent and percentage rent
- Three, 5-year options
- Corporate guarantee

Quick Casual Restaurant #2—Indianapolis
- Value-add deal
- $1,003,000 (4.50% cap rate)

- 4 years remaining on NNN lease
- Landlord collects base rent and percentage rent
- No remaining options
- Corporate guarantee

QSR Burger #2—Knoxville, TN (Under Contract)
- $2,060,000 (5.83% cap rate)
- 20 years remaining on NNN lease
- 5% increases every 5 years
- Four, 5-year options
- Franchisee guarantee

QSR Burger #1—Mansfield, OH (Under Contract)
- $1,100,000 (5.00% cap rate)
- 13.5 years remaining on NNN lease
- 7.5% increases every 5 years
- Two, 5-year options
- Corporate guarantee

NNN Lease Property Comparables

"Core" Properties

QSR Burger #3, National Chain—Costa Mesa, CA
- $4,500,000
- Lease expires in April 2019
- No remaining options to extend
- Value-add deal

Quick Casual Restaurant #3, Small Regional Chain—Buena Park, CA
- $4,500,000 (5.71% cap rate)
- 5 remaining years on lease
- No further options to extend

Quick Casual Restaurant #4—Apple Valley, CA
- $3,580,000 (4.90% cap rate)
- Lease expires 1/31/2024, three 5-year options
- Corporate guarantee
- 10% rent increases every 5 years

Convenience Store, National Chain—Bloomington, CA
- $3,722,000 (4.45% cap rate)
- New 15-year lease
- Four 5-year options
- 10% increases every 5 years
- Corporate guarantee

Coffee Retailer, National Chain—Santa Clarita, CA

- $3,060,000 (4.25% cap rate)
- 15-year lease
- 10% increases every 5 years
- Corporate guarantee

Convenience Store #2, National Chain—Highland, CA

- $2,950,000 (no cap rate given)
- No other info given

QSR Chicken #1, National Chain—Eastvale, CA

- $3,250,000 (4.00% cap rate)
- New 20-year lease
- Four 5-year options
- 10% increases every 5 years
- Corporate guarantee

Quick Casual Restaurant #5, Regional Chain—Ontario, CA

- $5,625,000 (4.00% cap rate)
- Lease expires 6/30/2033
- Three 5-year options and one 4-year options
- 10% increases every 5 years
- Corporate guarantee

QSR Burger #3, National Chain—Hemet, CA

- $2,950,000 (5.10% cap rate)
- 10-year lease
- No other info given

QSR Burger #4, National Chain—Fontana, CA

- $3,658,000 (3.23% cap rate)
- No other info given

QSR Chicken #2, National Chain—Pico Rivera, CA

- $3,225,000 (4.00% cap rate)
- 20-year lease
- Four 5-year options
- 10% increases every 5 years
- Personal guarantee

QSR TexMex #1, National Chain—Santa Monica, CA

- $5,000,000 (3.75% cap rate)
- 20-year ground lease
- Four 5-year options

- CPI % increases
- Corporate guarantee

Coffee Retailer #2, National Chain—Montebello, CA
- New 20-year ground lease
- Kick-out clause in year 10
- 10% increases
- Three 5-year options
- Corporate guarantee

Case 15

Let's Do This Again

If we take the offer, we can get right back in there and get our capital on the steep part of the return curve.

I. The Memo

Date:	January 11th, 2015
To:	"Englewoods" Development Team
From:	Thom C, Principal – La Poudre Partners
Subject:	Pre-Sale Offer Strategy Meeting
Deadlines:	Next Week – Finalize Strategy for JV Partner

I'm calling a meeting tomorrow to strategize our next steps at "Englewoods." Please review the notes from our last meeting below and familiarize yourself with the outstanding issues. The goal of our meeting is to identify and discuss outstanding issues and prepare you to generate strategy recommendations for next week.

To recap/update:

➤ After a difficult but successful rezoning we closed escrow in December 2013, pulled our building permits in January 2014 and started construction on the 245-unit Englewoods apartment project in February 2014. Construction has been delayed a bit due to weather and we've encountered some cost increases/change orders but overall we're in pretty good shape. Below is an updated Sources/Uses. Our first buildings are nearly complete and we start marketing units **next week** and hope to move our first renters in by mid-February of 2015.

➤ We continue to underwrite the project internally at a conservative market rent of $1.45psf without any premiums. But after receiving our most recent market analysis from the Property Manager we believe we can easily hit rents of $1.55psf. It might be possible to generate a little more revenue as well through other income: parking, storage, pets, etc. It's our expectation to lease up 25 units per month starting in February 2015 and hit stabilization January 2016.

Underwriting Commercial Real Estate in a Dynamic Market. https://doi.org/10.1016/B978-0-12-815989-7.00015-X

> ➤ The key issue for the meeting tomorrow: La Poudre Partners has received an unsolicited pre-sale offer to purchase the property once we hit 50% leasing for the apartments. The initial pre-sale offer is at a 5.75% cap rate, 50 basis points over current market cap rates of 5.25%. Construction completion guarantees will be required.

We need to decide the following: 1) is accepting the pre-sale proposal in the best interest of La Poudre Partners and 2) is this in the best interest of our JV Partner and 3) are the answers to 1 and 2 the same and, if not, how do we resolve this conflict?

And on a lighter note, if we do agree to the pre-sale agreement, we will turn over branding to the new owner. This will save us another argument about naming the apartments. I remain sure that the working name "Englewoods" is never going to appear on any monumentation there. We can do better than that.

Thanks, Thom

Attachments: Exhibit A – Current Budget/Sources & Uses, B – Term Sheet Abstract

II.   La Poudre Partners

La Poudre Partners (LPP) was established over 40 years ago by two entrepreneurs who began with the basic premise that "development isn't rocket science." Certainly, development was simpler 40 years ago than today, but the basics still held: the populations had grown in LPP's markets and the existing stock of real estate would continue to depreciate. That meant development would be necessary. There was no need to overthink starting a new firm. LPP focused on the needs of the market and improving execution—making it internally efficient and externally accountable. Focusing on these two priorities over the past 40 years left a legacy of goodwill for LPP in the communities where they build, among the partners with whom they develop, and among the investors who back them. The result is that LPP's reputation gives them an enormous advantage in doing business. People who find potential sites contact LPP because they know they'll be treated fairly in negotiations and, because once struck, the deal is likely to see completion. Cities can see a long list of LPP projects that improved their neighborhoods, while being completed as promised. And investors have enjoyed better-than-average returns with very few deals in which any principal is lost. Indeed LPP has given up its own return of profits to make sure that investors were made whole. Given their track record, LPP is viewed by key stakeholders as a firm that hits a lot of "stand up doubles"—meaning they got extra-normal returns without taking extra-normal risk.

LPP's founders brought mix of pragmatism and ambition to their firm. They saw growth as a regional phenomenon in the western United States and chose the name for La Poudre Partners from La Poudre Pass, which is the source of the Colorado River. As one of the partners points out, "Like development, it's not rocket science how the runoff gets to households so far away, but it doesn't happen without thinking hard about gravity and about where gravity won't get it there alone." The snowmelt from that pass supports growth in the all the markets in which they now develop: Colorado, Arizona, Utah, Nevada, and California.

III.   Core and Periphery

The basic business plan for LPP early on simply was to meet the needs of a growing market. This meant that they tried to be able to develop almost anything feasible when the opportunity came up. But LPP discovered that larger projects required more capital and more staff than they were willing to risk. So they focused on smaller projects, and in particular single tenant retail build-to-suits (BTS). Population growth meant a need for housing and those new residents needed groceries, pharmacies, and all the other basics that go with modern life. Over the course of several cycles, LPP refined its retail business, building deep relationships with numerous national chains that wanted to follow the same population growth that LPP foresaw. LPP became the merchant developer for many name brand companies, developing over 300 stores for one of the nation's largest pharmacy chains alone.

While stamping out repeat BTS work for corporate retail clients, LPP also figured out how to be successful at renovating and repurposing obsolete retail real estate. During this process, they often found it optimal to buy and assemble neighboring parcels to develop larger retail centers and mixed use projects. It was here that the current look of the firm came into view. Ground-up development on green field sites in the periphery became overly competitive over time with profit margins narrowing. And corporate clients there have started opting more often to self-develop their own real estate, slowing demand for our BTS services. Fortunately, LPP was one of the first firms to embrace infill development, updating and improving retail in larger urban areas where residents were increasingly looking to move back to the core. This sort of development and redevelopment required mastering a complex set of issues—neighbors and their fears about gentrification, cities and their concerns about tax revenue and infrastructure needs, lender concerns about comps, and their own understanding of the changing demographics of urbanization. These were not easy deals, but LPP brought its track record of execution and found ways to bring various parties to agreement. It often took many attempts to solve these puzzles, but LPP was frequently successful where others would not have even earned a seat at the table.

During and following the Great Recession, there remained enough infill projects to fill LPP's pipeline, but retail was beginning to slow, and LPP looked ahead at the impact of Amazon on its own business. LPP's core activities in recent years had been grocery-anchored infill centers. Once thought to be "Amazon-proof," even grocers were rethinking their space needs so LPP was looking for ways to diversify its business.

LPP has a long tradition of adjusting to market demand and recently the demand has been for apartments. Given the "it's not rocket science" mentality at LPP, the firm began a multifamily division, focused on ground-up, suburban apartment development. While there will be a learning curve to do ground-up apartment construction, nothing scared them about that part of the development—they knew about entitlements, permitting, and construction. What did scare them were the capital requirements. Building a 245-unit apartment building with modern common areas takes a lot more capital than LPP was used to funding.

IV. Funding the Basics and Moving Beyond Them

Of course all of LPP's projects require a lot of capital, but they have been good at cultivating a deep bench of friends and family investors that consistently fund whatever projects that make it through LPP's strict risk/reward filter and underwriting standards. However, success breeds challenge and because LPP has steadfastly paid its bills and repaid its investors' capital along with a good return, there is an excess demand by its investors to develop more and allow them to invest more. Second, even though it is relatively easy to raise equity, debt is still cheaper, leading partners to wonder should LPP borrow more? The same track record that generates so much equity investment interest would be just as attractive to lenders. Third, why not turn to institutional capital? LPP's traditional investors have been an extended set of "family and friends." But LPP's business model and consistent performance might make it an obvious candidate for a partnership with a private equity firm or family office to scale up to a much larger extent.

All of these issues arise out of LPP's success. Earning a safe 15% return over treasuries year after year has made it easy for LPP to raise capital. Indeed, the firm has such demand for investment that it has been able to create a capital structure that allows it to have zero basis after acquisition, while still retaining a healthy share of the profits going forward. Essentially, LPP pays for all the pursuit costs—search, site control, entitlement, preliminary design and engineering costs, and preliminary leasing costs. This means that if a deal does not close, LPP absorbs the full pursuit costs. The project is marketed to investors during this pursuit phase, giving LPP and its investors a chance to understand the project and its potential risks and returns. Typically, LPP will enter an option with an owner or several parcel owners with an agreement to close at an agreed upon price upon receiving development entitlements. At closing of the acquisition, it is investor cash that pays for the land and pays back all of LPP's pursuit costs. At that point, LPP has a zero basis, but can receive on the order of 20%–50% of the future cash flows after repayment of debt and investor equity with no preferred returns paid to investors plus LPP receives handsome development fees. This is a peculiar arrangement. It is typical for the sponsors (in this case LPP) to be paid last, or at least to have their promoted interest occur only after investors have received their returns first. LPP is able to do this because investors have made excellent returns over time allowing them to dictate their capital structure to their hungry and loyal investors.

The strength of this capital structure is abundantly clear to LPP and its investors. LPP is fully responsible for finding good deals and doing the necessary work to ready the site for development; investors avoid much of the worst problems of development, those associated with controlling and assembling the parcels and navigating the approval process. A weakness of this structure is the scale: their "family and friends" are not in a position to write very large equity checks. LPP could lever up to a greater extent to stretch its equity capital or it could turn to institutional capital for more equity, but personal observations about the risks of fast-growing companies have left the principals at LPP clearly committed to avoiding their two biggest concerns in real estate: over leverage and lack of control. Regarding debt, it's always tempting to lever up and drive for higher returns to equity. But even if the long-term strategy is right and real estate values will rise in the future, if a firm can't make debt service, it will lose the property and someone else will see the benefits of the recovery. LPP has never lost a property through loan default.

But regarding institutional capital, LPP has traditionally not been willing to cede control of its activities. It needs to be quick to enter a market when the opportunity arises and quick to exit when it feels fundamentals are shifting. In both of these circumstances, lack of control is risk. With its current capital structure, LPP is solely responsible for how it spends it time and pursuit costs. No investor has a vested interest in even monitoring projects at that stage. No institutional capital partner would allow for this structure as the "money partner." They would want full control of the project. A business plan would need to be vetted well in advance and an institutional partner would require sign off at every step—from site control to design on the way in, leasing and operations during a hold, and maybe even control of when to sell.

This explains why LPP is not bigger than it is and why it took 40 years to have the footprint it does. And this is why LPP is now wondering if it made a mistake when it finally accepted institutional capital when it wanted to try developing the large apartment complex in Englewood, Colorado. Understanding the importance of branding, the development team almost immediately latched onto "The Englewoods" as an internal joke. To date, nothing better has replaced it.

V. Capitalizing the First Multifamily Deal

LPP knows every bit of real estate in the great Denver area and knows how diverse its neighborhoods have been—and how they are changing. Much of the capital invested in apartments in Denver recently is in downtown and, specially, "LoDo"—Lower Downtown. Denver, like many metropolitan areas, is experiencing a renewed interest in its core. While developing downtown would have capitalized on Denver's urban renaissance and Millenial migration wave, LPP strategically focused its site selection efforts in supply constrained suburbs where land was cheaper and competing projects would be fewer than the urban land rush downtown. Of several suburban cities close to Denver, LPP found an appropriate site in Englewood. It was a big site, but a good deal and LPP anticipated that, because it knew the city, it would be relatively straightforward to obtain the entitlements. LPP developed a business plan for the site and built a pitch book to raise capital. (An abstracted version of the pitch book is below in the exhibits.)

The budget was well beyond the reach of "family and friends," so LPP finally returned a call from a Boston-based institutional real estate advisor called Newarks Investment Advisory. It was not a hard negotiation. LPP needed capital and wanted to get started. NIA offered what seemed like fair terms and a willingness to move quickly. LPP feared missing the cycle more than it feared missing small points in the joint venture agreement. The JV agreement LPP signed followed traditional institutional capital terms, which were significantly different than LPP's "friends and family" terms. NIA asked for more paperwork than LPP was used to, but NIA also did everything it was asked to, and the new equity partners closed on the land on schedule and began developing their first ground-up construction of an apartment complex. (An abstracted term sheet for the JV agreement are also in the exhibits below.)

VI.   Now and Next Steps

As noted in the opening memo, LPP and NIA have received an offer to buy the Englewoods once occupancy hits 50%. The offer is a presale, meaning that the actual sale price will be determined ahead of time. In particular, the potential buyer is willing to use the Year 3 stabilized NOI from the pitch book to establish the price. The memo from Thom in Section A suggests there are numerous issues to sort through. Your job is to underwrite the Englewoods under the current JV agreement with NAI and the presale proposal. You must figure out if the presale deal is good for you and for NIA. If it is not, then you should at least propose a counter offer. If the presale is beneficial to you and NIA, what would preclude agreeing to the presale? If there is a reason to believe that there are differences between the benefits to LPP and NIA, is there a way to overcome them?

The discussion between the principals at LPP last week ended with one partner urging the firm to capture the value they had created at the Englewoods and use the sale proceeds to get right back to work with a second apartment development. "If we take the offer, we can get right back in there and get our capital back on the steep part of the return curve. All we do by waiting is have our promote watered down." It would take some thinking to understand his statement, and it would also require some underwriting to check if he was right at all. Thinking broadly about LPP's future, what should the firm do with regard to the presale agreement? Please prepare an internal memo to the team ahead of next week's meeting.

Questions to Explore

a. La Poudre Partners seems to have a highly simplified view of real estate. Is real estate simple? If real estate really is this simple, how is it that LPP has been able to continuously outperform competitors? What factors have contributed to LPP's success? Are these factors easily replicated?

b. LPP is apparently already a significant success—note that they have completed nearly 500 retail projects! Why should LPP consider expanding further? It appears to have thrived under its current strategy and capital structure. Why gamble by getting bigger?

c. Newark Investors Advisory represents mostly pension funds and sovereign wealth funds, and has been operating a multifamily development program for several years. It is partnering with many other sponsors like LPP to place in excess of $500M of equity building infill apartments in the United States. Was it necessary for LPP to turn to an institutional capital provider rather than a private equity firm, a family office, or other syndicator? Understanding that there is wide variation among these capital providers, how would you define each? In light of LPP's norms and the size of the Englewoods project, what other options might LPP have considered? Or was NIA the best choice? Why?

d. Was La Poudre Partners right to move into multifamily construction? In particular, was it right to start this effort with such a large project? In retrospect, should LPP have found a smaller site and built a smaller complex, one that its "family and friends" investors could have funded?

e. The JV agreement with NIA (below) lays out the basic set of rights and responsibilities. Do you understand why they were structured this way?

f. What is a "promote"? Both "family and friends" and institution capital offer LPP "promoted" positions. What does this mean and how do the promote structures differ between the typical family and friends agreements and that of NIA? What do these say about the incentives for LPP with family and friends capital versus NIA?

g. How do you value the Englewoods Apartments? Given the pitch book pro forma numbers that will be used to set the presale price, are NIA and LPP receiving a fair price? If not, would you recommend rejecting the presale proposal and holding the property through the 3-year lockout?

h. We know that one of the partners at LPP thinks the Englewoods has been a success. Is it? Would NIA agree? Does the return to up until today matter? Or is it the return at the end of the lock out that matters? While Thom is focused on LPP's decisions, who is thinking about NIA and what would NIA want to do next?

i. What other exit options does LPP have? What would LPP like to do next? Can it? Should it?

In preparation for the meeting with Thom, prepare a brief memo that includes your suggested route forward for Thom and LPP. It should include both a well-argued, high-level plan for LPP at Englewoods and beyond and a concise set of suggestions for the particulars of a meeting with NIA. Understand that NIA is an institutional firm that will probably require more numbers than Thom might need, so please be thorough.

VII. Exhibits

Sources and Uses, Property Description, Valuation Year Cash Flows

Basic property description		Sources and uses		Pro forma cash flows for valuation	
					Year 3
Gross rentable area (sf)	229,627	**Sources**		**Rental revenue**	
Units	245	Loan	$29,213,625	Apartment rental revenue	4,079,061
Avg. unit size (sf)	937	Equity	$12,520,125	Concession	–
		Total sources	*$41,733,750*	Vacancy and credit loss	(203,953)
				Effective rental revenue	3,875,108
		Uses		**Other income**	
		Land price	$3,960,000	Storage	17,446
		Land closing costs	$115,000	Administrative income	90,866
		Development costs	$78,000	Parking	179,309
		Municipal fees	$3,125,000	**Total other income**	287,620
		Permits	$700,000	Vacancy and credit loss	(14,382)
		Design services	$1,102,500	**Effective other income**	273,239
		FF&E and marketing	$780,000	**Effective revenue**	4,148,347
		Bonds and insurance	$455,000		

Basic property description	Sources and uses		Pro forma cash flows for valuation	
	Developer contingency	$650,000	**Operating expenses**	—
	Operating deficit	$59,000	Taxes	237,831
	Financing fees	$515,750	Insurance	38,235
	Const loan interest reserve	$780,000	Payroll and benefits	313,270
	Property tax	$74,500	Repairs and maintenance	29,058
	Development fee	$1,200,000	Landscaping/contracts	37,470
	Hard costs	$27,307,000	Utilities	128,468
	GC fee	$832,000	Marketing/advertising	102,724
	Total uses	$41,733,750	Total make ready expense	26,254
			General and administrative	25,490
			Management fee	121,979
			Reserves for units	44,608
			Total expenses	1,105,386
			Net operating income	3,042,961
			Market rental rate per unit	1411
			Market rental rate psf/month	1.51

Abstracted JV Agreement Terms From the LOI

November 15, 2013

Summary of the Proposed Investment

Description: Development of approximately 245 apartment units in Englewood.

Type/hold: Equity investment—partnership's intent is to "build & sell" so the approximate hold period is projected at 3 years.

Structure: A to-be-created LLC ("Company"). Newarks Investment Advisory ("NIA") as limited partner and La Poudre Partners ("LPP"), or an affiliate satisfactory to as general partner.

Total capitalization: $44,982,235 ($183,600/unit) (LPP to send updated budget for by 10/29 and by 11/1)

Debt: $31,487,564 (70% LTC) (understands that the actual construction debt may range from 65% to 70% LTC)

Total required equity: $13,494,670

85% ($11,470,470).

LPP @ 15% ($2,024,201)

Development fee: $1,320,471 (not to exceed the lesser of 3% of total cost or 5% of hard cost) paid monthly in arrears based on% complete basis.

Management fee: 3.00% of total revenues for 2 years from completion; thereafter 2.75%.

Placement fees: NIA and LPP agree that a placement agent shall be paid an equity placement fee of approximately 2.50% of equity investment and a debt placement fee of approximately 0.70% of the construction loan subject to a separate agreement executed August 8, 2013 (and available upon request). Both fees will be a project expense and capitalized into the deal.

Preferred return: 11% cumulative preferred return, compounded quarterly

Cost overruns: Cost overruns (excluding interest reserve), if any, will be (i) paid first from development fee then Developer's own funds and (ii) guaranteed by LPP or an entity acceptable to In any event, such amounts paid will be forfeited by Developer.

Additional capital: Proportionate to Residual Splits, with the exception of capital contributions to extend, resize or refinance debt, Force Majeure and changes to scope approved by the partnership. Funds for these purposes will be funded per initial capital contributions (85%/15% NIA/LPP). Any capital contributions to extend, resize or refinance debt will be at the sole discretion of NIA.

Cash flow distributions:

(1) Debt service

(2) 100% to pay return of/on default contributions; then

(3) 100% to pay return of/on additional contributions; then

(4) 100% to pay preferred returns pari passu; then

(5) 100% to return Initial Capital Contributions (pari passu); then

(6) 70%–30% to LPP until NIA has achieved a 16% internal rate of return per annum, compounded quarterly, on its total capital contributions; then

(7) 60%–40% to LPP until NIA has achieved a 21% internal rate of return per annum, compounded quarterly, on its total capital contributions; then

(8) 50%–50% thereafter

Lockout period: 3 years from the effective date of the partnership agreement.

Approvals for closing: Prior to closing, LPP shall have obtained all discretionary governmental and quasigovernmental approvals to develop the Project.

Dispute resolution: Disputes between the Partners shall be resolved by a buy-sell provision or forced sale with right of first offer. The structure of these provisions shall be mutually agreed upon by Partners, however, the acquiring Partner shall be given no less than 90 days in total to close.

Outside activities: There will be no restriction on the ability of either party to pursue, own and invest in properties similar to this Project except during the Lockout Period LPP may not develop or lease a competing asset without first offering the opportunity to invest in the competing asset if the competing asset(s) are within a 5-mile radius of the Project shall have 10 business days to indicate its initial interest.

Governance/major decisions: LPP will be the General Partner of the JV and will control all day to day activities. NIA will have approval of "Major Decisions" including financing, sale or refinancing, material changes to the capital budget, selection of third parties, admission of new partners, etc.

Part IV

Iteration and Integration: Development and Redevelopment

The final set of cases are organized around real estate development and redevelopment. These are among the most challenging and fun cases to teach because the range of options is so large. Implicit in all the other cases was the option to redevelop. It might not have been easy (in fact it likely would have been complicated and costly) but as the owner of land one generally retains the opportunity to pursue redevelopment of the property. That said, in all of the earlier cases in this book the protagonists were fundamentally engaged in buying an existing asset for the purpose of using it as is and perhaps making small changes at the edges. In this section, the cases address more explicit conversations about how to fundamentally change a property. This means that the range of options is potentially quite wide, even though local land-use policies and the market will likely push developers in certain directions. In the first two cases, we look at significantly repositioning existing assets. Both cases feature older, tired real estate, but the developers in these cases actually see this as opportunities to make a good return. The question becomes which direction to take these properties. The third case may be the largest and most complex deal among the 20 cases in this book. It involves potentially 2 million sq. ft of development in the downtown of a gateway city. This case has been taught with our advanced graduate real estate students, but also with the introductory undergraduate students. It is as good for both populations but for different reasons. In the former, there are rich conversations to be had about the JV structure and sharing risk and control. In the latter, this case can be used to teach how development works and allow students to see that there is a structure that is common to both the large complex deal as well as four-unit bungalows found in the first case in this section. The last two cases are among the most successful we've had the last several years. Both of them are fundamentally about thinking through the secular trends at work in metropolitan areas and in examining whether or not they can be exploited to create profitable investments. But even more fun and challenging is that these cases introduce the reality of the business of real estate as much as the fundamentals that drive values; while late cycle fundamentals suggest caution, many real estate firms depend on deal flow to stay in business. This tension is problematic and something students should understand.

Case 16

Huntington Flats

Lily Foster thinks of herself as a developer. She just hasn't developed anything yet. She has put a great deal of time and effort trying to find her first deal, but any number of things have stopped her from moving forward – pricing seems expensive, the deal is too large or too complicated, or the property is outside her market. But now she has found a candidate for her first project. Your job is to put yourself in Lily's shoes and help her make a well-reasoned decision about how to proceed. The numbers and information that Lily accumulated while investigating her options are included. To the extent that Lily has omitted numbers you think necessary, feel free to augment them in your analysis and be ready to defend your choices in your underwriting of Lily's project.

I. Introduction

Lily Foster walked the site feeling a little overwhelmed. She had looked at a hundred sites for her first project and had found reasons to reject all of them. On the 101st look she was beginning to wonder how anyone ever built anything. And yet there she was at the intersection of Huntington and Main and all she saw in every direction was buildings. In fact, it was this array of buildings that kept her walking the site. It was an attractive neighborhood in Northeast Los Angeles, near the borders of South Pasadena and Alhambra. The site was in Los Angeles, but Lily thought the amenities just up the street in these two nearby cities would be attractive to residents. But which residents would end up here? Would they live in the units already there? Would there be new renters? Would they own the units? Would they be renovated? Lily was going to be a developer and if this was going to be her first development, she had these and many other questions to answer.

After all the other sites she had looked at, Lily thought she had finally found something that met her criteria: a scale that would be manageable, some potential to make a profit—without exposing her very-limited equity to excessive risk—a middle-market project that wouldn't require subsidies, and an opportunity to get her started up the development learning curve. Her bid for the property would be required by the close of business in just a few days. With so much to do, the next couple of days would be busy. She decided on a provisional project name: "Huntington Flats," and got started on her analysis.

The next morning Lily started with a round of phone calls. First was the seller's broker, who told her that the asking price was $650,000, and that—given

Underwriting Commercial Real Estate in a Dynamic Market. https://doi.org/10.1016/B978-0-12-815989-7.00016-1

the demand for land zoned for residential—the owner would probably not settle for anything less. The second set of calls were to contractors, all of whom were able to give her a general idea about some costs, but were fairly insistent that they'd need more details on what Lily wanted to build before they could give her specific numbers as to time or costs for her project. This forced Lily to focus on what she intended to do with the property. The site was approximately 12,500 sf (and zoned RD1.5-1, for up to eight units); it had four units that were currently operated as rentals—two structures of two units each, with garages connecting the units within each structure. Her original inspiration had been to find exactly such a set-up, to "condoize" attached units, renovate them, and then sell them as owner-occupied bungalows. Her logic relied largely on the market's optimism regarding owning a home. Specifically, interest rates were low, the local economy was robust, and new development had been limited in core areas. All of these factors meant that owner-occupied units sold at prices that seemed to make this a viable plan. This option would require funds for acquisition, funds for renovation, and funds to change the structures to owner-occupied units. The transformation of the units from rentals was the unknown part of this plan and would probably require extensive time on legalities and possible upgrades to the units to meet current building codes. This would be Plan A, but Lily knew that it would be foolish to jump into this option without first considering other alternatives.

Plan B was the path of lesser resistance. It would involve buying the property and running it as-is or with some simple upgrades—making her less a developer and more a property investor and manager. This had many benefits. First, equity requirements would be lower. While some funds would likely be needed to clean up the place, they would be smaller than the renovation costs associated with turning the units into condominiums. Perhaps the best feature of Plan B was that no approvals from the City would be required (approvals for renovations would be required from the Department of Building and Safety if they were anything more than cosmetic). Lily had heard all the stories about how painful dealing with the City could be and avoiding that morass would be a big plus for operating the property as-entitled. She would also be learning about asset management and finally get that first deal under her belt—she might even make some money in the process. And while all of these advantages got her thinking that this might end up being the best choice, she also did not want to let her fear of the unknown guide this decision. She would undertake her analysis as objectively as possible, letting the numbers guide her.

While the two obvious choices were to buy and run as-is or buy and subdivide, the developer in her also recognized a third option. The parcel adjacent to the one for sale had two structures on it: an owner-occupied home and a rental duplex. With the two parcels combined, the larger lot could be developed at a higher density, perhaps a 16-unit apartment building. This was a very intimidating prospect, but an exciting one that she wanted to consider. This option would require assembling the two parcels, getting approvals from the City, building a new structure, and marketing the project in a more formal manner; it would require more capital and more complex debt structures. In short, it would be a larger scale project on every level. Lily again found herself wanting to make sure that whatever decision she made that was based on sound thinking. If this option really was the best, then her fears about failing on her first project should not prevent her from trying.

With these three plans in mind, it became much easier to form her questions for the contractors. She had three options and for each there were specific questions. She needed to know how long it would take and how much it would cost to go from the existing set up to the "highest and best" use. She would have to talk with bankers about acquisition and development loans. She also needed to talk to brokers about rents and prices for the various products she was contemplating: she needed to know what they would provide in terms of revenue. With only 3 days to model the options, she would be busy. So she went back to the phones. She would spend the morning gathering all the information she could and then she would start crunching numbers on the three options.

Your job is to put yourself in the Lily's shoes and a) decide which option represents the "highest and best" use of the property(ies), and b) how much to bid for the property(ies).

II. The Property(ies)

The property is located on North Huntington Drive at the north-eastern-most corner of the City of Los Angeles, half a block south of the City of South Pasadena and directly across the street from the City of Alhambra. The 12,520 sq.-ft property includes four small residential "bungalows" built between 1949 and 1952. Four covered single-car garages connect the buildings into two separate duplexes, accessed by a common driveway. The property includes approximately 4000 sf of yards and patio space. (See Exhibits for property photographs and the site plan.) The units are currently operated as apartments, with three of the four bungalows occupied.

The adjacent 12,370 sf parcel contained two structures, a duplex and an in-law unit. Both properties are zoned such that all the plans discussed are "by-right." That is, the R1.5-1 zoning in place allows for up to eight units on each parcel. The combined parcels could then be developed to a total of 16 units. This "right" is with regard to the density of development—no variance is needed. Subdivision—needed in the plan to sell condominium units—will not require a variance either, but will require a variety of entitlement steps and processes required by the City and State. These are outlined below.

III. (Re)Development Options

The broker was pitching the property as a "buy-and-hold" strategy. His story was simply that prices were rising and that the cash flow would cover holding costs while the new owner reaped capital gains. It was a nice story, but Lily would do her own underwriting. Clearly, show would look into the broker's suggestion, but she would also try to think about what else could be done with the property if she bought it. She came up with several different plans and started assessing them in order.

Plan A: Operate as a Rental

The first numbers Lily obtained were the operating rents and expenses from the seller. From her own research, from other brokers, and from the many sites and projects she'd considered, she thought the property was performing about as well as could be expected given the limited attention paid to operating the property. Lily thought the current owner had placed too high a premium on low turnover and had skimped on basic maintenance. This led to steady, but low-rent tenants. In fact, the asking price was very high given the cash flow the property produced: the broker's comments aside, Lily recognized that this property was no bargain as a simple acquisition to buy and hold as is. The asking price was $650,000 and the rents flows were as follows (Unit 4 is currently vacant, the rent in the Exhibit is projected):

Exhibit A1: Current monthly operating rents

	Size (sf)	Rent/month
Unit 1	805	721.00
Unit 2	900	850.00
Unit 3	720	594.00
Unit 4	775	800.00

Exhibit A2: Current operating expenses

	Annual ($)
Insurance	2000.00
Water	1425.00
Other utilities	2475.00
Gardening	800.00
Maintenance	1800.00
Property taxes	1171.67

Lily thought the property was underinsured and also noted that if she were to buy the property her property taxes would rise significantly. The assessed value would rise to whatever Lily paid for the property, and new taxes would be assessed at 1.25% of the purchase price. She adjusted the expenses she received from the seller to reflect her assumptions for expenses in the future.

Exhibit A3: Revised expenses for "as-is" operation	
	Annual ($)
Insurance	3000.00
Water	1425.00
Other utilities	2475.00
Gardening	800.00
Maintenance	3200.00
Property taxes	1.25% of price

While there were no major structural problems, Lily felt that the age of the structures would result in ongoing maintenance that would require significantly higher funds than currently allocated. Lily was not impressed at the level of maintenance, and there was no explicit source of funds for capital expenses. The first calculation Lily needed to do was to determine the market value of the property as an acquisition to be run as it was currently operated. She would need to update the property taxes—after acquisition, they would be 1.25% of the purchase price. The new sale price would also require higher insurance coverage. She left everything else as is but expected higher rents. During her underwriting, Lily had discovered that the current rents were about 10% below market. Fearing tenant turnover, the current owner had simply let rents stagnate. With at most year-long leases in place, it would not be long before Lily—as a new owner—would be able to move them up to market. She assumed a 10% increase. At this higher rent, she felt a safe allowance for turnover vacancy would be a month-and-a-half per unit per year. Finally, she used an average cap rate from the last four similar deals she had seen sell, about 6.25%.

Question A1: What is the market value of the property under these assumptions?

These phone calls also revealed that there were higher rents to be had from even simple repositioning. Lily learned that newly renovated units could generate a 30% premium over current rents. She got a couple of bids for simple renovations: some kitchen updates including some new appliances, door knobs, sink faucets, a variety of other fixtures, a fresh coat of paint, and refinished hard wood floors. Outside, new planting and irrigation would be installed. This sort of face-lift would put the units in a different class of rentals made possible by the proximity to the amenities in South Pasadena and easy access to the rest of Los Angeles. As for the cost of the renovations, several bids had come back in the $60,000–$90,000 range; Lily assumed the midpoint: $75,000. She was then able to repeat the same calculation as before but with some new assumptions. Rents would be bumped by 30% over current numbers. And, even at these higher rents, she thought the renovations made this a tighter market segment and that turnover vacancy could be lowered to 1 month per year per unit.

Expenses would be higher and lower—insurance, gardening, and maintenance would all have to be higher, but utilities would be slightly lower given the newer appliances. Of the lower utility costs, only the lower water costs would help the owner, since the tenants would be responsible for the other utilities. Expenses would be revised according to Exhibit A4.

Exhibit A4: Expenses for "renovated" operation	
	Annual ($)
Insurance	3500.00
Water	1375.00
Other utilities	2225.00
Gardening	1200.00
Maintenance	4000.00
Property taxes	1.25% of price

Question A2: Repeat the static analysis using Lily's assumptions. What is the market value of the property under these assumptions? Was this a better option than the previous strategy she considered—buying and operating "as-is"? Would you recommend either option to Lily? What should she do?

After tinkering with these numbers, Lily felt that they were not telling her the whole story—something was missing from the static analyses, something that might change her valuation.

Question A3: What assumptions has Lily made in using these static valuations?

Lily learned more about the market from her conversations with local brokers and from a variety of sources about the local economy. She thought not only would rents get a bump with renovation, but so too would rent growth. She decided she needed a discounted cash flow (DCF) analysis to make use of this insight as to the future of rent growth. Based on a 10-year holding period, she would model rents, expenses, debt, and equity in order to get a better handle on the value of the property. To build the DCF model, she needed to make a forecast of rent growth. Lily was quite optimistic about rents. Housing prices were rising quickly, making the affordability of entry-level housing an issue that could result in higher rents. With local unemployment low, a robust and diverse local economy would be likely to continue to grow. These units would be apartments with parking and no shared walls—no one walking overhead, no one complaining from below. They were too small for a family with school-age kids, so the location was perfect for young households not eager to pay the premium for access to South Pasadena's schools, but eager to take advantage of the restaurants, retail, and other local amenities there.

Lily thought that rents would be 30% higher at the beginning of Year 2 when the existing leases rolled over. With the robust economy and the difficulty of building in California, she thought rent growth would be a 10% for another 3 years before settling at 5%. Vacancy would be low throughout the holding period, with the exception perhaps of the time needed to make the renovations. So Lily would model Year 1 vacancy and collection loss at 10%, but keep it at an equivalent of a month-and-a-half per year per unit for the remainder of the holding period.

On the expense side, Lily saw no particular reason to think her expenses would rise any faster than inflation. She thought 3% per year would be a reasonable forecast for expense growth. She would use the assumptions in Exhibit A4 as a starting point, with the addition of one further expense. She wanted to be able to move on to other projects and this desire, combined with the fact she would be an inexperienced manager, led her to include a small fee for a professional asset manager to make sure that the property generated all the revenue it could, while also being looked after to protect its value. In addition to the expenses in Exhibit A4, she added a property manager who would cost her 3% of the effective gross income.

In terms of assumptions about acquisition and disposition, Lily assumed 2% costs of sales for purchase and 6.5% of the sale price at sale—these assumptions covered a number of miscellaneous costs: brokers, legal, entity set-up, etc. Cap rates for apartments in this area were about 6.25%, but Lily thought they would be back up to 6.75% by the end of the holding period. Lily, of course, had been in touch with lenders. And, while there was a great deal of variation in the loan packages, Lily assumed a "typical" set of loan attributes.

Exhibit A5: Loan terms

	Annual ($)
Loan to value ratio	75%
Loan term	10 years
Amortization period	30 years
Interest rate	6.50%
Points	1.00%

Recognizing the added value of the renovations, the lenders had allowed the 75% (loan-to-value ratio) LTV to be calculated on value equal to the purchase price plus the $75,000 in renovation funds.

Question A4: Build a 10-year discounted cash flow using Lily's assumptions. Calculate the before-tax internal rate of return (IRR) and the before-tax net present value (NPV) of the cash flow after debt service using a 12% discount rate. If this is Lily's hurdle rate, is the plan to buy, renovate, and operate a good option?

Plan B: Subdivide

Having analyzed two options for continuing to operate the property as a rental, Lily returned to the original inspiration: creating owner-occupied dwellings from the rental units. Lily suspected that the demand for entry-level owner-occupied stock was high, but single detached units were too expensive for most in this neighborhood. In fact, she thought that condominiums were not widely viewed as a good first choice for owner-occupation because of the shared walls and common areas. That is, while more affordable than comparable detached homes, many condos felt like expensive apartments. Subdividing the units on the Huntington site had the advantage of creating affordable entry-level units while retaining the feel of detached housing. A new ordinance just adopted by the City of Los Angeles provided for the development of fee-simple single family housing on much smaller lots than previously allowable. While the ordinance was envisioned for use with ground-up development, no mention of new versus existing construction was included in the ordinance. Lily had the idea that the ordinance might be an appropriate way to convert Huntington Flats into ownership units, making them a step below traditional single-family homes, but more desirable than condominiums.

The existing units were in reasonable shape, but extensive renovations would be needed to transform the physical structures to be acceptable both to the market segment Lily had in mind and to the officials from the City, who would be interested in seeing that the renovations included updating the structures to meet current codes. Lily also wanted to exploit the opportunity to expand the two end-units, adding a small bedroom to one and a bedroom/bathroom to another (Figs. 1–9).

FIG. 1   Front of property.

FIG. 2   Unit 2.

FIG. 3   Unit 3.

FIG. 4 Unit 4.

FIG. 5 Back patio.

FIG. 6   Back yard Patio.

FIG. 7   Common driveways.

FIG. 8   Attached garages.

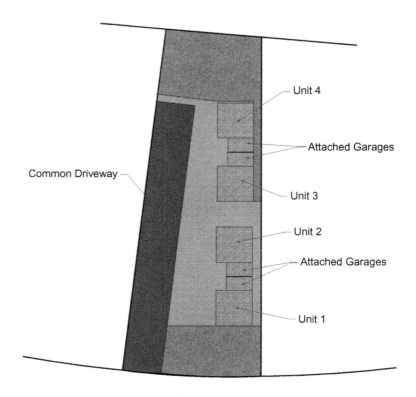

Huntington Drive

FIG. 9   Site plan.

Renovation and landscaping of the four units would be fully permitted and performed by a licensed contractor. The preliminary scope of work would include:

- Front porches and side or back patios for all units.
- Substantial landscaping and fencing to create lush private yards for each unit and attractive plantings throughout the property.
- The addition of one bedroom and one bathroom to the front-most and back-most units to create two bedrooms, two-bath homes of approximately 1200 and 1400 sf. The middle two units would be sold as one-bedroom, one-bathroom homes of approximately 800 sf.
- Interior upgrades such as:
  - ○ Installation of sliding glass doors onto patios and yards
  - ○ Refinishing existing hardwood floors
  - ○ Renovation of kitchens, including appliances and cabinetry
  - ○ Replacing some tiling in the bathrooms
  - ○ Installation of laundry hook-ups in the three units without them
- The replacement of two garages with new, free-standing carports. (The garages currently physically connect the units together into duplexes. However, the homes must be completely free-standing to be sold separately without invoking onerous and costly condominium requirements.)
- Miscellaneous repairs and upgrades to windows, gutters, water heaters, and other small items currently in disrepair.

Lily had talked with numerous contractors and had estimates of the total costs of the physical improvements—a large number that would require some careful underwriting. She was sure that the construction numbers could be known fairly accurately. After all, wasn't this a simple renovation? What she was unsure of was the cost of the entitlements/approval process required to convert from rental units to ownership townhomes. There would be two types of costs. First, there was the need for surveying and subdividing the property.[a] Second, there was the cost of relocating tenants. She was able to get a list of fees from the City, including the relocation schedule. The list of estimated fees and expenses for the subdivision came to about $25,000—though she had already heard how unreliable these could be; relocations would be $3200 for a childless

---

[a] Subdivision into smaller lots is a legal process governed by the City of Los Angeles Planning Department and the State of California, with some guidelines set by the California Department of Real Estate. After preliminary meetings with City staff, a subdivision application is submitted for approval, with required revisions made if needed. Subdivision of the Huntington Flat units is "by-right," meaning the City does not have the authority to decline the application. The City may impose certain conditions of approval such as an increase in the number of required parking spaces or the required width of the driveway. Tenant Relocation is a process governed by the City of Los Angeles Housing Department and Los Angeles' Rent Stabilization Ordinance. Specific City requirements include: 120-day advance notification of intention to remove the buildings from rental housing use and mandatory relocation payments of $3200 for childless households (two existing tenants) and $8000 for single-parent households (one existing tenant).

household and $8000 for households with children. With one unit vacated, Lily would have to relocate two childless households and one family with a child. In addition to these costs, there would be the usual constructions costs, as listed below.

Exhibit B1: Construction costs

	Annual ($)	
A&E/landscaping	8000	total
Renovation costs	60,000	per unit
Building permits	5000	total
Contractor fee	9000	total
Project insurance	7500	total
Contingency	10%	of total costs

Lily thought the subdivision could be completed in 12 months and the renovations could be completed in 8 months, getting started on the nonintrusive parts of the development while allowing the property to continue to generate rents over the first 6 months of the 20-month process. Of course, Lily would need financing for the development—an acquisition and development loan to cover as much of the costs as possible. Her equity partners were the most common sources for first-time developers: family and friends. Getting these people paid would be her highest priority.

The Acquisition and Development loans were varied, many of which were variable rate and had ceilings and floors, rate locks, indexes, margins, and other elements that Lily thought were beyond the scope of analysis at this point. She wanted to figure out a ballpark valuation number before diving into more details, so she based the financing costs on the simplest A&D loan.

Exhibit B2: A&D loan terms

Loan to costs	75%	of total A&D costs
Loan fees	1%	of loan amount
Loan term	20	months
Interest rate	8.50%	annual rate

In order to calculate the interest carry for the loan, Lily thought the average outstanding balance during the construction period would be about 70% of the loan amount. Of the remaining 25% of the A&D costs, she would turn to family and friends for 20% and she would fund the last 5% with the entirety of her personal savings.

Finally, Lily needed to project revenues. She had entered this process thinking that there was a niche market that was underserved by larger condo builders who built attached, mostly stacked product. If she pulled this off, these would be owner-occupied units of minimal size, but using very little of the most expensive input in terms of costs: land. The strength of her plan was the niche-aspect of the product type; the problem was that there were no direct comparables for Lily to use to estimate prices. Her best comparisons were two higher-density developments that had sold out earlier in the year. The first was in South Pasadena with an average price at about $480,000 per unit; the second, in Los Angeles (down the street about a mile), had sold out quickly at $340,000 per unit. The units were of similar size—some with better amenities, some without. The big difference was the market's perception of school quality, which was that South Pasadena's public school ratings far exceeded those of Los Angeles. Lily thought the way things were going in local housing markets, she could sell out quickly if she set the price at the low-end of this range. But she also thought that her products were advantaged by their detached-, lower-density-feel. At a higher price, it would take longer to sell out (and would require higher carrying costs). She assumed that it would take a year to sell the four units at an average of $440,000. She would have to pay the buyer and seller broker's fees and the transfer tax. She thought 7.5% of total sale price would be about what these costs would come to. Beyond that she would include $2000 for general marketing costs. She knew that she would have to pay 10% on any equity funds she used and was hoping to clear a profit for herself as well. Something in the neighborhood of 15% of gross sales revenue was optimistic, but she thought she would start there.

> *Question B1: Build a static analysis of the "Building residual"—calculate the net revenues from sale less the costs associated with generating the sales by using the lower average sale price assumption.*
>
> *Question B2: Calculate the building residual under the higher average sale-price and sale-time assumptions—which strategy maximizes the residual?*
>
> *Question B3: Is subdivision a viable development plan given Lily's assumptions?*

Plan C: Acquire Two Parcels and Redevelop the Larger Lot

When Lily walked the site on an earlier visit, she came up with the idea for the third option: during the visit she met the neighbor, an elderly woman who lived in a single detached home on the parcel adjacent to the Huntington Flats parcel. The neighbor's parcel had a duplex, with the second unit currently vacant and an in-law unit that had been rented out for some years. The long-time resident of the in-law unit had just announced that he would not be renewing his lease. The combination of the upkeep in her own home—which was large and on the older side—and the prospect of finding an acceptable tenant led her to mentioned half-heartedly to Lily "If you don't like that one, you ought to come take a look over here. As eager as you are to get in to real estate, I am to get out."

Given the zoning, Lily knew that the option to acquire the adjacent parcel and redevelop the combined lots as a 16-unit apartment building would not require entitlements—the parcels were zoned for the use and density. However, Los Angeles rent control law prohibits the relocation of sitting tenants for the purposes of building a new apartment building. One fleeting thought Lily had as she contemplated assembling the parcels was higher density condominiums. But she ruled out that idea almost as soon as she had it. As a first time developer, she was willing to consider the entitlement/approval risk of subdividing the existing units or the development risk of constructing the larger apartment building, but not both.

Exhibit C1: Subject property descriptions

Huntington Flats parcel		Adjacent parcel		
Asking price	650,000	Asking price	579,000	
Existing units	4	Existing units	3	
Site area	12,519 sf	Site area	12,370 sf	
Zoning	RD1.5-1	Zoning	RD1.5-1	
Allowable units	8 units	Allowable units	8 units	

The numbers for the redevelopment of both parcels were more than she bargained for. She had asked a couple of friends for numbers from their recent projects and they were very forthcoming. She filtered through the numbers, editing and combining as she went. The project would begin with a 3-month acquisition period. She would then operate the rentals on both parcels during the predevelopment process, something she thought would take about a year. During this period she would be incurring the costs associated with planning and relocation. As long as tenants were there, of course, they would be paying rent. The acquisition and development plans are given in Exhibits C1 and C2.

Exhibit C2: Development scenario

Project description			Project schedule		
Apartment units	16	units	Property acquisition	3	months
Average unit size	1200	sf	Project approval	12	months
Parking spaces	2.00	per unit	Construction	12	months
Guest parking spaces	0.50	per unit	Holding period	8	years
Total parking required	40	spaces			

Exhibit C2: Development scenario

Project description		Project schedule	
Apartment area	19,200 sf	Total project timeline	10 years
Parking garage area	11,200 sf		
Parking stall size	350 sf/stall		

After acquisition, approvals, and planning were complete, Lily planned on a year-long development schedule. She was particularly grateful to her friends for their numbers; she felt she had a much better handle on the development costs than she would have otherwise. The details of the debt coordination were still a bit uncertain, but as she planned it, there would be three loans. The first would be an acquisition loan to assist in the purchase of the two properties. The second would be a construction loan, but would take out the acquisition loan as well as supporting the development of the 16-unit apartment building. Any equity requirements would be funded by family and friends, who would earn a cumulative 12% return until operation began. The third—permanent—loan would take out the construction loan and pay off the accumulated equity returns.

Lily used her friend's numbers as best she could in developing Exhibits C3, C4, and C5. Where there were no comparable numbers, she made calls, and talked to brokers, bankers, builders, etc. She would have to build a more complicated cash flow analysis to make use of all the information. She would first have to pay attention to the details needed to build the models, and then think hard about what answers they provided.

Exhibit C3: Property acquisition assumptions (in dollars unless noted)

Acquisition costs (excluding properties)		Acquisition financing	
Ownership entity	3377	Apartment purchase price	1,229,000
Investor relations	500	Appraised value	975,000
Misc. closing costs	2964	Loan amount	75.00% LTV (appraised)
Total	6841	Loan term	10 years
		Amortization period	30 years
Project planning/approvals		Interest rate (fixed)	5.78%
Survey	7500	Points	1.25%

Exhibit C3: Property acquisition assumptions (in dollars unless noted)

Acquisition costs (excluding properties)		Acquisition financing		
Soils report	7500	Equity return	12.00%	IRR
Architect (Inc. Engineering)	171,840			
Landscape architect	10,000	Operating cash flows (existing property)		
Permit submittal fees	5000	Existing monthly rent	5725	PGI/month
Total	201,840			
		Maintenance ($300/month)	3600	per year
Relocation assistance		Property manager	5.00%	of EGI
Childless households	3200	Property taxes	1.25%	of PP
Single parent households	8000	Insurance	5541	per year
Total relocation cost	14,400	Utilities ($500/month)	6000	per year
		Gardening ($100/month)	1200	per year
Total planning/approval	223,081	Capital reserves (N/A)	–	

Exhibit C4: Construction/development costs (in dollars unless noted)

Hard cost			Construction financing	
Building hard costs	185	psf	Property value	975,000
(Includes demolition)			Hard + soft costs	5,249,200
Garage hard costs	60	psf	Interest reserve	500,000
Total hard costs	4,224,000		Total project cost	6,724,200
Soft costs			LTC	70.00%
Building permits	115,000		Loan fees/closing costs	2.00%

Exhibit C4: Construction/development costs (in dollars unless noted)

Hard cost		Construction financing	
Contractor fee	358,000	Construction interest rate	9.00%
Project level insurance	75,000	Construction period (months)	12
Total soft costs	548,000	Average outstanding balance	65.00%
Construction contingency	10.00% H&S costs	Equity return (IRR)	12.00%
Total	5,249,200		

Exhibit C5: Operation/disposition (in dollars unless noted)

Rents (new development)		Permanent loan	
Average rent per unit	1800	Loan amount (%LTV)	75.00%
Lease up period (months)	3.0	Interest rate (fixed)	6.75%
		Amortization period (years)	30
Annual operating costs (new development)		Points/fees	2.00%
Property manager (% of EGI)	5.00%	Valuation cap rate	6.25%
Property taxes (% on purchase price)	1.25%		
Insurance	12,000	Disposition assumptions	
Utilities ($500/ month)	6000	Going out cap rate	6.75%
Gardening ($200/ month)	2400	Cost of sales (% of sale price)	6.50%
Maintenance ($500/month)	6000		
Capital reserves ($2000/month)	24,000		

Question C1: If warranted, build a discounted cash flow analysis of the acquisition, development, operation, and disposition cash flows. Should Lily pursue the development strategy of acquiring the adjacent parcels and developing a 16-unit apartment building on the combined properties? Why or why not?

Having answered the smaller, component questions, you face the Big Question:

What should Lily do?

1. *You have explored three broad strategies for acquiring and developing this property: which is the most likely to succeed? Why?*
2. *Of the less successful options, is there any reason to pursue further analysis? Why or why not?*
3. *With regard to the "best" strategy, would you buy the property at the asking price? If not, what is your highest feasible bid? If yes, how much higher would you go?*
4. *At your highest feasible bid, would you advise Lily to proceed? Why or why not? Would you advise her "family and friends" to invest in Lily's project? Why or why not?*
5. *Given the preliminary nature of the analysis, where would you spend your time doing more research to make your underwriting more accurate?*

Case 17

Leaning Into Headwinds: Grocery-Anchored Retail in the Era of Amazon

I. Uncovering Value in the Age of Amazon

It is the age of Amazon, and many real estate investors are concerned—maybe even frightened—by the impact of e-commerce on "bricks and mortar" retailers. Major bankruptcies loom, vacancies are up and rental rate growth has stalled despite a strong national economy well into its recovery. Yet even in the face of these headwinds, Pat Pilich, co-founder and head of asset management at Precision REI, wasn't convinced that all was doom and gloom in retail. A classic contrarian investor, he felt confident that the general sentiment against retail was overblown and the pendulum had swung too far to the "retail is dead" end of things. Retail was experiencing serious headwinds, but it—like all real estate—wasn't simply a commodity. Buying opportunities were out there for those with a keen eye, patient capital, and sufficient fortitude. If he looked past the "headline risks," Pat knew he would find a deal. Indeed, the broader market's panic about Amazon worked in Pat's favor: retail might be oversold. If he remained disciplined, he could create value and earn solid risk-adjusted returns in retail.

II. Company Background

Precision REI (PREI) was founded in January 2014 by Pat and his partner George Wicker. They worked together at a large real estate investment fund manager that had $35 billion of assets under management. While at the fund, Pat and George were charged with buying core and value-add investments in all four major product types (office, retail, apartments, and industrial) in all of the eight major MSA's in the western United States. After years of investing on behalf of billion-dollar pension funds, Pat and George finally made the decision to own real estate themselves and to invest on behalf of a group of close friends and family. They were confident that owning real estate themselves was a path

Underwriting Commercial Real Estate in a Dynamic Market. https://doi.org/10.1016/B978-0-12-815989-7.00017-3

toward building long-term wealth, and that they would be more personally and professionally satisfied working with people whom they knew and cared about.

When developing Precision's strategy, they drew on their experience as institutional investors and looked for market inefficiencies to exploit. They knew big investors had plenty of "dry powder," which meant that prices on large deals were consistently bid up and returns were relatively thin for deals over $30 million. They also knew wealthy individuals and family offices had ample capital to buy real estate under $10 million. But they remained confident that the $10 million to $30 million niche was one where it was difficult to raise equity, there were fewer competitors, and thus potentially strong returns could be found.

They also realized that as sponsors, they needed to have a deep level of expertise in their core investment focus. No longer could they "fly at 30,000 feet," like at their previous firm. There, they were focused on diversification and spreading investments around to capture broader trends. At Precision, the ground-level details would be essential. In order to identify and create value, Precision needed to know everything that was happening in their local market. That would require developing an extensive network of relationships with brokers, lenders, appraisers, property managers, and tenants. They decided a sponsor could either be an expert at one market and operate in multiple product types, or could focus on one product type and operate in multiple markets. They researched the risk and return characteristics of each property type and, as contrarian investors, determined retail was too far out of favor and good opportunities could be found provided a high-level of discipline and patience. They further identified two markets in which they wanted to operate: Southern California and Arizona. Each market was convenient for them, but were at different stages in its economic recovery following the Great Recession. As the larger, more mature market, Los Angeles offered greater safety and stability, but also lower prospective returns. Arizona was on its way to recovery and its population was beginning to grow again. Phoenix, specifically, offered the chance for much higher long-term growth, but had a reputation as a "boom and bust" town, so PREI would need to stay aware of potential risks and market conditions.

Once Precision had developed its investment thesis, it approached a select group of high net worth friends and family investors and immediately received positive feedback. Through an iterative process of meetings and market research, the partners determined they could make money while also generating acceptable returns for their investors by structuring investments with an 8% preferred rate of return on invested equity, and a 70/30 split (favoring investors) of all cash flow and net sales profits. Additionally, the firm would receive an acquisition fee of 1% of the purchase price and a 2% lease renewal fee anytime a nonanchor tenant extended or renewed their lease. This structure worked well for the group and by late 2016, the Prescott Towne Center (PTC) became the firm's ninth acquisition. The firm's total portfolio was valued at nearly $185 million.

III.   Prescott and Prescott PTC

As the biggest and most well-located shopping center in a tertiary market, Prescott PTC (PTC) fit squarely into the category of "overlooked and unloved," but maybe a great value. Built in phases during the 1980s, the 163,000 sf shopping center was located at the premier retail intersection in Prescott, Arizona, was in good physical condition, and was occupied by several strong, nationally recognized tenants. As part of a 10-year renewal, the grocery anchor had recently invested substantial capital to renovate the store and was enjoying an exceptional 35% increase in year-over-year sales.

The previous owner of PTC passed away unexpectedly several years ago and his surviving family members, all of whom lived in California, weren't in a position to become "hands on" managers. There had been some mismanagement with respect to tenant relations and marketing the center to new prospective tenants, and as a result, the center's occupancy rate had dropped to 81%. Included in the vacancy were several prime, high-visibility pads that Pat knew would be appealing to high-credit single tenant NNN tenants (in Pat's opinion, a shining star in retail capital markets today).

Prescott is a small but vibrant and quickly growing town in Northern Arizona. It has a strong population base of retirees and affluent second home owners who frequently make the short trip to escape Phoenix's legendary summer heat. A potential catalyst for future growth, Northern Arizona University is in negotiations to construct a satellite campus a few miles outside of town on 210 acres of land it recently purchased from the State of Arizona Land Bureau. Tourism is also a strong driver of the local economy. The town benefits from its proximity to Sedona and the Grand Canyon and is surrounded by hundreds of square miles of beautiful forests that provide world class hiking, camping, hunting, and fishing.

The town has five multitenant anchored shopping centers, as well as a smattering of single tenant "box tenants" and "pad tenants." The single tenant "box tenants" include corporations like WalMart, Ross, and Petco, but also some local retailers who covered souvenirs, chocolates, and gifts to sell to tourists passing through town. The "pad tenants" were similar to what one would see throughout the country: Burger King, Dairy Queen, Del Taco, Popeye's Chicken. The box tenants tended to be in single-story buildings of from 10,000 to 20,000 sf, while pad tenants were all manner of smaller format structures—but many are fast food franchises—that range from 1500 to 3500 sf.

Compared to the competing retail centers in town, PTC was widely considered the premier center: it is located at the primary intersection of the region, and it has the best visibility and ingress/egress. Its status as the top center was validated by the fact that the rent roll consisted of more sophisticated "national" tenants than any other center in the area, and during Pat's due diligence process he spoke with several brokers who said their clients in Prescott would like to relocate to PTC if their space requirement could be accommodated. Because retail shopping centers are not homogenous in the way office or industrial assets are, he liked to break down local vacancy rates into three segments: anchors (spaces larger than 10,000 sf), in-line shops (suites up to 10,000 sf), and the pads tenants that often are located on a center's outbuildings. Vacancy rates for anchors and pads were very low, sub-3%, but the in-line shops (that were mostly filled by low-credit local mom-and-pop tenants) was concerningly high at 16%. Because of these figures, Pat decided to account for the tenants by broad categories: he assumed healthy market rental rates and rent growth on the PTC anchor and pad spaces, but remained conservative on both market rents and lease-up schedule of the in-line vacancies.

Despite the positive attributes and recent growth, Prescott is a tertiary market—a small-town whose fundamentals would prohibit most big institutional investors such as "core" funds, pensions, and REIT's from pursuing investment there. Furthermore, high net worth investors and syndicators were generally "scared" of retail, especially a retail asset in tertiary Arizona that would require substantial time and effort to manage. Indeed, Pat had several conversations with investors from out of state who were concerned by the burden of owning a property that was a two-hour drive from Phoenix Skyharbor airport. They knew that retail could be a management-intensive business and they were worried about their ability to check in regularly.

While these dynamics made Pat's life more challenging than it would have been in Phoenix, they made the pool of bidders for what was an otherwise strong asset very small. Precision REI capitalized on the opportunity and paid approximately $22 million for PTC. Precision also invested an additional $500,000 for an adjacent vacant land parcel. This land parcel was excluded from the primary loan used to acquire PTC, meaning Precision owned the parcel free and clear. Pat felt this price gave Precision a very low basis at only $135 psf, well below replacement cost. To assemble the necessary capital for the PTC, Precision hired a mortgage broker to arrange a $15.5 million CMBS loan and then raised the required $7.5 million dollars of equity through a private syndication of friends and family investors. This $7.5 million dollars in equity would also cover closing costs, fees, and reserves.

While Pat knew the available pads would generate strong interest from new tenants, he was pleasantly surprised at the swift pace of leasing of the in-line shop spaces. There was substantial pent-up demand from local tenants for good quality space in a professionally managed center. Pat's first order of business to stimulate interest was to change brokerage firms and require the new team to canvas the town door to door to market the vacant in-line shops directly to prospective users. This strategy produced immediate results and, to generate "word of mouth" interest around town and induce even further demand, he actually "broke" his pro-forma numbers, quickly signing three new leases at slightly below market rental rates. While not hitting his anticipated rents, he filled the vacant suites earlier than expected and it paid off in other ways almost immediately. When word got out around town, he was flooded with interest from new tenants and was able to sign multiple renewals of existing tenants as well as new leases at higher than expected rental rates at an accelerated lease-up pace from his original underwriting assumptions. Within 12 months of acquisition, he had signed new leases for Suites 252 and 254, as well as all 4 suites that were vacant between the Dollar Store and Sports Store. (See the parcel map below.)

Prescott Towne Center–Exhibit A

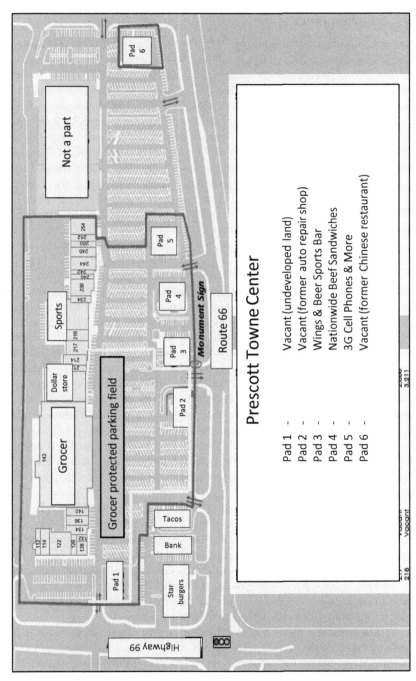

Prescott Towne Center

Pad 1 - Vacant (undeveloped land)
Pad 2 - Vacant (former auto repair shop)
Pad 3 - Wings & Beer Sports Bar
Pad 4 - Nationwide Beef Sandwiches
Pad 5 - 3G Cell Phones & More
Pad 6 - Vacant (former Chinese restaurant)

IV.   Puzzle Pieces

Now 12 months after purchasing PTC, Pat found himself in the office scratching his head and trying to figure out how to best execute the second half of his strategy to capture as much value as he could from the PTC. The first half of the strategy spanned acquiring the PTC through to filling the vacant in-line suites. Pat viewed this as a success. The second half would be to getting to a new equilibrium—taking whatever steps were needed to squeeze the property's efficiency. Since starting PREI, Pat had already learned that many older retail properties were typically run only well enough to hit some previous benchmark, but were not optimized on an on-going basis. And, PTC clearly showed signs of hands-off management from the previous owners. But, he had also figured out how much time it took to find and close on a new deal. Once he got his teeth into Precision's next acquisition, he would likely spend less time in Prescott. This was the time to think hard about how best to run PTC.

What Pat was considering was how to reposition the shopping center. In larger metropolitan areas, retail centers like this were being redeveloped with vertical elements—like towers of apartments and sometimes office towers—being added in the largely underutilized parking fields. In Prescott, land prices made such a strategy implausible, but there could be other, less-dramatic changes that could help Precision's cash flow and improve the value of the property.

Pat would want to think through all of them but would have to be mindful of his use of time. There was always more one could do on a site with as many moving parts as the PTC, but every hour he spent tinkering on minutiae was an hour he wasn't spending looking for his next deal. For Precision, the plan has always been to accumulate enough cash flow to support itself and allow their anticipated appreciation to create longer-term wealth. Right now, Pat felt Precision had not yet acquired enough real estate to fully support them, and he did not want to wait until the next cycle to continue acquisitions. If there were management decisions at the property that could materially help cash flows now and/or appreciation later, then he would take the time to explore them. But he would have to prioritize.

Of the six pads (shown in Exhibit A) beyond the grocery and inline shops, three were occupied, two were developed but vacant, and one was raw, undeveloped land. As Pat looked over the site plan of the center he puzzled over a number of issues: (1) where to locate each interested tenant; (2) how to finance the construction, renovation, tenant improvements, and leasing commissions; (3) which tenants are offering the best lease terms; (4) how prospective leases and financing decisions relate to his (and his investor's) bigger picture and longer term strategy of risk tolerance and holding period?

Pad 3 housed a sports bar. Pad 5 housed a cell phone store. Pad 6 had been part of other earlier tenant negotiations with two restauranteurs at PTC: one wanted more space, the other had too much. The two will be switching locations. This left three pads to "solve." Below are details regarding Pat's first take on his options and some of the givens and assumptions.

Pad 1—Undeveloped Land

This pad has received strong interest from a high-credit tenant called Seattle Café. Seattle Café requires a "Built to Suit" (BTS) project including a drive-thru. This means Precision would construct the shop to the Café's specification. Precision would use either debt or equity capital to construct the building "shell" and would provide the tenant an improvement allowance as a contribution toward the Café's interior design, construction, and fixturization costs. The Grocer tenant, however, has approval rights over any new development within the area designated as its protected parking field in Exhibit A and will not approve because of concerns about high demand causing lines to form in drive-aisle, thus impairing ingress for grocery customers. Seattle Café has asked Precision to find another location with less impact on grocery customers.

Based on these conversations, Pat assumed lease and construction numbers as follows:

- 10-year lease
- $110,000 NNN rent per annum (no escalations)
- Site work costs: $150,000
- Hard costs: $600,000
- Soft costs: $200,000
- Tenant improvements: $90,000
- Leasing broker: 6% of total base rent paid during years 1–5; 3% of total rent paid during years 6–10
- This pad is owned free and clear (no debt), and Pat assumes a pad land basis: $500,000
- Resale cap rate 5.50%

Pad 2—Vacant Auto Shop

The existing structure is a 1400 sf former auto repair shop that includes oil wells and hydraulic lifts. The prior use was somewhat noxious and there may be a need for environmental remediation if a change of use occurs. Precision acquired this pad at the same time it purchased the rest of the PTC and is included as collateral for the existing CMBS loan. Encumbered by the existing loan, this pad cannot be sold or used as collateral for secondary loan.

Pat has received interest from a local auto repair firm for this pad. The potential tenant has been in business for 18 years, has a strong reputation and is well known in town. This potential tenant lacks substantial assets or credit, but is willing to take the existing vacant auto shop building in "as-is" condition. Precision can save substantial money by leasing to this tenant because it does not have to invest additional capital or provide an improvement allowance to this tenant. He is not represented by a broker.

- The tenant proposes a 5-year lease, with $35 psf/year NNN rent and 3% annual increases.

- Tenant willing to pay percentage rent of 6% of sales in addition to the base rent. Based on operating experience, the tenant anticipates sales of $200,000 on the low end and $300,000 on the high-end.
- Again, the pad cannot be sold because it serves as a portion of the collateral for the loan of the entire shopping center, but if it could be sold the market cap rate would probably be between 8.5% and 9%.

Pat has also had interest from a national fast-food hamburger and fries franchisee for a "reverse build-to-suit," in which the tenant designs, constructs, and pays for their building, while the landlord contributes a predetermined fixed amount to these costs. Precision likes this type of lease structure because its costs are fixed and predetermined, while the tenant performs all the work and accepts the risk of any construction cost overruns. The franchisee lives out of state, but has six other locations in Arizona and plans to continue growing in the market. All the other locations are performing well, but Pat is slightly hesitant because he would be entering Prescott, a small market with seven other fast food hamburger providers in town already. He is unsure if there is enough demand to support an additional operating in this space. Another consideration is the Grocer's approval rights and how their preference for one tenant versus the other could influence Pat's decision. The franchisee proposes:

- A 20-year ground lease, with a personal guarantee during the initial 10 years
- Precision would deliver Pad 2 prepped (existing structure demolished) and ready for development, including utilities stubbed to the site. This may require substantial environmental remediation because of prior "noxious" use. Pat's estimate of the contribution and costs:
  - Landlord contribution: $700,000
  - Demolition: $50,000
  - Remediation cost: $100,000
  - Site prep: $75,000
  - Leasing commission: $75,000
- $100,000 NNN rent per year, 10% increases every 5 years

Pat thought the franchisee would be a strong tenant, but not a national credit tenant, with a market cap rate if sold of 6.5%. Pat thought there might be two options to fund this change to Pad 2. First, he could make a capital call to investors to raise additional equity. Second, he could accept an unsecured 5-year loan at a 10% interest rate. The loan would come with full recourse if it was an interest only loan, but would be nonrecourse if it the loan payments were amortized over a 15-year term.

Pad 4—Nationwide Sandwiches

A nationally recognized sandwich chain store is the existing tenant on Pad 4. It has been successfully operating on this 2200 sf site at this facility for more than 30 years. With the lease signed in 1986, the building is overdue for a major renovation to meet the tenant's current national proto-type format. This franchise is owned by a franchisee that has total control over the entire Arizona territory. She owns and operates 44 stores, and has a strong track record for success and an equally strong balance sheet. The lease she signed had four 5-year extensions and the final option has already been used. The lease will end in 12 months. At that point she will have no rights to occupy the space. Given the nature of fast-food, she is keen to stay on the site and is proposing a new, 20-year lease, but wants Precision to contribute half of the estimated $500,000 in remodeling costs. She also suggests a new lease: $36 psf NNN with 10% increases every 5 years. Pat is confident he can achieve approximately $40 psf and perhaps less of the remodeling budget. Pat assumes $425,000.

V. Deliverables

Your job is to help Pat organize his thinking about next steps at PTC. He and his partner have a lot to do at the PTC, at their other properties, and at any number of candidate properties that might become the eighth property in Precision's portfolio. What should Pat do? If you were in Pat's shoes, how would go about assembling a business plan for the PTC in light of the data you have? What would you like to know before you commit to any one option?

Precision already owns PTC and it is fully up to Pat and George how much time they want to put into a property they already own and that is already doing fairly well. Many real estate properties face this issue every day, but it is often not thought about as an active choice. That is, there is a lot of real estate that is operating as it is simply because that's the way it was operating yesterday. Should Precision let the PTC roll along and earn a return on the momentum it has now? This would allow Pat to spend close to 100% of his time on the next deal. If not, what would you have him do at the PTC? Suggest a prioritized list of next steps and what you anticipate the return to be from them. To be clear, suggesting that Pat spend more time gathering data is reasonable, but whether it be a recommendation to act or to investigate more, articulate the logic and, where possible, use some numbers to estimate the returns to the effort.

Some issues you may find helpful as you organize your thoughts include:
a. What's your top line summary of the state of retail? Is it relevant to PTC? How so? While there appears to be anecdotal evidence of retail doing well in the urban markets, Prescott is far from a big city. Is there any reason to compare A-list properties in the Gateway cities to the performance of PTC? Likewise, there are so many B- and C-quality centers around the country that are clearly suffering. Should Prescott be compared to them?
b. Given that Pat and George already own PTC, is the preceding question even relevant? Will digging into that issue just reveal they may have overpaid or underpaid? That is, should the larger question about the relative value and position of retail influence how Pat chooses to manage PTC?

c. List all the various options Pat has available to him. Which pads should be leased to each tenant? Is there any way to best match particular tenants with locations within the PTC?

d. How does tenant use, credit quality, leasing costs, and factors outside of Precision control (such as approval rights of other tenants) influence your recommendations?

e. Who are the stakeholders at the PTC? Who has to say yes to any one of your suggestions? Are there obvious conflicts that you should mindful of? Are these significant conflicts or are they concerns? For example, are the grocer's concerns valid? How will the grocer respond if Pat tried to find a way forward? What are the grocer's long term interests? Do they correlate well with Precision's?

f. What do you think about the other junior anchors? Do the Sporting Goods and Dollar Store help or hurt the overall value at PTC?

g. A major strategic element for Precision is improving current cash flow. Which of the options above best helps achieve this? What is the best way to finance these plans? Assume that Precision's base cost of capital is 8% (it might be higher if the center does well). Do your answers to these consider longer-term appreciation as well? What is the best way for Precision to balance these two goals? Are they in tension?

h. More mechanically, how did you go about evaluating what's "best"? How did you rank Pat's options? What is the best metric to inform these decisions? That is, should Pat use return on cost? Contribution to overall IRR? And if IRR, which one: levered or unlevered IRR?

i. Calculate the total profit and profit margin of the proposed Seattle Café development. Assuming Precision made a capital call and used equity to construct the building, how much of the profit would be paid to investors and how much would Precision receive? If Pat decided to hold the building for the long-term, how much money would Precision receive annually?

j. Calculate the Return on Cost (RoC) for the proposed auto repair and fast hamburgers and fries leases. What do these numbers tell you? Is it a "good" return? Against what benchmark would you compare it? Should you, can you, use the RoC to make other choices?

k. If the Vacant Auto Shop pad could be sold, what would be the sale value of the auto repair lease? What about the Burger and Fries lease? Which option has a higher profit margin? Is using the "unsecured loan" option or making a capital call to fund the Burgers and Fries lease more accretive to returns? Considering this parcel must be held long-term, if Pat decided to use the loan, which structure is more accretive to returns and why? How does each loan options change the risk profile to Precision and is the benefit worth the risk?

Case 18

Anyone for Extra Innings? Let's Play Two? Late-Cycle Underwriting for Irwindale Reliance and the Olympic Plant

Originally written in 2016, the case asked which of two properties were worth pursuing as late cycle development projects for the Kearny Real Estate Company. At that point, the general consensus was that the real estate cycle had matured; both cranes and capital could be readily found throughout the region, and prices reflected the accumulation of years of optimism. But as of late 2018, the "imminent" downturn still has yet to materialize. Of the two deals Kearny considered 2016, one was subsequently sold at a price well beyond the valuation that Kearny estimated. The second deal remains unsold. The current case now adds several new questions in light of the duration of the current cycle. What was the "right" way to underwrite the deal Kearny lost in 2016? Should Kearny revisit its underwriting of the second deal that remains open? At issue are differences between short-term and long-term fundamentals and how to underwrite them when they don't agree.

I. Looking Under Rocks in "Late Cycle" 2016

As one of the so-called "gateway" markets, metropolitan Los Angeles has been a significant target for real estate investment since capital started flowing again after the housing bust in 2008. By 2015, cap rates were lower than anyone thought possible and aggressive pricing was pervasive. But it was not just the primary markets that were setting records. The "search for yield" resulted in capital flowing further afield, making all the obvious deals very competitive. While local fundamentals were often used to explain pricing, there was a sense that though long-term fundamentals were strong, current land pricing felt risky. That did not mean there were no deals to look at, but they were neither cheap nor simple. You could hold onto your capital and wait for a correction, but you would earn neither fees nor a return while waiting. So while there was risk in

Underwriting Commercial Real Estate in a Dynamic Market. https://doi.org/10.1016/B978-0-12-815989-7.00018-5
199

moving forward with another investment, this would have been just as true at the end of 2014, when the chatter about "late cycle" first started popping up.

The National Bureau of Economic Research defined the last recession as beginning in December of 2007 and lasting until June of 2009. In June of 2016, it would be a full seven years of recovery. While many real estate professionals looked at prospective numbers to underwrite their deals, there were also some who thought about market cycles—especially real estate cycles—as a natural phenomenon like tides or the seasons. This sense that natural laws guide real estate seems to reappear every cycle. An interesting conversation at a prominent conference in the fall of 2015 involved five panelists from premier capital shops. The consensus among them was that they were "tapping the brakes." They mentioned the traditional business cycle was about seven years old; therefore, "we are due for a correction." There was lengthy conversation about the usual suspects that would lead to a correction, with a one new generic worry to be added: the "wall of CMBS maturities that would hit real estate soon." But the moderator kept pushing them to link these worries to impending softness in real estate. The moderator not only uncovered that they were they still actively investing, but that they couldn't name a single fundamental was signaling a slowdown. "If you believe there's an imminent slowdown, then why are you still placing capital?" the moderator asked. They hesitated, and so he continued: "Okay. I'll let you off the hook on that one. But at least give me one solid fundamental that we should worry about." Again, no one wanted to take the microphone. A brave panelist finally spoke up: "Okay, fine. We don't know. It just feels late. And we lost a lot of money the last time we waited too long to get careful."

If you had "tapped the brakes" in 2015 you would have been in good company. But that strategy would have left you and your investors out of another year of solid recovery. Of course there are risks and opportunities at every point in the cycle. A developer's job is to discern one from the other and make good trade-offs. And you now face just such a choice. You are a project manager at Kearny Real Estate Company. It is now early 2016 and your firm is looking at two potential investments. The first is the Irwindale Reliance Business Park, a 91.5 acre aggregate pit adjacent to the 210 freeway at the Irwindale Avenue on/off ramp. The second is in Downtown Los Angeles in a neighborhood now being marketed as the "Lower" Arts District. This 26-acre site, at the intersection of 8th & Alameda Streets, includes the Los Angeles Times' printing press facility.

Both deals are complicated, but either may be your firm's best chance to find a site for redevelopment that isn't attracting the same amount of capital and pricing that simpler deals are. Your job is to analyze both opportunities and make an argument for the deal you feel has the best risk-adjusted returns.

II.   Irwindale Reliance Business Park as of 2016

Reliance II is a 91.5 acre site owned by Calmat (Vulcan Materials Corp, NYSE: VMC). The site is a former aggregate pit located in the City of Irwindale in the San Gabriel Valley. The filling process is expected to be completed in mid-2020 and will result in a 91.5-acre infill site that is ideal for development.

The Seller—Vulcan Materials Corporation

Vulcan mined the Reliance II pit for aggregate that was used in construction. They are now in the process of mining an adjacent pit in a $300M project. As they excavate the adjacent pit, the excavated material is being used to fill Reliance II.

The City/Entitlements

In an initial meeting between city staff and Kearny, the city called the Reliance II pit the "crown jewel" of Irwindale. The 91.5 acre site is the largest site that can be developed. The city has stressed the need for the development to create jobs and generate revenue for the city.

While retail use would provide jobs and revenues for the city through sales tax generated at the site, the market demand for retail in this location is low. Warehouse and distribution uses would create jobs, but historically have not created much sales tax revenue. With current market conditions, industrial land is worth roughly twice the amount of retail land. Of course, housing is in perennially short supply in the city and region, but housing appears to be out of favor because it won't create permanent jobs or long-term revenue for the city.

Irwindale is embarking on a specific plan for the local area and the buyer is expected to be part of that process. That is, the developer should expect significant negotiation with the city about land uses before acquisition because the city wants to coordinate the final design with the revised specific plan. In addition to these negotiations, the site will require an environmental impact report (EIR) along with the development plan.

A plan for the development suggests that this is indeed a long-term project. Kearny is used to large scale projects that span years, but this pushes the anticipated sales 8 years in the future—even if everything goes according to plan. You have been able to get some informal numbers about rents and prices now, but what number would you put in a pro forma when you're going to market with your brand new industrial building in 2022? You think the retail land is not worth as much, and retail could be relatively weaker by 2022. The very same industrial buildings the market seems inclined to build are as likely as any to be occupied by Amazon distribution centers that are undermining the economics of retail as we speak. This is why Kearny was sure there would be less competition: it will be very hard for most credit committees to say yes to anything this speculative.

At the same time, what do you think the world will look like in 2022? Will businesses still be looking for more industrial space? If not, what about housing? Is there a shortage of land in Los Angeles? This is a gravel pit, but relatively soon it will be raw land within a major metropolitan area and at the intersection of key freeways. It must be worth something…but what?

The seller has requested the last round of offers for the site and has asked for offers for two scenarios. The first is an immediate sale, one in which Kearny would be required to pay the full $70 million price under the current entitlements—that is, as an exhausted gravel pit. The second scenario is for Kearny to close on the full amount of $95 million upon receiving entitlements. Under either scenario, assume the seller has offered a leaseback until the gravel pit has been filled. It will pay rent in the amount of 6% per year on the agreed price.

Proposed Timeline

Development schedule	Months	Start	Completion
Due diligence	4	Mar-16	Jun-16
Purchase—Buy now		Jul-16	
Entitlement	18	Jul-16	Dec-17
Purchase—Postentitlement		Jan-18	
Backfill/leaseback	48	Jul-16	Jun-20
Horizontal development	12	Jul-20	Jun-21
Retail land sale	1	Jul-21	Jul-21
Industrial development	24	Jul-21	Jun-23
Industrial sales	24	Jul-22	Jun- 24

Market Comps

After years of multifamily being the "hottest" real estate segment, industrial is surpassing it now. With the evolution of e-commerce and the fervor for "omni-channel" strategies, there is far more demand for industrial space than in the past. With growing globalization, the Ports of Los Angeles and San Pedro are setting records for shipments. With a third or more of the goods for the entire country coming through these ports, the need for transshipment facilities and storage is high.

The local food movement and the demands for food preparation and cold storage have also grown significantly over the last several years. These alone might have made for excess demand without the advent of Amazon's model of quick delivery. All of this means that industrial space need will grow in aggregate, but the nature of the growth will also mean more than just million-plus building in the exurbs where land is cheap. Being closer to the ports and closer to customers will require proximal land, which is already in limited supply.

For all the new focus on industrial real estate, there has been some divergence in the way it is underwritten. While industrial is one of the major real estate "food groups" and can appear from the outside like a commodity, a growing number of developers, logistics firms and consultants have been astonishingly aggressive in optimizing something that had been thought of as relatively generic. For some users and investors, every feature of a building contributes to or retards efficiency and therefore demand. A building that is one additional stop light from the freeway is penalized. A clear-height that is 4 ft below current standard is penalized. Those without enhanced fire suppression are penalized. Ask an expert about what makes for a great industrial building and you'll get an earful about truck parking, number of dock doors and their spacing, driveway tilt down for unloading on one side and tilt down again for loading on the other side—but the floor inside must be essentially perfectly flat to allow very high inventory stacking. There is a science to modern industrial buildings, but this science makes underwriting that much more difficult to evaluate from afar. The data below gives a sense of rents and prices nearby, but should be viewed with some caution without a site visit. Clearly, much of what makes an industrial building valuable is not included in the data.

Market lease comps	City	sf	Year built	($/sf NNN)	Lease start	Comments
1223 W 10th Street	Azusa	343,699	2016	0.56	Jan-16	10-year deal
4775 Irwindale Avenue	Baldwin Park	127,440	2003	0.58	Sep-15	
17651 Railroad Street	Industry	65,599	2015	0.60	Nov-15	

Sale comps	City	sf	Year built	($/sf NNN)	Date sold	Comments
15025 Proctor Ave	Industry	128,581	2015	145.00	Dec-15	In escrow
13001 Temple Ave	Industry	56,496	2015	153.00	Apr-15	
5150–5160 Rivergrade	Baldwin Park	54,860	1987	145.00	Sep-15	Class A bldg.; heavy power

Land comps	City	Acres	Status	$/sf	Lease start	Comments
Safeway El Monte	El Monte	92.06	In escrow	35.00	In escrow	2-year leaseback; resi; school
17300 Chestnut	Industry	30.00	Sold	32.11	Jul-14	
CT Azusa Center	Azusa	8.35	Sold	22.00		No demo required

Property pipeline—For lease	City	# of bldgs	sf—Low	sf—High	($/sf NNN)	Comments
Irwindale Canyon BP	Irwindale	2	85,042	87,421	0.64	Small units ~17K sf
Arcadia Logistics Ctr	Arcadia	6	150,000	375,000	0.65	In talks, rents ~60's
242 Live Oak	Irwindale	1	77,000			Start 4Q 2016
Arrow Hwy BP	Irwindale	1	133,800			Divisible

Pipeline buildings—For sale	City	# of bldgs	sf—Low	sf—High	$/sf	Comments
CT Azusa Center	Azusa	3	30,598	107,402	160–190	Site on other side of 210
Magellan Gateway	El Monte	5	52,448	164,284	145–190	In escrow for $145 psf
Irwindale Canyon BP	Irwindale	2	85,042	87,421	165	Units as small at 17K sf

Development

Development could not begin for several years, but you were able to get some estimates of what it would cost if you were building today. Construction costs are a moving target just like rents and cap rates. Currently, you are planning to sell whatever retail land is required by the City (if any) and so you didn't spend much time underwriting the retail development costs. That said, the land development budget includes infrastructure and pad preparation for all 91.5 acres of the site.

Rough development budget	
Land development	4,000,000
Hard costs	
Building shell	35.50
Office buildout	3.50
Soft costs	25% of hard costs
Development fee	4% of hard costs
Contingency	5% of total

Notes: 1. Leasing commissions are 6% on 5-year deals (if going with a for-lease program). 2. Sale costs (incl. commissions) are 5.5% for 1-off building sales; if selling as a leased investment use 1%.

While many details are missing, would you want to use today's details even if you had them? If you were able visit each of the comparables and find the most appropriate matches, would you have a better sense of the value of the Vulcan pit? While having more data would be nice if it were free, it is not. It takes time and often money to get more. Would having more information about today's market help you decide to pursue this project? Given the numbers you have been given, can you ballpark a reasonable preliminary bid? What return would you expect on a deal like this given the risks? At your valuation, would you expect to be able to win the bid?

III.   LA Times Olympic Plant as of 2016

The second project that is on the market is the Los Angeles Times printing facility at the Olympic Plant. When the Tribune Company emerged from bankruptcy in late 2014, they split into two companies—Tribune Publishing (TPUB; later the company changed its name to tronc), which focuses on print media, and Tribune Media, which took ownership of the company's real estate, TV, and radio assets. Tribune Publishing (NYSE: TPUB) has seen their value decline dramatically as print media has fallen out of favor. To cut costs, newspapers have been merging and operations consolidating. During initial due diligence, Kearny learned that the Olympic Plant is now one of only a handful of remaining printing presses in Southern California and nearly all newspapers distributed in SoCal are printed in the TPUB facility (WSJ and USA Today are examples). This printing facility and its parcel are now being marketed for sale.

The Site

The LA Times Olympic Plant is a 680,000 sf building on 26-acres located along Alameda Street with visibility from the I-10 freeway. The site is south of the emerging Arts District, an emerging submarket east of downtown Los Angeles. Once a thriving manufacturing center, when manufacturing still a major industry in downtowns, it has become more famous for raves in cavernous industrial buildings and for short cuts on vacant surface roads when the local freeways are jammed. The Arts District now has significant momentum with 23 residential projects under construction and more than 13,000 housing units in the pipeline. Creative office and retail have followed the rise in the local population. But the vast majority of this new investment has been north of the Olympic Plant. When asked if he would consider the Olympic Plant to be in the Arts District, a broker replied, "the Arts District isn't a well-defined place, it's a state of mind." Your boss enjoyed that one: "Spoken like a broker." There is investment heading toward the "Lower Arts District" and the Olympic Plant, but at this time it remains surrounded by more traditional industrial and manufacturing uses than those in the more energized and maturing Arts District to the north.

Tenant and Lease Overview

Tribune Publishing is the sole lessee of the buildings, situated on the back 19 acres of the site. The seven acres along Alameda can be parceled off and split from the TPUB lease. The "Remainder Property" and west half of the "Licensed Area" make up the remaining seven acres. TPUB has 7 years left on the initial lease they signed for the property. The lease also provides TPUB with two 10-year extension options at a determined Fair Market Value (FMV) rent. There is no insight into whether TPUB will want to extend after the initial lease term, but during due diligence Kearny determined that their current rent is below market.

During initial underwriting, Kearny received the following information on market rents. These rents are for the as-is re-use of the building:

- Industrial rents in the immediate area are in the $0.90–$1.00 NNN range. However, the average downtown industrial tenant is 10,000–50,000. The printing plant is over 650,000 sf and does not easily demise for multiple tenants.

- Two brokers gave ranges of market lease rates for the building of $0.70–$0.85 NNN without being able to provide much rationale for why.
- Rents at several larger buildings in Vernon/Commerce (the closest meaningful industrial market) with large contiguous available industrial spaces are leasing at $0.60–$0.70 NNN.

There is also the question of how much square footage would be considered in the market lease rate determination. There is more information on land comps and creative offices comps in the exhibits below.

Building Overview

The printing plant used to be one of three that was printing papers at full capacity for the LA Times in the 1990s. Where the facility once employed over 1000 people, peak employment is now just 45. The building was built specifically for TPUB and while the paper storage area and distribution areas are functional industrial space, the central press section would be a challenge to repurpose for an industrial tenant. The 13′ clear on the first floor would be a challenge; the third floor mezzanine 27′ above the second floor would be another. In the fair market rent determination, a broker would need to make a determination for the rent for those areas as well.

A conversion of the building to creative office is possible. The printing plant is a steel frame building and has a central clear height of nearly 70′ that can be converted into office space. Similar projects across the Arts District are under construction financed by numerous institutional investors.

Arts District Market Overview

The Arts District has drawn tremendous investment in the past decade, with top restaurants and shops coming to the area along with the influx of residents. Large residential projects have been completed with a number of other projects planned. There are also a half dozen adaptive re-use projects, turning old manufacturing properties into residential lofts and creative office spaces. While there has been an absorption of the residential space, the office absorption has been much slower with very few large tenants making the move to the area so far. The Olympic Plant sits outside of the Arts District, but recent investments have made the distance between the two shrink.

The theoretical highest value for the LA Times land would come from residential use or adaptive re-use to creative office, but entitlement issues cloud the potential to achieve residential entitlements across the site. From a market supply and demand perspective, your boss is skeptical about the viability of this location for residential use or creative office. Additionally, there is 2MM sf of creative office space coming online with limited leasing to date. The Row, an adaptive reuse of industrial manufacturing buildings across the street, has 1.5MM sf coming online without any new leasing.

Entitlement Issues

All of the development activity in the Arts District has resulted in fewer readily developable parcels left and a growing backlash against the rapid pace of change here. The scarcity of land and rising rents means that land prices are rising, but so, too, is the entitlement risk. A site as large as the Olympic Plant would be worth a considerable amount if it could be developed to its highest and best use. For now, the LA Times has a lease that on the plant itself and some immediate parking. There is, however, a remainder parcel that could be developed now, and the Olympic Plant itself could be renovated or razed to allow for other uses once the owner regains control of the site. In short, there are several entitlement issues to be considered that will depend on the long-term plans for the site.

In the near term, an owner could split the larger site and sell the seven acres of remainder land along Alameda Street. This would require a parking variance from the City that would acknowledge the limited parking needs of the printing press and enable limited parking for the back area of the site. In the longer term, an owner could then redevelop the plant area. If it were to be renovated for creative-office, it would face one set of entitlement issues; if it were to be used for residential it would face another. Both are hard to underwrite because of the politics of land use in the City, but the most pressing issue is an initiative on the ballot in November that would greatly limit development across the City. The "Neighborhood Integrity Issue" will raise the bar for attaining entitlements for meaningful developments. The Initiative would put a moratorium on large residential developments for two years and require a general plan amendment for large projects that do not conform to in-place zoning. While the November ballot may fail, there is a growing antidevelopment sentiment in Southern California which could limit the future development potential of the site.

Status of Offer

The seller has requested the best and final offer. In order to secure the deal, you need to be able to offer $120MM.

8TH & ALAMEDA COMPARABLES

Land comps (unentitled)

Property	Buyer	Size (ac)	Price ($mm)	Price (psf)	Date	Comments
6th & Alameda	Suncal/MSD Capital	14.57	130.0	205.0	Mar-15	Current income; plans for 240 units
1525 Industrial	Camden Property Trust	2.50			Jun-15	
668 Alameda	Avalon Bay	3.83	46.7	280.0	In Escrow	2-year escrow
2110 Bay Street	Bay Capital	1.75	11.5	151.0	Mar-15	Add'l cost of $650K ($8 psf) to buy out tenant
695 Santa Fe	Boluor Associates	2.30	43.0	429.0	Dec-15	Entitled for 240 units
520 Mateo	Greystar	1.84	21.5	268.0	Oct-15	Confirming buyer

Adaptive re-use office comps

Property	Buyer	Size (ac)	Price ($mm)	Price (psf)	Date	Comments
The Row (Alameda Sq)	Atlas	1,300,000	na	na	Oct-14	Part of $357 mm buyout
At Mateo	ABS/Batteis & Schnur	130,000	32.5	250.0	Jun-14	$60 mm development incl. 400 car garage
405 Mateo	Hudson Pacific	130,000	40.0	308.0	Aug-15	Purchased vacant
Ford Motor Factory	Shorenstein	254,000	37.0	146.0	Apr-14	Purchased vacant
Coca-Cola Factory	Hudson Pacific	150,000	49.0	327.0	May-15	Purchased vacant

IV.   Extra-Innings in 2018?

The original case was written in 2016, and was about underwriting these two unique deals, assembling business plans and establishing prices that Kearny would be willing to pay for them. Both were live deals at the time the case was written. At issue now in late 2018 is the deal in Irwindale, which remains unsold. But before diving into this valuation, the owner of the Kearny Real Estate Company, Jeff Dritley, wants you to make sure he is thinking about late cycle deals the right way. That is, he and his team floated bids for both deals in 2016. Kearny was not close to the accepted price at the Olympic Plant of $120MM. Jeff would like you to reverse engineer various paths from a purchase price of $120M to a 14% unlevered return. One could imagine a number of options for redeveloping the site, but could any realistically earn the target return? Given the amount of capital looking for deals in 2016, he was not surprised that someone stepped up and met the asking price, but Jeff was never going to stretch that far to be competitive at that price: he was simply too worried about too many risks. His real priority for you is underwriting the Irwindale deal, but first he wants you to explore any plausible way he could have missed something that would have allowed him to improve his offer to acquire and redevelop the Olympic Plant.

Then Jeff would then like you to underwrite bidding for the Reliance II Vulcan gravel pit. To complete both tasks, you should understand who your boss is and what he is looking for in these undertakings. Jeff Dritley is the founder and managing partner of Kearny Real Estate Company. He has made a career of finding large and complex real estate deals. Since starting Kearny as an operator/developer that focuses on value-add and opportunistic office, industrial, and land development projects in Southern California, the firm has over $4.5 billion of transactional experience, over $720MM of equity with an average return of 46% weighted average IRR. Kearny typically invests in these projects with average hold periods of 3–5 years. These investments are usually underwritten to a 20%+ IRR, but clearly have consistently outperformed this benchmark.

Surprisingly, Jeff does not believe that Kearny's 46% IRR is the product of sophisticated financial engineering, but rather of Jeff's central approach to underwriting: a good investment should have a simple narrative about how it will be profitable and some basic numbers to back it up. Counterintuitively, while the financial sector is investing heavily in AI, Big Data, and other technological advances, Jeff is locally famous for kicking junior analysts out of his office if they show up to a meeting with a complex excel model before justifying the need to build it in the first place. Jeff enjoys mentoring young professionals, but has found it more and more difficult to get them to focus on basics first and only then turning to the elaborate spread sheets. He is more than willing to engage in as much financial sophistication as needed, but he wants to see the "need" part first.

As you assemble your memo to Jeff about your the two assignments, he would like you to hold to his "Crayon Test." That is, he is not yet interested in a formal investment committee memo or an elaborate waterfall to pitch to an equity partner. At this stage, Jeff is "looking under rocks." And so, he is looking for a rigorous—if largely qualitative—story that could then warrant a more thorough underwriting. For the backward look at the bidding on the Olympic Plant, think first about the paths that might be followed by the buyer. He or she put up $120 million dollars to own an old printing press with a long-term lease—and potentially a very long lease. There are likely many nuances one could explore, but what are the basics business plans that the new owner was likely to follow? While it might be useful to have all their costs numbers, you don't have them and won't get them. But, what can you use to estimate cash flows under a number of basic strategies? Do the best you can with the numbers you have and be resourceful. If you asked Jeff about the costs associated with transforming the existing plant into creative office, he might guess $250–$350 psf. He might suggest $3.50 a sf per month for a NNN lease, but also be quick to add "No way they get to charge rent on all the square feet under that big roof. Maybe 80% of the square feet could generate the $3.50 rent." This casual approach reflects his knowledge of the market, but more importantly it is honest about the fact that it may be decades before an owner would be able to control the site and begin renovations. Even the current owner is still figuring out the costs of renovation because he's still just starting. If he doesn't know, how would anyone else know? This is where the Crayon Test reveals its power. There is no perfect data for the questions being asked of these large, complex, and singular deals. But that means that you have to be resourceful. This may be hard, but the alternative is just guessing or going back to competing with all the others who are chasing simple deals.

Please read over Jeff's "Crayon Test" and prepare a response that will not get you thrown out of his office.

Crayon Test

Don't turn a computer on until you have thought through these issues.

Goal of this is to help us all to <u>Turn</u> <u>Lots</u> of <u>Rocks</u> Efficiently.

We need to turn 100 rocks to find something interesting under 10 rocks. If we close one of those 10 that's pretty good.

- How are the "stars and moon" aligning to allow Kearny to be successful buyer and then make value/add or opportunistic returns? What are the "Deal Dynamics"?

- What chance do we have to win the deal?

- How is Kearny adding value? Will we get good bang for the buck with Cap-X improvements?

- Who is the Seller? Optics of buying from some can be tough.

- Is it good real estate – what are the "bones" – location, market, adequate parking, good access, visibility, bay depths, loading, etc.?

- Are we serving the capital's needs or does Kearny have capital relationships (equity & debt) that would be interested in the opportunity and does Kearny experience give us credibility?

- Will we bid the opportunity with a partner or alone as Kearny?

- Does the opportunity line up well with where we are in the cycle?

- What is "whisper" price and exit sale price psf; how do they compare to replacement cost and are they compelling?

- What is the spread between yield on cost and sales cap rate?

- What are the other assumptions that will "drive" the model and why are they good objective base case assumptions? These assumptions drive the answer the model spits out – remember GIGO. Get sign off on assumptions before turning on computer.

  - Market Rent
  - Rent Growth
  - Expenses
  - Capital Expenditures

  - Tenant Improvements
  - Absorption period
  - Debt Assumptions
  - Exit Cap Rate

KEARNY
Real Estate Company

2·28·18

Exhibit A—The Crayon Test.

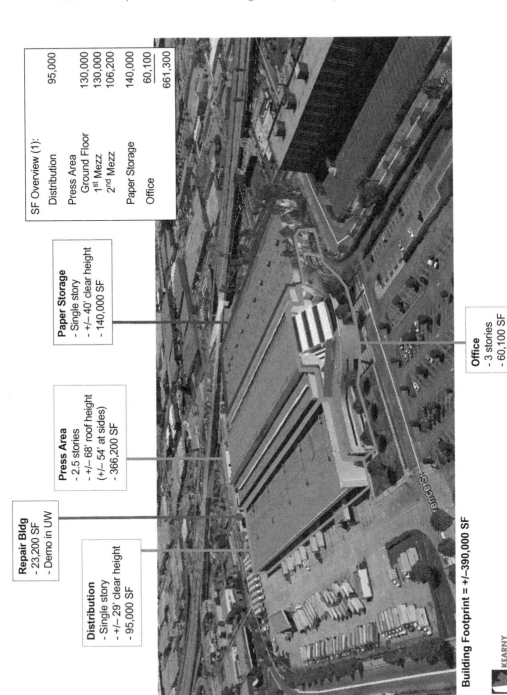

SF Overview (1):

Distribution	95,000
Press Area	
Ground Floor	130,000
1st Mezz	130,000
2nd Mezz	106,200
Paper Storage	140,000
Office	60,100
	661,300

Paper Storage
- Single story
- +/− 40' clear height
- 140,000 SF

Office
- 3 stories
- 60,100 SF

Press Area
- 2.5 stories
- +/− 68' roof height
  (+/− 54' at sides)
- 366,200 SF

Repair Bldg
- 23,200 SF
- Demo in UW

Distribution
- Single story
- +/− 29' clear height
- 95,000 SF

Building Footprint = +/−390,000 SF

KEARNY

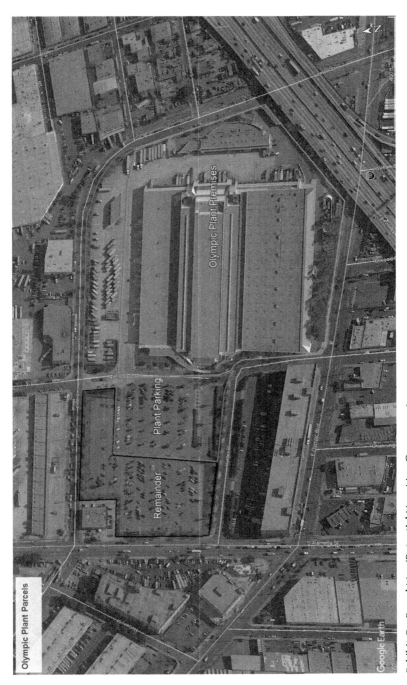

Exhibit C—Parcel Map/Potential New Map Components.

Case 19

The Minnifield Parcel

It's the third developer who makes money. I'm just not sure if we're number two or number three.

I. Prologue

Sitting at the intersection of two prominent major streets in the core of a gateway city, the "Minnifield parcel" had seen plenty of suitors over the years—but no wedding. The last engagement started when Minnifield Properties tied up the site in 2005 with the intent of developing the acre-plus parcel. But Minnifield missed its chance at success with the downturn in 2008. Minnifield hadn't been in the practice of buying unentitled land, but the market in 2005 was white hot and the seller at the time would not budge on more time for due diligence, let alone a risky and time-consuming entitlement process. Minnifield closed anyhow and then spent considerable time and money on design and entitlements, but couldn't complete them in time to avoid the downturn. By the end of 2008, all work had stopped. First, because valuations dropped significantly, the construction lender stopped allowing draws from the construction loan. Then because Minnifield was unable raise more equity to fund work or remargin the construction loan, there were no funds to keep moving forward. Minnifield held off the inevitable by declaring bankruptcy. But in the end, Minnifield couldn't find a way to reorganize and opted for a straight liquidation. This meant that the sale of one of the best parcels in downtown. Every real estate professional in the region was familiar with the drama, and the site became known as the "Minnifield Parcel."

Unlike previous downturns, the lender on the Minnifield parcel did not immediately start foreclosure. The site was at the intersection of a great location in the CBD of one of the so-called "gateway" cities. Even though valuations were down, they weren't down as far as those of other cities. The lender didn't want to hold the parcel on its books and was hopeful that Minnifield could find more equity given the premier location. This had been a costly acquisition and had only been possible due to optimistic underwriting by all the capital providers—making an oft-quoted truism apt here: "Have trouble with a small loan? It's your problem. Have trouble with a big loan? It's the bank's problem." The 2005 acquisition loan was very large and significantly impaired by 2009. And so after

Underwriting Commercial Real Estate in a Dynamic Market. https://doi.org/10.1016/B978-0-12-815989-7.00019-7
217

some delay—and despite the bankruptcy filing—the bank was allowed to engage a third-party developer to continue processing the entitlements in an effort to add value to the collateral backed by the loan.

By 2012, the progress made on the entitlements and interim market recovery would allow the bank to be fully repaid. Now the bankruptcy judge is close to agreeing to terms to sell the Minnifield parcel to Turner Partners, with your firm, Morrow Investments as the equity partner in a joint venture, on the condition that the loan and all unsecured claims within the bankruptcy be repaid at par. Turner is a well-respected regional developer. Morrow is a private equity firm that has had a great run since spinning off from a blue-chip Wall Street firm a decade earlier. Chris Corbett is a managing director for Morrow and it is his responsibility to shape the terms of the deal between Turner and Morrow.

II. The Development

Turner and Morrow have agreed in principle on the development plan. The acre-plus site has been upzoned for residential and commercial use of up to 2,000,000 sf. The partial entitlement that Minnifield obtained with help from a City-sponsored environmental impact report (EIR) means that the remaining approval process should take 24 to 36 months to complete. Turner and Morrow would then face a decision about whether to develop the site themselves, partner with others, flip the property, or find other exit points going forward. Based on some current market analysis, the unlevered annual IRR for a development of residential and office uses is about 20% and a 2.2× equity multiple over a horizon that had them seeing through the entitlement and selling the residential land piece after three years and the office land after five years.

The estimates behind these returns included land costs at about $62 psf of buildable square feet, needing about $75 psf of buildable sf to finish design and entitlements. The cost of the land and the hard and soft costs to develop the property would be in the more than $750 psf of buildable area. Given the land basis, the untrended yield on cost for the office development was 7.8%, while the residential development yield would be just about 7.1%. Both of these are in excess of market yields today.

III. The Joint Venture

Turner is a good partner, bringing local and regional development experience to the table. It has a history of successful large-scale developments—not a large as this one, but enough to suggest that the firm is capable of developing the Minnifield site. Turner would be the sponsor and developer of the site. Turner would put up 5% of required equity, and would be asking for significant developer fees and some elements of control. For its purposes, Morrow will be writing a very large check to close this deal and fund the design and entitlements necessary to create value on the site. In providing 95% of the needed equity, Morrow wanted to have control of essentially everything.

Having two parties be at odds over issues of control is typical with millions of dollars at stake. Chris Corbett had seen a lot of these negotiations, but knew each was unique because of variations in the cycle, the property, the location, and the principals involved. The control issues they needed to agree on included: who would control the decision to obtain debt on the property; who would control the decision to proceed with the vertical construction; who would be the developer if going vertical indeed happened; who would earn fees in the process, and, last but not least, who would control the decision (the date and the amount) of a sale. Turner and Morrow saw the fundamentals the same way: there was a good return to be had. The tension, inherent to these deals, was about sharing risk and return along the way to a good outcome.

IV.   The Challenge

Your role is to help Chris Corbett think through how best to navigate the joint venture agreement between Turner and Morrow. As an employee of Morrow and a co-investor in the Minnifield property, Chris is motivated to maximize his return. But he knows that if he pushes too hard, he runs that risk that he will lose his partner and perhaps the bid for the Minnifield property as it exits the bankruptcy process.

Your job is to think through the elements of a joint venture agreement that enshrines a thoughtful and thorough negotiation with Turner. Chris is already aware of several key issues. You should address these, and go beyond them as well.

Chris has identified two broad categories of control:

General control

- What are the elements of control that need to be agreed upon?
- What are the natural tensions between these two partners?
- What sort of agreements exist typically? Is this market or property typical? Is Turner "different" in a way that would suggest that an atypical JV agreement is warranted?

Specific control issues

Understanding that "control" is all-encompassing, how would you think through these issues in particular?

- Development fees, acquisition fees, management fees
- The use and terms of debt in the development and entitlement phase
- The decision to sell early if the chance arises
- The decision to delay selling if the need arises
- The ability of the partners to invest more if needed
- The terms of the equity waterfall as cash flow warrants

Your charge is to rethink the Minnifield development plan and help Chris make sure he has considered the components to the joint venture agreement with regard to control. In the same way that a general contractor has a "punch list" to make sure he/she doesn't forget anything in completing a structure, Chris needs a guide for completing his joint venture agreement with Turner: a comprehensive set of control issues, an explanation of why they are relevant, a guess as to which party will care more and why, the set of issues that either party might consider nonnegotiable, and an estimate of the compensation that either party will need to agree to a deal. This is a qualitative exercise, but feel free to make use of the numbers from the land residuals below.

In the end, Morrow needs to decide if it will invest 95% of this very large project. To do this, it will need to understand the return that can be expected and a full understanding of the risks it faces in buying the Minnifield parcel in partnership with Turner.

Questions/issues to explore as you construct your "Punchlist"

a. Do you understand the development process? The development of the Minnifield parcel would be an enormous project. The Minnifield parcel is unique in the same way every parcel of real estate is inherently unique. It stands out because its size, its location, and its recent history, but how is it different than any other development?

b. Who controls the site now? Can they develop it now? Why don't they?

c. It appears that Turner initiated the deal and sought out conversations with Morrow. Does Turner need Morrow? Does Morrow need Turner? What role will each play as partners? Which role is more important? Should either side earn an outsized return? Or should this deal be *pari passu*—"shoulder to shoulder"—with Turner and Morrow sharing proceeds in proportion to their investment?

d. Given that Turner "found" the deal, should it control the project? Given that Morrow is considering writing a check for 95% of the deal, should they control the project?

e. Who is bearing more risk? Turner is a much smaller firm and its 5% coninvest may represent a much bigger stake of its worth relative to Morrow's. Clearly Morrow is writing a bigger check, so more is at stake in absolute terms, but it is also a very large private equity firm. Does this matter?

f. It might be useful to return to the structure of development and generate an anticipated timeline for events and decisions. As you develop this timeline, consider what might go wrong at each point.
  - Who will be responsible for closing on the purchase? What if one of the two parties fails to provide their share of the equity?
  - What if there are additional costs prior to closing? After closing? During construction? Who is responsible for covering them and what will the return be for the additional costs? For example, if Morrow is asked to cover cost overruns, should Morrow get those funds paid back before dol-

lars are distributed to the partners? Aren't cost overruns under control of Turner as the sponsor/developer? Why should Morrow pay when Turner should have kept on budget?

- Once closed, who will decide on the entitlement plan and timing? What if the controlling party decides to pursue an aggressive reentitlement of a much larger project? What if the controlling party decides to forego the final steps of the remaining entitlement issues so as to avoid any entitlement risk and begin development now? Given the purchase price, this might make for an attractive return, but a return that is likely to be significantly smaller than under the current plan of 2 million square feet. Who benefits from taking the safe route?
- Who decides when the property is developed? Sold? Refinanced? Etc.

Again, build the development timeline and consider options along that path as well as surprises from other stakeholders, the site, the weather, and the market.

g. It might also be useful to explore some scenarios. These need not be comprehensive, but should allow you to begin to see the issues that a JV structure needs to consider. The land residual analysis below should provide rough numbers to allow for explicit modeling of the scenarios below.

(1) "Sprint to Make the Cycle"—here the partners decide to push hard to get everything built quickly. Who would make this possible? If Turner's developer's fee is based on time, wouldn't this result in a smaller fee to Turner? Is this "fair?"

(2) Endless design—The Minnifield parcel is a large, complex urban site with lots of issues to resolve. What if the design team—which is essential for a large project like this—is slow to resolve design issues like massing and materials, even…maybe even especially…finishes? It may produce a great outcome, but it may also cost a lot of time. Who suffers for the delay? Who suffers from cutting off the design discussion and applying for building permits?

(3) Foreign buyer—A year into an 18-month entitlement process, what if a foreign buyer approaches Turner and Morrow to inquire about an all-cash deal? Assume the price would give the partnership a 20% IRR to date. This would remove a long list of risks. Who benefits from the quick offer? Think about how each party in the JV is compensated. What happens to each to them if they sell to the foreign buyer?

(4) Market slowdown/pick up—What if the recovery is illusory and real estate prices fall by 15%? Should the partnership continue development? Who suffers for the delay? What if the current recovery is just getting underway and the project becomes more valuable? Who should earn an extra-normal return? Does either scenario suggest a different plan going forward?

(5) Go vertical—Perhaps the simplest issue on this list, both parties have long track records of breaking ground and commencing the building

phase. But do both parties feel the same about when it's time to start demolition and site preparation? Should that happen before receiving entitlements? Before getting permits? Who bears the risk of either choice? Is there an upside to starting early? Who benefits?

(6) Lever up—Another issue that is very familiar to both parties, but getting debt on a property is not simple. Which loan? What type? What term? Is there recourse? Who benefits from debt? Who bears additional risk?

This may seem like a large and complex deal, and it is. The key to helping Chris will be first, understanding how development works in principle, and then revisiting that framework with the particulars of the Minnifield parcel, the sponsor Turner, and the equity partner—Morrow. The goal is to reach the best deal possible that is acceptable to both parties. It might be best to take turns putting yourself in both Turner and Morrow's shoes and asking if each is being paid according to the skills they bring and the risks they bear.

The deliverables for this exercise are:

(1) A brief memo that provides a JV "punch list," enumerating key issues and how the partners should share the risks and returns for each.
(2) The top three key risks for Morrow. Chris is your boss and he will need to be made aware of these and why you see them as such.
(3) A prospectus on the chances of finding agreement with Turner. Can Morrow and Turner find a JV agreement that allows both of them to say yes and for both to succeed?

Exhibits–Office/Residential Land Residuals

	RSF	GSF
Office area	1,317,457	1,442,365
Residential area	473,950	557,635
Total area	*1,791,407*	*2,000,000*

	Office	Residential
	$ Total	$ Total
Land basis	93,105	23,276
Hold-out parcels	17,770	—
Entitlement costs	6031	2332
Hard costs	414,997	189,588
Soft costs	101,852	17,319
Tenant improvements	92,814	995

	RSF	GSF
Leasing commissions	31,619	1147
Site/permit/impact fees	72,156	12,050
Vacation of streets	790	197
Tenant buyout costs	247	31,600
Demolition	3455	–
Total unlevered costs	*834,836*	*278,504*
FSG rent	98,809	29,576
Other income	–	118
Parking	931	444
Total gross rent	*99,740*	30,139
Operating expenses	(15,792)	(4364)
RE taxes	(14,351)	(4788)
NNN rent	70,497	20,987
General vacancy	(4987)	(1205)
NOI	65,510	19,782
Untrended yield on cost	7.8%	7.1%
Market development margin	7.0%	6.0%
Implied land value	218,710	77,000
Implied land value per GSF	151.63	138.08

Case 20

Do Cycles Die of Old Age? Or Is 10 the New 6?

I. Introduction

At the end of 2017, almost 10 years into the current real estate cycle, Edgar Waite faced a big decision. He had been working for an office/industrial operator focused on Southern California since finishing graduate school four years earlier. Edgar learned a lot, took on a much larger role over time, and became an integral part of the conversations senior managers were having about key investments. While Edgar felt ahead of schedule with regard to his understanding of real estate, he didn't feel like he was ever going to be a partner on the senior management team. His classmates were doing well, but most didn't have the responsibility he had on projects that could cost $100M dollars. These were big, complex real estate deals and Edgar was integral to every phase. Yet when the time came for a "go/no-go decision," Edgar was asked for advice, but had no voting power.

Edgar understood this was how it would be from the beginning of his time at the firm. His mentor had been terrific, investing time with Edgar and giving him as much responsibility as he could handle. But control always remained with the principals, who had different goals than Edgar. They were later in their careers and beginning to ask questions about wealth preservation; for them the prospect of a home run deal would be welcome, but not enough to make up for a significant loss. Earlier they had focused on taking "good risks." It had not been about the level of risk because the principals were comfortable with all sorts of complex and messy deals. Rather, it had been about making sure the expected returns would compensate them for it. They were disciplined about not over-extending themselves and were able to find success where more conservative investors would never go. Edgar felt the principals' definition of a "looking for good risks" had recently evolved into simply avoiding risk.

Edgar's growing frustration was rooted in the fact that the principals were getting more patient and more selective in the projects they chose to pursue because they believed that the real estate cycle was growing old. His boss had told him early on that "Most cycles don't get killed, they die of old age. You can look for a smoking gun, but it's just time. By about six years, I start seeing gray hairs." It would be several years before he had the confidence to push back, but

Underwriting Commercial Real Estate in a Dynamic Market. https://doi.org/10.1016/B978-0-12-815989-7.00020-3

had started to when they began to get cautious. Edgar spoke up: "Cycles might die of old age, but maybe we're living longer." Referring to his boss's benchmark 6-year cycle, he ventured "Maybe '10' is the new six. Maybe we have a couple of good years ahead of us." Edgar fully understood the logic behind increased caution, but it had beginning to cost him financially—his compensation has always been dependent on acquisitions and execution on the deals they acquired. Being passive would have a longer term impact as well. Deal flow and fees paid the bills at the firm, and without positive fee income there would be a much smaller bonus. Edgar had also been able to negotiate for the ability to coinvest with the partners' equity, and it was the promoted interest from those investments that Edgar saw as the key to his own financial security in the future. He could live frugally if necessary, but it hurt him to see time pass without having funds invested in creating long-term value.

Edgar's classmates have gone through their own adjustments; like Edgar, many had used their first four years after graduation to dive in aggressively to master their respective roles. But, like Edgar, many were also looking for their next steps after a few years. Edgar's classmates stayed in touch and it felt that every time they got together one of them would declare a need for a change. Some got the promotion they wanted, but others moved to jobs with competitors, some set up their own shops and replicated their experiences in other cities—often in the cities or towns where they grew up. Others changed direction entirely, with one friend returning to brokerage and another joining a pension fund advisory firm. Both realized that the developer's business model was just not for them. The "eat what you kill" approach to life made it too stressful. And while his friend who returned to brokerage would have the same basic structure, he was just more confident that he would be more successful hunting there.

Late last year, it was Edgar's time to feel the itch and find his own next step. It didn't take long. Several quiet lunches and coffees later, a classmate put him in touch with a new private equity firm. The founder was one of the managers at a big institutional private equity firm on the West Coast. She, too, found herself looking for a next step and decided to start her own firm. She announced she would be leaving and starting looking for a small team that would have to be able to do everything. She would have a deep set of investors and lender connections and some seed funding, but would quickly have to get some deals rolling if she was going to have any operating cash flow. It sounded risky, but also perfectly matched Edgar's perspective on investing.

The founder and Edgar hit it off and he received an offer. The work would be similar to what he'd been doing and enjoying at his previous firm, and compensation would still be tilted toward closing deals and executing on them. But, the control of major decisions would be shared. The investment committee would be comprised of four real estate professionals. Because he was not a founder nor could he invest as much as the others, Edgar would not have an equal vote, but he would have a significant one. And just like that, Edgar was off. It all happened almost too quickly. He had been talking about changing jobs with his wife for some time, but the considerable risk made the two of them wrestle with what it could mean for their family. With kids and a mortgage, there was real risk to their current income and quality of life. But staying at his previous firm posed a different risk. They both felt that this was the right time to be aggressive. Maybe later, he'd find himself with his old firm's principals emphasizing preservation, but for now he was interested in wealth creation.

Today, Edgar is a director at the new firm. He has a broader mandate and a much larger scope for investment. He will cover more product types than before and be able to reach more markets across the West Coast. Given how lean the new team will be, he will also have a fair bit of autonomy. Importantly, because the firm is just starting, it won't have the luxury of sitting out the rest of the cycle; Edgar and the team will need to show investors that they're active and good at finding opportunities—even in what feels like the waning years of a long bull market.

II.   Allocator Funds Versus Operators/Developers

In a typical real estate transaction, there is an operator (also called a developer or sponsor) that runs the acquisition and manages the day-to-day operations of a project, and an equity partner who (as the name suggests) provides the bulk of the equity but has much less say in the day-to-day operations. In the large majority of cases, the equity partner provides 90% or more of the equity and retains control over major decisions (financing, major leases, holding period, etc.). The sponsor and the equity partner play different roles, invest differently, and are compensated differently. It is common for the equity partner to get a preference in terms of timing of repayment, but it is also common for the sponsor to earn an outsized return if the deal goes well. If the sponsor invests, say, 2% of the required equity, it can earn many multiples of its equity when the project exceeds its pro forma numbers. The equity partner and sponsor form a joint venture agreement that outlines many of the rights and responsibilities of the project. Among them is a so-called "waterfall structure" that is negotiated at the outset of the project. For example, if a project achieves a deal-level 20% IRR, then a typical equity partner might receive an 18%–19% IRR while the sponsor can hit a return of 30% or more. In this sense, the sponsor is working for "the promote"—a return in excess of the share s/he originally invested.

Different joint venture (JV) agreements are structured differently in terms of fees and operating income that goes to pay employees and cover overhead. Operators can typically receive an acquisition fee, some sort of management or development fee, and hopefully a promote from successful deals. Promotes are hard to rely on as sources of business operation costs, so typically operators are focused on fees to cover their expenses. The promote is where the majority of real estate wealth is created, and principals can keep it for themselves (as they are typically the ones who put in the required coinvest) or split it with key employees. But because of where the bulk of the wealth is created, operators are focused on projects that can return a meaningful promote. They will take on fee deals to "keep the lights on" but they are looking for upside—not an opportunity to become fee developers.

Real estate private equity funds are structured a bit differently. Of the money raised through funds, a private equity firm can charge a fee on committed capital—the fund equity actually invested in real estate. As the equity group grows and invests more, there is more fee income to go around. Equity funds also typically structure their compensation with fund investors using a waterfall, but these deals typically involve a fund-level waterfall, with every property in the fund contributing to the total cash flows throughout. If things go well and there is a promote, it can take seven or more years to pay out because it won't be clear if a promote has been earned until the final properties in the fund are sold. Another important feature that is typical of these types of fund structures is that fees are earned only on committed capital—on actual equity invested in a property. There is a natural tension in these funds: on one hand there is a desire for equity groups to continue deploying capital to earn these fees; on the other, investing capital into a bad deal may result in bad outcomes in the future. Of course, the fund managers are heavily incentivized to find good deals because of the waterfall and the embedded promotes. But, if they can't find a good deal, there still is a temptation to invest anyway, earning the acquisition and management fees today and worrying about returns later.

Between these two models, individual compensation will vary greatly. Operators typically offer lower annual compensation but with larger bonuses if promotes are earned. Positions at private equity funds typically offer higher annual salaries and bonuses, but with a lower likelihood of hitting it big in any given year.

III. Edgar's Firm and Its First Fund

Edgar was new to the firm, and the firm was also just getting up and running. In addition to all the challenges of starting a new enterprise, it also faced an immediate need to find equity. While the bulk of the fundraising responsibilities would be with his new boss, Edgar would need to support her work by convincing investors that they could earn a better return with the new firm than with any other—including the firms they all just left. The team planned to target opportunistic and value-add type returns. Strategically, it was looking to move away from the intense competition in larger deals, targeting as little as $5M per transaction where most of the larger equity groups impose a minimum of $20M.

Edgar's boss was able to attract a first investor to back her desire to start the new firm, so the team started halfway to its goal of $100M for its first fund. Other potential investors might listen to what they planned to do but soon they would ask about their track record. In this regard, Edgar will be asked on every one he proposes: "how will this deal perform in terms of returns and in terms of fundraising?" As much as they needed to find good deals to generate fee income, they also needed to book some wins that they can use to market themselves. Deals that may seem promising to the team but that may be poorly received by investors might need to be ignored. Indeed, submarkets, certain product types and certain types of deals will need to be turned down if they make potential investors too nervous. Edgar left a conservative firm to find good investments, taking risks his previous firm would not. But while his new firm was ready to be more aggressive, it still had to convince its equity partners that the risk and return trade-offs were good ones.

Edgar did the basic math: the investors were comfortable with some risk and wanted a target net return in the range of 13%–15% IRR. So with those target investor returns in mind and an eye to the fund waterfall structure, Edgar estimated that he would have to find deals that earned something close to an 18% IRR in order for the fund to achieve a promote. 18% IRR deals do not grown on trees.

IV. Current Economic Overview

Edgar reviewed the team's notes on the current market:

- Unemployment hit a cycle-low of 3.7%, but employment growth was not exceptional relative to the last 8 years. And wage growth is still under 3%, with the majority of wage growth occurring in the upper end of the distribution, though there were some signs that low-end wage earners were beginning to catch up.
- Inflation had finally reached the Federal Reserve Board target of 2% annual growth. Despite a decade below the threshold, the Fed was keen to prevent inflation from getting any serious momentum and was on pace to raise rates four times over the year, for a total raise of 100 basis points. The 10-year treasury was just over 3.0% and the yield curve flattened significantly over the year.
- Construction costs have risen over 10% annually for the past 2 years, driven by labor shortages, material costs, and tariffs.
- GDP growth in 2Q18 was 4.2%, spurred by corporate tax breaks. GDP growth is expected to revert to 3% over the balance of the year.
- Stock market continues climbing with strong corporate earnings.

Overall, the feel is that growth has been slow and steady during the 10-year recovery since the last recession, but also that the United States is overdue for a correction. In real estate, there are numerous headwinds given the cost of construction and rising interest rates. New development is getting harder to justify and across the industry, people feel that their base case pro forma for many projects will only be hit if everything goes well, that there is no longer some upside case that can deliver stronger returns.

V. Investment Options and Deliverables

With the larger context in mind, Edgar's job was to source new investment opportunities. Clearly, there were a lot of boxes to check to make a deal possible, but added to this was the pressure of having some "early wins" to help convince investors that this fund would outperform its peers this late in a cycle so that Edgar's firm could look ahead at Fund II and a deeper flow of fees to grow the firm. In his old position at the office/industrial operator, he would have been able to stay on the sidelines if the deals he found weren't really good ones. But he now needed to show his investors that he was earning the fees they were paying. It would be important to find a deal, and soon. There are a few investments gaining traction internally, but each one still feels like you're stretching to hit your target returns.

Edgar very much liked the new management approach to sourcing deals. Given their flexibility, it was almost paralyzing to figure out what to do next. There were so many deals and so many markets to underwrite that he needed help prioritizing them and developing some investment strategies to help focus his search. The four professionals at the new firm would meet weekly to handle nuts and bolts issues to move underwriting along, but they always spent significant time thinking about the big trends that shaped real estate. While it was easy to get caught up in recent deals, it was here—thinking about larger fundamentals—that Edgar needed help.

As a hypothetical fifth member of the team, your task is to help Edgar respond to last week's team meeting. They had agreed to four basic areas of potential investment that could largely satisfy their capital partners. The four areas are not necessarily specific deals, but rather broad investment theses. There are particulars, but consider them representative of the four options. Edgar wants to lead the conversation on these potential areas of investment. How would you prioritize them? How do you assess and mitigate strategic risks for each? Do you think following any one of them will lead to investments that will advance Edgar's new firm?

Edgar would like to lead the discussion about strategic directions at the next weekly investment meeting with the team. No matter which direction they choose, they will look of relative bargains using all the usual tactics, but they now face a higher-level question about investment fundamentals. Assuming they get fair pricing on any individual deal, which submarket is the best bet? Which product type? They can readily see which of these have performed well looking backward, but which will continue to do well and which are already overinvested? The underlying structure of this task is essentially about beating the market: which strategies do to the market fundamentally have wrong? If markets were efficient, the team could pick at random, right? But, recent history says that while markets may tend to efficiency, they may never get there as other fundamentals keep shifting before reaching equilibrium. Edgar has to find a market that is out of equilibrium and one in which he can exploit to find an extra-normal return. If their investments outperform, his firm will be able to raise more capital in the future and allow Edgar to begin to create his own wealth. Below are the four that the team started with and their summary notes from last week's meeting.

Southern California Multifamily Development

This cycle has been good for multifamily development. Rental growth since the downturn has been strong and there were plenty of opportunities and sites earlier in the cycle. In recent years, rents kept rising, but construction costs went up even faster. Yet projects that are being completed or are nearing completion still seem like they'll do fine given how compressed cap rates have remained. You have friends who work for other groups who made investments in 2015 and while you'd think the deals would be hitting it out of the park, given the final construction costs, only modest returns are expected.

Looking into the future, big questions about rising interest rates and the continued growth of construction costs might be having an impact and resulting in fewer development deals getting done.

That said, your firm is still seeing an ample supply of multifamily development opportunities in and around Los Angeles. Generally, these deals all show the same metrics: the return on cost ranges from 5.5%–6.0% depending on the location, but typically around 100–125 bps above current going-in cap rates. But nobody feels good about projecting flat cap rates 3–4 years into the future as these projects are complete, and any increase in cap rates would negatively impact project returns. Rent growth is slowing so it feels like achieving rents above pro forma is unlikely.

When you analyze these opportunities, it will become immediately obvious how sensitive returns are to changes in costs or exit cap rates. With only modest changes in either one can quickly lose profitability. Yet the fundamentals also tell you that Southern California still has a shortage of housing and that the market should be able to absorb additional projects coming online.

San Diego Infill Industrial Development

Industrial has been booming due to the huge demand from the shift to ecommerce. Southern California has historic low vacancy rates even with strong development activity across the region. Many submarkets have recorded sub-1% vacancy. As demand has risen, supply has struggled to keep up and rents have been growing at 10%+ annually in many markets. On the sale side, institutions are hungry to add to their industrial portfolios and cap rates have been pushed to record lows, even hitting sub-4% for Class A product. Both these factors have driven developers to pay record-setting amounts for industrial land.

Similar to residential development, all the increased demand put strains on contractors, labor, and materials—so costs to construct new projects have been growing substantially and consistently.

Your fund's investors are aware of the macro trends and would love to be able to invest in the industrial space in San Diego. This is much harder to do when looking for mid-teens returns, so any industrial investment almost certainly means building smaller buildings to sell.

As an example of deals Edgar might find consider an opportunity to develop in Sorrento Mesa in San Diego County. San Diego industrial is a bit different from the larger SoCal distribution market and is driven more by biotech and manufacturing than straightforward distribution which is the main catalyst in Los Angeles County. That said, the industrial market in San Diego has been on fire as well and there are limited opportunities for developable sites.

The site you are reviewing has a gross area of 25 acres, but the site is on a hillside and the net area is only six acres. This site has been on the market for over 25 years and nobody has ever been able to make sense of the grading work and costs needed to prepare the site for development. Once the 6 acres are completed, the site allows for three small buildings totaling 84,000 sf, intersected by a fairly steep ramp into and out of the site. Not only are the grading costs substantial, but building smaller buildings is much more expensive than the big boxes being built in the Inland Empire due to lost efficiencies in construction.

The net cost to finish the land is $35 per land ft and the finished cost for the buildings would be $225 per building sf. While you feel good about the location (land in the South Bay of Los Angeles is trading at $60 per land ft and although far superior compared to the subject, Sorrento Mesa is the best market in San Diego), the basis in the building feels terrible. Even though they are small and could be offered for sale, very few areas in Southern California are getting close to these prices on user sale buildings. And you'd need to exit at $290 psf at rents of $1.40 NNN to hit your returns. Both that rent assumption and the sale price feel extremely aggressive.

While getting an industrial project under your belt in Southern California would be great for fundraising, you need to weigh the risks to future returns of investing in this project today.

Las Vegas Office Investment

For many in the institutional world, "Las Vegas" has terrible connotations. Many investors lost huge sums in the City in the Great Recession, and the memory is fresh in many minds. But Las Vegas has diversified and is one of the fastest growing cities in the United States. Affordable housing, low taxes and jobs are bringing many new residents and businesses to the City. A contact in Las Vegas sent Edgar a lead on a deal there that could be reflective of a creative way to enter than market.

An operator has tied up seven office buildings in Las Vegas from different owners and is looking to assemble the needed capital to close the deals. He is optimistic about the future in Las Vegas and is asking for Edgar to provide equity capital above a 70% acquisition loan to back the seven purchases. In particular, Edgar and his firm would provide equity between the 70% loan and 90% position in the capital stack with the operator funding the remaining 10% with his own equity.

Two of the office acquisitions are completely vacant, but they are not, in fact, stand-alone office buildings. There two acquisitions are office components within a larger mixed use project that has been condoized. These office properties are in two- and three-story buildings, both with retail on the ground floor, in which the retail is owned separately and not part of this acquisition. The other five properties would be purchased from a well-known institutional group who bought a very large office portfolio in 2012 at the bottom of the market and have made extraordinary returns on their investment. Currently, these five buildings are 85% leased in aggregate, with the vacancy in just two of the projects. The fully occupied three buildings of the five have new leases. The operator feels that there is some room to flip out of these leased buildings, to book some gain but also to lower his basis on the remaining four properties. It would be the vacant condoized offices and the two partially occupied office buildings that the operator would aim to fill with good tenants at high rents and then sell.

The investment is a bit of a headscratcher because there are so many moving parts and has taken a couple of phone calls to understand. The crucial parts of the deal are the operator and a continued improvement in the office market in Las Vegas. The operator has a history of out-hustling the competition and getting leases done with large companies, many before even closing his deals. And he is in talks with some very large corporations on leases for some of the vacancies in the seven-building portfolio while in escrow. But he is also paying top dollar for these assets and will need to sell them at record high pricing and record low cap rates in Las Vegas for him to earn a return. If you were to invest in his portfolio, the optics could be terrible. You would be buying five of the buildings—which have a very limited value-add story—from a partnership which has done extremely well on the investment, and the two vacant office condo interests were bought six months prior for half the price that is currently being offered. The current seller of the office condos bought these properties in auction but has done nothing with the property and will still double their money. Where would the "value-add" be for you if the previous owner has already extracted a lot of value?

All that scares Edgar and makes him skeptical about spending any more time on a deal as messy and one that looks more like gambling than value-added investment, but the reason this it could make sense is that the joint venture agreement would give Edgar's firm priority in terms of earning a return. Of the $100 MM of capital needed for the project, a senior lender would be providing roughly 70% and then your investment in the portfolio would not be as the owner but as a capital provider to another operator. Your offer would be the capital from the 70% loan up to 90% of the capital stack. The operator will be coming in with his own money (and some money he has raised from friends and family) for the final $10 MM of the stack. You have provided terms that would see you get your investment back and a 15% return before the operator would get any of their money back. Plus you would share in 10% of the cashflow after your preferred investment (plus accrual) is repaid. With this structure, the operator can get wiped out very quickly, but would also make even more money if he executes as planned. So, while this is not an investment Edgar would like to make as the operator, in this deal he doesn't have to.

While this deal is actually an option for your now, Edgar is beginning to find that there are other optimistic operators in Las Vegas who share some enthusiasm for better fundamentals going forward. If you could argue that they are right, then there's likely more deals to be done like this one.

Preferred Equity/Mezz Options

The creative or risky option of providing equity to others is a broader category Edgar and the team want to consider further. On many investments, underwriting seems very aggressive and it is uncomfortable to invest at current pricing. It is late in the cycle and it is getting hard to find deals, but there really is no choice. Instead of passing, you could offer operators preferred equity or mezzanine debt. Similar to the position on the Las Vegas deal, this allows the operator to put more money in, but keep more of the upside. And in any potential downturn, any losses would first be borne by the operator. By not taking this "last dollar risk," you're still able to make investments with a lower basis. And if the market really takes a turn, you could end up owning the property at a discount to what the original operator bought or developed the property for. Typically, you can offer to go up to 85% of the capital stack.

The problem is that the typical rate for these investments don't hit your returns. The market is still competitive with lots of groups looking to deploy capital and this space can be filled by other equity groups or higher leverage lenders. The rates for these types of investments are typically 12%–13% with a 1% origination and exit fee. On a 3-year hold, this typically gets you to a 14%–15% IRR, which after the fund management fees and promote, net your fund investors a 12% return. While this may be great for a 2018-vintage fund, it's not what you're promising your investors and won't earn any meaningful promote for the fund. Of course, it things go badly and Edgar ends up taking over for the operator, he will essentially have purchased the deal at a significantly lower price than the operator paid. Maybe the upside could be from the recovery on the next cycle. This might not help Edgar earn a promote and might not keep investors happy either.

VI. Conclusion/Recommendation

These are the broad investment directions on the table. While several are actual deals that could be considered, there are a ton of details to go through with regard to them. And those will only be necessary if the team feels that one of the broader investment theses is worth pursuing. However, the deals above can be used as examples of what Edgar and his team might find in each. Certainly, they can be used to explore risks and returns. And, this trade-off is the crux of the question Edgar is posing to you. Which is the best bet? Among the four very broad investment theses, how would you rank them? If you found a fair deal from any, what's the expected return? How bad could things be? Importantly, what are the upside risks for the four?

The team needs to show that it is active and pull the trigger on some investments in order to attract future investors to the fund. At the same time, they can't mess up on the first fund and overpay for an unnecessarily risky asset. The success of these help investments will determine whether or not a second fund is possible and if the business will succeed.

The data in the four theses are scarce. You will need to make some assumptions, but this level of analysis is almost easier than underwriting a specific property because so many 10,000foot level summaries of activity are available online. Find some and then see if you can understand recent trends and can anticipate which trends should persist. Then ask if these trends are already priced in? Edgar is looking for a brief white paper with an executive summary in which you rank the four, identifying key risks and opportunities for each. This is largely a qualitative exercise, with key numbers used to support your analysis. Use the rough numbers you have to explore return scenarios, testing how robust your conclusions are to the key assumptions you make. For example consider:

- In the SoCal multifamily strategy, model a 5.5% return on cost development and look at the sensitivity of higher costs and higher cap rates on returns. Given this sensitivity, how would you rank this type of investment? Again, use aggregate data from several submarkets or even find some template-type deals to use as examples. Build some pro forma and test returns against movements in rents, costs, cap rates, debt, and other key variables as needed.
- Similar to the multifamily scenario, run sensitivities on rents and cap rates in the San Diego industrial strategy to see how sensitive returns are to the rents and exit prices. Assume development over two years to start, but if other holding periods offer better outcome, use them and defend your assumptions.
- To explore the Las Vegas strategy, assume the all-in basis for the seven-property portfolio at $250 psf. Then you would have two types of exit—piecemeal or as a flip to another portfolio investor. What would sales have to be to earn the kind of returns Edgar needs? How soon would he need to start selling? Could you defend such price appreciation? Again, at this level of analysis, use submarket aggregates to help model rents and pricing.

- In the case of the preferred equity strategy, consider how far asset prices would have to fall for Edgar to lose money. Is this choice really a lot safer than the others? If Edgar's firm does end up owning the property, how long would they have to hold to see a positive return and what range could the investor expect, and what could Edgar's firm expect? Could you convince the investors to be happy with this strategy?

These are really hard questions, but Edgar's firm has to be able to invest soon to generate the fees that will keep the firm operating, all while still being able to defend the deals in the short run and earn good returns in the next couple of years. They need a plan; this is your task.

Index

Note: Page numbers followed by *f* indicate figures and *t* indicate tables.